BEYOND POSITIVE ECONOMICS?

The "positivist revolution" in economics dramatically changed the character of the subject, by emphasizing the importance of *testability*: is the proposition in a form that renders it capable of rejection? Can it in fact be disproved? But there is increasing dissatisfaction that the tests that economists use are themselves convincing: many, for example, treat all data as a record of fulfilled expectations which is not the way actual decision-makers would see the problem.

The purpose of the volume is not to reject positivism or testability, but to ask for a more relevant description of human behavior and its environment as a starting-point. The introductory paper (Wiseman) attempts to specify the problem. The next set (Shackle, Littlechild, Katouzian, Shearmur, Coats) debates the intellectual issues and their history. The following papers (Loasby, Jefferson, Hey, Earl) consider practical questions and possibilities for a "new" (but less intellectually arrogant) positivism, and a final paper (Hutchison) reviews the contribution of the BA to the development of thought in the relevant areas.

BEYOND POSITIVE ECONOMICS?

Proceedings of Section F (Economics)
of the British Association for
the Advancement of Science
York 1981

Edited by
Jack Wiseman

Professor of Economics and
Director of the Institute of Social and Economic Research
University of York

St. Martin's Press   New York

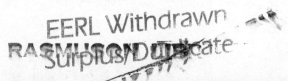

Printed in Great Britain
First published in the United States of America in 1983

ISBN 0–312–07780–7

Library of Congress Cataloging in Publication Data

Main entry under title:

Beyond positive economics?

   Includes index.
   Contents: Beyond positive economics: dream and
reality/Jack Wiseman — The bounds of unknowledge/
G. L. S. Shackle — Subjectivism and method in economics/
Stephen Littlechild — Towards the progress of
economic knowledge/Homa Katouzian — [etc.]
   1. Economics—Congresses. I. Wiseman, Jack.
II. British Association for the Advancement of
Science. Section F (Economics). III. Title: Positive
economics.
HB21.B49   1983   330   82–16874
ISBN 0–312–07780–7

Contents

Acknowledgements

I should like to acknowledge particularly the help I had in preparing the programme from Dr David Reisman, Recorder of Section F, and from my secretary Miss B. Dodds.

I am also most appreciative of the ready response of my associates, and of the efforts of the British Association officers of Section F and their colleagues at the University of York, which contributed to an occasion which was socially as well as intellectually memorable.

J. W.

Notes on the Contributors

A. W. Coats is Professor of Economic and Social History, University of Nottingham. He was formerly Reader at the University of York and has taught at a number of American universities. His main publications have been in the history of economic thought, with special reference to the development of the economics profession and the role of economists in government.

Peter Earl graduated from the University of Cambridge with first-class honours in 1977 and was awarded the Wrenbury Scholarship. He was subsequently appointed Munro Research Scholar at Queen's College, Cambridge. Since 1979 he has been Lecturer in Economics at the University of Stirling. He is co-author of *Money Matters: a Keynesian Approach to Monetary Economics*.

John D. Hey is Senior Lecturer in the Department of Economics and Related Studies at the University of York. He has also been a lecturer at Durham and St Andrews Universities and an econometrician with a London firm of stockbrokers. His main research interests are in the economics of uncertainty. Among his recent publications are two books in that area, *Uncertainty in Microeconomics* and *Economics in Disequilibrium*.

Terence Hutchison is Emeritus Professor of Economics at the University of Birmingham. A graduate in economics of Cambridge University, he was nine years at the London School of Economics before moving to Birmingham in 1956. He has been Visiting Professor, or Fellow, at the Universities of Columbia, Virginia, Yale and California, and also at the Australian National University, the University of the Saarland and other universities. He has published a number of books on the history and method of economics, including, most recently, *The Politics and Philosophy of Economics*.

Michael Jefferson is Head of Planning for Shell International Petroleum in Europe, and Head of Supply Appraisal, based in The Hague. He is responsible for the supply and trading of a significant proportion of Scandinavia's oil requirements, where economic uncertainty and decision-making are ever present. Previously he was Chief Economist of Shell International Petroleum in London. He studied economics at Oxford and the London School of Economics and has published in the fields of industrial economics, inflation, economic and social history, and social fiction (including 'The Concern with Inequality in Victorian Fiction' at the 1975 British Association meeting, published in Aubrey Jones (ed.), *Economics and Equality*).

Homa Katouzian was Assistant Lecturer in Economics at the University of Leeds from 1968 to 1969. He then moved to the University of Kent at Canterbury, where he is now Senior Lecturer in Economics. He was also Visiting Professor of Economics at Chiraz, Visiting Fellow at St Antony's, Oxford, and Visiting Associate Professor of Economics at McMaster University, Canada. He has written numerous articles for international journals and *Ideology and Method in Economics*.

Stephen Littlechild is Professor of Commerce and Head of the Department of Industrial Economics, University of Birmingham. He is the author of numerous papers and books, including *The Fallacy of the Mixed Economy*.

Brian Loasby is Professor of Management Economics at the University of Stirling, where he is Joint Director of an interdisciplinary graduate programme for scientists and engineers. His principal research interests are decision-processes in organisations and the development of economic ideas – making use in both contexts of theories of knowledge. His publications include *The Swindon Project* and *Choice, Complexity and Ignorance*.

G. L. S. Shackle was formerly Brunner Professor of Economic Science at the University of Liverpool. He is the author of many influential books and articles, including *The Nature of Economic Thought*, *The Years of High Theory* and *Epistemics and Economics*.

Jeremy Shearmur, BSc (Econ), MSc, is a temporary lecturer in philosophy at the University of Edinburgh. He was previously assistant to Karl Popper in the Department of Philosophy, London School of

Economics. He has published on a variety of subjects from political philosophy and the philosophy of history to the sociology of religious sectarianism, and he is at present engaged in a study of F. A. Hayek.

Jack Wiseman is Professor of Economics and Director of the Institute of Social and Economic Research at the University of York. His interests in economics have always been diverse, consistent with a conviction that 'specialisation' in economics is inconsistent with a subjectivist view of human behaviour. He has consequently published in a variety of fields, with some concentration on industrial economics, public sector economics and economics of human resources. Publications of special relevance to the theme of this volume are 'Uncertainty, Costs and Collectivist Economic Planning', *Economica*, 1953; 'The Theory of Public Utility Price: an Empty Box', *Oxford Economic Papers*, February 1956; 'The Political Economy of Nationalised Industry', *The Economics of Politics*, IEA Readings, no. 19, 1978; and 'Costs and Decisions', in Currie and Peters (eds), *Contemporary Economic Analysis* (proceedings of AUTE, 1978).

Introduction

JACK WISEMAN

It is a signal honour to be invited to be President of Section F in the 150th anniversary year of the British Association. I don't fool myself that the Association's return to its foundation city had nothing to do with the invitation. But my kind of economist sees the subject as concerned with adaptation to, or exploitation of, previously unforeseen opportunities: and that is also how I viewed this invitation.

It is perhaps fair to say that the topics treated by Section F are predominantly related to issues of currently practical importance. This is not to say that the meetings have made no contribution to the intellectual foundations or methodology of the subject. Terence Hutchison's survey (Chapter 11) provides adequate contrary evidence on that score. But methodological debate emerges at intervals after periods of relative quiescence. This is as it should be: a continuous involvement in methodological debate is debilitating, but a periodic incursion may be refreshing and illuminating. Indeed, one of our contributors has elsewhere suggested that methodology, like sex, is the proper pre-occupation of young men: in which case I suppose I must be an example of arrested development?

In any event, I chose to use my presidency to stimulate debate not upon a particular topic but upon the nature and method of the subject: this seemed to me appropriate in the light of both the occasion and the state of the subject. The academic equivalent of crying wolf is crying crisis. All intellectual disciplines are in a state of continuous crisis, and need to remain so. But there is more than one kind of crisis: there are crises that need no more than a shift in intellectual attitudes, others that render a whole stock of intellectual capital obsolete, or at the least greatly devalue it. This latter state is what I think (though I'm not sure) Kahn would call the need for a 'paradigm change'. Not everything in economics is wrong, not everything in positive economics

1

is wrong: but the intellectual constructs we use are wrong, or, more precisely, increasingly irrelevant, in ways that demand a major re-thinking of the methodology of our subject. These are large claims, but I believe that this volume sustains them. I make no secret of the fact that the contributors are persons with whom I am intellectually sympathetic: though the observant reader will notice that they do not always agree with each other (or with me). That is as it should be: the world we are trying to explain is confusing and unmanageable. We can hope to agree about its relevant characteristics: that would be a great advance. It will take much longer before we agree about explanations of economic phenomena, if indeed we ever can. But this volume, like the meeting from which the papers emerged, starts from a belief that we can do better than positivism: or at least than the positivism we have now.

The first essay offers my own statement of the issues. It was written when I had seen drafts of the papers of only the most punctilious of my colleagues, and is a personal statement rather than a summary: the latter is the purpose of this Introduction. The next nine papers, once assembled, divided happily into two groups (perhaps there really is a 'co-ordinating principle' at work?) The first group (Chapters 2–6 inclusive) offers perspectives on the nature of the economic problem: the papers are concerned with philosophy, conceptualisation and methodology. The second set (Chapters 7–10 inclusive) attacks practical problems from a subjectivist standpoint. Their contribution is important because they confront in different contexts the question so often asked of subjectivist critics of received doctrine: you make telling criticisms, but what contribution do you yourself have to make to the better explanation/understanding/control of real-world phenomena? The question is not entirely fair: it is not valueless to point out that the king has no clothes, even if one cannot also offer means to cover him. But these contributions do suggest some directions for future develop-ment. The final chapter (11) was not part of the proceedings of Section F, but a 150th anniversary review lecture which helps place the debate in the evolving history of economic thought.

Chapter 1 (Jack Wiseman) is an attempt to provide a context for what follows: it is for this reason, and not from any conviction of its intrinsic merit (nor because of the property rights of the editor), that the précis here is fairly long.

The chapter accepts that the development of positive economics has revolutionised the subject in the past fifteen or twenty years. Positiv-ism consists essentially in subjecting theories about the way the economy works to the test of prediction: a theory is falsified and rejected if the results it predicts do not eventuate. The emergence of positivism has accelerated the use of mathematical techniques in economics, and with this the emphasis on mechanistic rather than conceptual questions.

The theme of the paper is that this is now beginning to produce an unwelcome and damaging bifurcation which needs to be remedied. This is not because the notion of positivism is wrong, but because the underlying model leaves out fundamental aspects of economic reality, and this emasculates the practical utility of positive testing, however sophisticated the techniques.

The core of the problem is that the received doctrine treats the future as known, either with certainty or within a finite set of possibilities to which probabilities can be assigned. In the world we live in, the future is unknowable. In the accepted model, the trains always run at the times advertised in the timetable. In the real world, they do not, but people treat the timetable as a forecast in deciding when to go to the station.

The chapter makes suggestions as to ways in which the model might be improved, including a reinterpretation of the human decision (planning) process, the concept of efficiency, and the future development of mathematical and quantitative techniques.

A final section gives examples of how and where immediate progress might be made: the substitution of bounded possibility for objective probability, the rejection of mechanistic 'rules' for the behaviour of public enterprises and the study of such enterprises in terms of the changes they necessitate in decision-processes and individual property rights, the direct study of consumer and business behaviour, and the simulation of the latter in ways that combine subjectivist/uncertainty ideas with computer modelling; and the improvement of the study of comparative economic systems.

G. L. S. Shackle, the author of Chapter 2, has been undervalued by his generation: his time will come. The perceptiveness of his thought is well illustrated by a comment offered on my own contribution: 'In the case of an unique event (i.e. a self-destructive experiment)', he asks, 'what *question* is answered by a statement of probability? Does it tell what *will* happen? No. Does it tell what will *not* happen? No (unless it is zero or unity). What *does* it tell?' Yet unique events permeate economics.

Shackle's style is so lucid, and so compact, that it is almost impertinent, as indeed it is difficult, to present his argument in summary.

I shall content myself with a statement of what the chapter is about. If you want more, read it. It rejects the use of probability to 'explain' economic events, and examines the potential of concepts of *possibility*. I can do no better than to quote the specification of the nature of choice with which the paper concludes:

> It is an attempted answer to the question: What can the action-chooser, the decision-maker, *know*, and with what content can the word 'know' be used when describing his business of choice?
>
> I have suggested, in effect, that he can tell himself where possibility reaches its limits, he can trace upon his thought map of imagined things a boundary-fence beyond which, given his resources, given his time-horizon for reaping the fruits of action, no action of his can reach. In a sense which has some degree of paradox, his knowledge is of the non-possible. It is beyond the fence that everything can be tagged with effective certainty as not belonging to the attainable. Unknowledge, for him, consists in *the plurality of rival possibles*. The bounds of the possible are bounds of unknowledge.

If this stimulates your imagination, read the chapter.

Stephen Littlechild (Chapter 3) offers a most perceptive evaluation of what such terms as 'positive' and 'normative' actually mean. 'Subjectivism' means different things to different people: its essence is concern with the 'human factor' in economics, and this leads naturally to the extension of the problem of scientific methodology to other intellectual disciplines: the work of authors such as Kuhn is as relevant to economics as to physics, as is the observation that the choice of subjects and investigatory methods is itself subjective: economists and physicists are also people. This introduces a crucial problem. What constitutes a satisfactory positive test, and a convincing result? To believe that hypotheses will be accepted or rejected in the light of 'the empirical evidence' is to believe that economists have no subjective differences about the nature of the issues. Similar strictures, argues Littlechild, can be levelled against the uncritical mathematical formalisation of economic relationships, against dogmatic *a priorism*, and, indeed, against the view that human behaviour can be explained, or fully explained, in terms of the acts of a 'rational man', acting alone and uninfluenced by society. This is a paper offering much food for thought.

In the next chapter (4), Homa Katouzian attacks the issues from a different but not intellectually unsympathetic direction, by relating the current methodological and philosophical debate in economics both to the *history* and to the relevance of such debate. He concludes that although logical and ideological issues are of theoretical as well as practical importance, they do not constitute the most urgent problems of modern economics. These arise from 'a methodological outlook which – by sacrificing substance for form, reality for appearance – homogenises economic categories and phenomena, mechanicises the associated problems, and universalises the results of their study'.

This diagnosis, argues Katouzian, implies its own prescription. But the move from puzzle-solving to problem-solving will be not a leap but a process, and some characteristics of the way 'beyond positivism' can be identified. First, the aim is not to replace analytical depth or empirical precision by 'descriptive general knowledge', but to construct more rigorous and relevant models, and use available techniques more effectively. Second, we must escape the confusion of *historical knowledge* with historicism. Abstract data are merely records (symbols) of past or present events, capable of manipulation and interpretation in diverse fashions. Third, the acquisition of social and historical knowledge can be as useful to an economist as the acquisition of competence in mathematics or statistics, and like the latter, need not turn the economist into something else. Such a shift in the balance of specialisation would raise the substantial (as distinct from the formal) quality of teaching and research in economics. Finally, he argues, we need a little help from our professional friends: not least the *eminente* who are themselves not unwilling to condemn such irrelevancies as equilibrium economics, but yet continue to acquiesce in a career structure that is clearly hindering the development of the subject.

So far, the authors show a clear intellectual empathy, though not, let it be emphasised, a complete harmony either of viewpoint or interest. They share the view that a new direction is needed, and that this must involve recognition of subjective choice related to an unknowable future as the core of the problem to be studied. But subjectivism means different things to different people, as Littlechild points out, and the authors would differ, for example, as to the extent to which methodological individualism implies a rejection of empiricism (as seems to be the position of some members of the Austrian School), the need for a new kind of empiricism, or emphasis on the need to 'marry' subjectivist insights and the existent behavioural and institutional economics. Jeremy Shearmur (Chapter 5) introduces an even more substantial dissent. After a lucid and thorough evaluation of the positions of the positivists and their critics, he concludes with a warning. The working economist must recognise subjectivism as a fertile source of substantive ideas, but should be wary that the subjectivist contribution 'would debar us from making any real contribution to many major problems in economics'. What Shearmur invites us to explore is the possibility that the 'natural selection' approach, exemplified by the works of such writers as Alchian, Friedman and Becker, is not capable of extension to embrace the subjectivist insights. This is clearly a different and more embracing integration than anything envisaged by earlier writers.

The Shearmur contribution is intellectually stimulating and, unsurprisingly, provocative. It is of interest that the most emphatic rejection of his position came from Michael Jefferson (Chapter 8, below), who saw no way that such an integration could be achieved in a fashion that would improve the economists' contribution to an understanding of business decision-making.

A. W. Coats's paper (Chapter 6) is really a watershed within the volume. I earlier placed it in the philosophical/methodological set. But in fact Coats sat through all the papers, and his own contribution draws on them, on the discussions, and on his own broader scholarship. It thus provides a link between the methodology-oriented and the issue-oriented papers. It is also, or again, an extremely difficult paper to encapsulate. Coats concerns himself not only with what subjectivist economics *is* (in regard to which he takes up and expands upon the questions raised in other papers), but also with its history and, specifically, with the explanation of its revival. This latter he sees in: 'autonomous' developments in the subjectivist movement itself, including the emergence of a contingent of neo-Austrians interested in behaviouralism; dissatisfaction with the reigning 'professional consensus', which opens the doors to all kinds of heterodox groups; developments in other intellectual disciplines and their philosophical foundations; and developments outside the academic world, in economic policy, performance and the public reputation of the economics profession. These related 'explanations', and the implied forecasts for the future of the subject and its practitioners, are elegantly and persuasively developed in the concluding section.

Brian Loasby's contribution (Chapter 7) is also in a sense transitional. In one sense, it is clearly a contribution to the methodological debate. In another, it is a commentary on the making and evaluation of public policy, and so 'practical' in the sense that critics invite subjectivists to be. There are two particularly intriguing aspects of the paper.

First, his use of Adam Smith's contribution to the methodological debate in his *History of Astronomy*, which is also referred to in Shearmur's discussion of philosophical/methodological issues to illustrate the difference between methodological positions and practical behaviour. Second, Loasby's explicit introduction of psychological concepts into the discussion of economic behaviour.

Many of the critical issues in contemporary economics, says Loasby, turn on the assumptions made about knowledge; but these assumptions rarely go beyond the manipulation of probabilities. He adopts the proposal by an American psychologist, George Kelly, that we analyse people as scientists, and therefore apply to their behaviour such understanding as we have of the developments of scientific knowledge.

Our world is far too complex to be comprehended directly. We have to impose our own patterns, which we then use to select and interpret information, and to guide decisions. What does not fit may be discarded, or it may lead to some modification of the pattern. Because it is imposed, no single pattern can claim unique validity, and, even if modified, may eventually cease to be adequate. What Loasby proposes is an alternative pattern for economists.

An economy, like science, depends on specialisation, on the development and continued testing of many different patterns of knowledge. Each firm is likely to be at an advantage in handling a particular set of problems, and in perceiving certain opportunities; these advantages evolve with its own interpretation of its own history. Its organisational structure imposes a framework on its managers, defining the information which is relevant and the way it is handled. Reorganisation implies a redefinition of both; that may be necessary for effective decisions, but it may be hard to achieve.

The economist's concept of perfect competition requires firms to be alike; but if competition is a process of discovery, it is important that the competitors should have varied experience, and varied frameworks for interpreting it. Some organisations may be unable to adapt to new circumstances, and may need to give way to others. Attempts by public policy to preserve what exists are liable to impede the adaptation of the economy, with painful results for most of us.

There is no doubt about the thrust of the next paper (Chapter 8). Michael Jefferson was educated as an economist, has contributed to the subject's journals, but in his everyday life is involved in taking the kind of decisions that economists theorise about. In that sense, he is a 'consumer' of the output of academic economists. It is heartening to those of us who press for change, but challenging to the discipline as a whole, that he finds little support from 'mainstream' economics, and looks to the subjectivists (the 'nihilists') for useful help. The chapter incorporates an illuminating exposition of the 'scenario planning' practised by the Shell organisation: it is useful material for academic economists from this point of view alone. It also incorporates Jefferson's critique of the contribution of economics (or economists) to the resolution of his own problems. These contributions are best described by Jefferson's own summary of the content of the paper:

● Uncertainty is endemic, but its true nature is rarely understood.
● Persistent efforts are made to propound theories, hypotheses and techniques as if uncertainty did not exist or could be effectively eliminated.
● Traditional economic theories, notably those relating to general equilibrium and perfect knowledge, buttress erroneous ideas concerning uncertainty and have few counterparts in the real world.
● The objective and pursuit of positive economics – theories that provide valid predictions – in particular are a will-o'-the-wisp.
● Academic contributions to the nature of business decision-making have been of rather modest value. There is a pressing need fully to accept the true nature of uncertainty and not to act in a manner which implies a greater degree of certainty and knowledge than the nature and circumstances of many business problems will admit.
● One widely adopted approach is to attach probabilities to future possibilities, and thus to unknowledge, which is liable to be a snare and delusion.

But

● There is a long tradition, especially in British economics, of some economists having a better understanding of uncertainty and the economics of the real world than the profession in general. It is regrettable that so many academics try to by-pass this work and ignore its exponents.
● In recent years this subjectivist tradition has been represented by such economists as G. L. S. Shackle, J. Wiseman, B. J. Loasby, H. Katouzian and S. C. Littlechild.
● There are important links between these developments in economics and parallel developments in the physical sciences, where uncertainty, time, change, order in chaos and chaos in order are matters of intensified interest.

● In living without certainty we must not be paralysed by hesitation. We need a conceptual framework to cope with uncertainty; a framework of ideas and elements which encourages awareness of uncertainty, change and future possibilities while also leading to appropriate action. Shell's experience suggests that the multiple-scenario approach provides an excellent framework for these purposes.

● The chapter sets out the relevant scenario elements, some of the factors required for the proper functioning of a scenario team, the importance of qualitative assessments, and some of the perspectives needed for success in these assessments.

● The history of scenario planning in Shell since 1971 is summarised, with appropriate illustrations. Links into strategy formation and implementation, and into shorter-term business decision-making, are discussed. While the story contains many successes, some failures are also indicated. Because relatively little has been written about Shell's experience in the application of multiple-scenario planning, this chapter is the fullest survey hitherto publicly available. However, it is such a large topic, involving so many ideas and people for more than a decision that no definitive survey is possible.

● There have been few academic contributions to the frameworks discussed, yet they have proved extremely valuable in coping with the turbulence of the past decade and encouraging the necessary resilience and adaptability. There have been recent signs of academic interest in modelling uncertainty, change and disequilibrium which suggest continuing search after some illusory Philosopher's Stone.

● The value of much general theorising is questionable. The chapter stresses rather the importance of context: time, place, circumstances, tradition, institutional framework, industry norms and corporate cultures.

What a fascinating contrast: a philosopher who sees the possibility of positive economics embracing subjectivism, and an industrial decision-maker who finds 'mainstream' positive economics irrelevant to his problems.

We come now to John Hey (Chapter 9), and to another change of pace. His interest in uncertainty began in an orthodox (probabilistic, simple decision-making) fashion. As his paper explains, he no longer takes this view.

To quote:

> Positive economics assumes that the world is sufficiently simple for humans to behave infallibly. In contrast Double Negative economics assumes that the world is *not* simple, and that humans are *not* infallible. While positive economics has reached a highly sophisticated level of development, double negative economics is merely in its infancy.

Thus, what Hey calls *Double Negative economics* attempts to rebuild economics around the truisms that the world is *not* simple and humans are *not* infallible. The paper argues that there are two ways of approaching Double Negative economics: from positive (optimality) economics and from random economics.

A number of very recent developments (including the work of Kahneman and Tversky, Machina, Sugden and Loomes and Fishburn) have signposted the way forward from positive economics. The way forward from random economics is less clear, but some indications have been provided by experimental evidence and work done by psychologists.

The main question mark hangs over whether these two separate lines of enquiry will 'meet in the middle'. Hey's position on this is optimistic but uncertain: he sees us needing

> some higher-level theory, which shows how rules are modified in the light of experience. Of necessity, this learning process would have to be non-Bayesian; but equally it could not be one of those rather depressing psychological theories of learning which imply that people never behave optimally however much experience they have. What this new learning theory will look like, I do not know; but there are rich rewards to be gained from it.

We should be clear about what he is saying: not that he has 'solutions', but that the useful modelling of decision problems is not beyond the wit of man. In this sense, he is concerned with the development of the empirical counterparts of the philosophical 'marrying' discussed earlier. It is easy to see why this 'modelling' approach might be unappealing to someone like Michael Jefferson (Chapter 8), but it is equally easy to see, conceptually at least, how the two formalisations of the problem might converge, and economists actually begin to contribute to efficient business decision-making.

Peter Earl, in Chapter 10, meets the challenge 'what would *you* do?', head-on. He challenges the orthodox theory of demand as unable to help those concerned to *predict* demand behaviour, and suggests ways in which subjectivism can make economics more relevant to an understanding of actual consumer behaviour. Earl's contribution is both critical of positive economics, and offers a constructive alternative, in the area of consumer behaviour theory. He argues first that conventional consumer theory, based on the notion of utility-maximisation, can tell us little more than the man in the street, viz, the Law of Demand, that if relative prices are lowered consumers will buy more of the products – except when they do not. In situations of structural change, where new products are being launched, or oligopolistic markets, even the very notion of a demand-function is open to question. Consumer theorists ought to be able to explain to firms how they can affect their sales at prices set in response to competitive pressures, but it is not possible to do this without a deeper understanding of consumer motives.

The subjectivist alternative sees consumers as attempting to cope with a complex and mysterious world by a process akin to normal scientific behaviour. That is to say, they form theories about how things are and then attempt to test them to see how they fit. They can only test a limited number of theories so they choose the most interesting ones. They will be afraid to choose activities which place them in situations which they cannot comprehend, particularly if they might have to justify their choices to others, or if the results of their theory-testing destroy their previously cherished beliefs. They will be especially worried about preserving their self-images, their theories of themselves.

Earl then uses this view of human behaviour to consider how consumers may be encouraged to change their behaviour, paying particular attention to ways in which firms can exploit the emotions of anxiety, hostility and aggression (for which he gives subjectivist definitions). The theory is also used to analyse the nature of 'keeping up with the Joneses' and sudden shifts in consumer durable purchases, along with consumer persistence in activities seemingly because of, rather than despite, sunk costs which conventional theory finds hard to explain.

The subjectivist view is particularly helpful in explaining the nature of clashes in tastes and why consumers of particular products, be they economic theories, styles of dress or drinks, react with hostility towards those who choose differently from themselves. Conventional theories, for all their displays of technical virtuosity, cannot say any more than that 'people choose different things because they like different things'. They cannot suggest why people might prefer others to like what they like and pressurise them to do so.

Terence Hutchison's concluding paper (Chapter 11), was not a part of the proceedings of Section F (Economics), but a general review of the Section over 150 years (though he did know that we planned to publish it). His paper is an overview of the history of thought, encapsulated in the form and content of the BA meetings, that obliges reading of itself. As to the content of our anniversary programme, let Terence Hutchison's words speak for themselves:

> So, in 1981, the moderate programme of the economist founders of Section F, 150 years ago, seems to retain its superior validity against its two competitors: that is the programme of rejecting the pretentious claims and hopes for epistemological parity with the advanced natural sciences, in terms at any rate of explanations and predictions; and of seeking to continue building up the often-changing empirical foundations of the subject, in accordance with, and in acceptance of, the disciplines of scientific method, common to both social and natural sciences.

1 Beyond Positive Economics – Dream and Reality

JACK WISEMAN

INTRODUCTION

> What song the sirens sang or what name Achilles assumed when he
> hid himself among women, though puzzling questions are not
> beyond all conjecture.
>
> (Browne, Sir Thomas, *Urn Burial*, Chapter 5, 1658)

The purpose of the series of lectures of which this is the first is not to
attempt to destroy or reject the notion of a positive economics, or to
deny that important insights have emerged from the exposure of 'mainstream' (neo-classical) economics to positivist ideas. Rather, it is to
argue that a new kind of positivism is now needed, if the subject is not
to become increasingly sterile, and divided between ever more sophisticated but practically unhelpful mathematical modelling on the one
hand, and an unsatisfying institutionalism or unsupported conceptualisation on the other. The essential reason for this division lies in the
growing importance of the inadequacies of the underlying behavioural
model (the set of propositions concerning man acting in his 'economic
environment',) used by economists; and allied with this a natural
reluctance to accept the obsolescence of a considerable stock of
intellectual capital, particularly as the kind of new model that is needed
lends itself easily neither to mathematical exposition nor to econometric sophistication. Its claims rest more upon relevance than upon
formal beauty, at least for the present.

These are bold claims: but the British Association is the place for
that. You will find them supported in particular contexts in other

13

papers. In this general introduction, I shall try to summarise what I believe to be wrong, and then make some suggestions as to directions of development that seem to me to be desirable.

THE DOMINANT ORTHODOXY AND ITS DEFICIENCIES

The core of the neo-classical explanation of 'economic' behaviour is the *exchange relationship*: humans transact one with another to their mutual benefit. The essential transaction is a two-person exchange. Money enters as a convenient *numéraire*: but the essence of the logic of choice is contained in Edgeworth's exposition of the transactions between peasant-with-corn and peasant-with-wine. Inevitably, other types of transactions have to be admitted: multi-person firms involve transactional relationships not easily comprehended by the Edgeworth direct exchange, as indeed do trade unions, families, governments and other social groups. But while these group-involvement activities are acknowledged and analysed in the specialist literatures, they are generally seen simply as extensions of the logic of choice developed around two-person exchange. This logic of choice is the basis for the accepted model of human 'economic' behaviour that I wish to examine. In its naive form, it treats the future as predictable, and has no place for group behaviour: 'firms' and other groups are simply combinations of human and non-human resources, co-ordinated by an entrepreneur who has perfect knowledge of all (future) factor and product prices, and whose choice of a 'best' plan of action never results in an unexpected outcome. As a description of the economic decision-process, this is not only naive but logically inconsistent. If the future is known, as it must be if future input and output prices are known, then in what meaningful sense can entrepreneurs make decisions (choose between alternative plans of action), since that choice must affect the prices concerned? The professional economist is well aware of the problem, and is normally cautious in the use of this naive model in his own work. But it is the general point of departure: and it is what thousands of students who study only a little economics are left thinking that the subject is about. Also, there are whole specialist literatures that have been developed on the assumption that choosers are fully aware of, and certain about, the future implications of their present choices.

More sophisticated formulations admit that the future is uncertain. But they deal with the resultant difficulties by assuming that the number of possible futures is finite, and is in an operational sense 'known'. If the risk-attitudes of decision-makers are also known, then their choice between plans can be deduced from this knowledge, together with the assumed knowledge of the (objective) probability attached to each of the outcomes within the finite set of outcomes considered. This formulation lends itself to great technical sophistication: models can be developed which permit entrepreneurial predictions to be disappointed, and the resultant 'learning' used to modify subsequent decisions. But the 'learning' is written into the model in advance: the 'clockwork Bayesians' programme information in a specified fashion until the process has run down and no further 'improvements' can be made.

The greater sophistication of this formulation must not be allowed to conceal the fact that the model fails to deal with the fundamental problem. If the future is unknowable (as it is) then the assumption of a finite set of possible future outcomes, known to someone (who? how?), and of a predetermined re-planning process ('learning' can only change plans in the programmed direction) reduces to a mechanistic system a decision-process whose essence is that it is *subjective* and *ignorant* (in the sense of depending on judgements about matters concerning which the decision-maker can have only opinions based upon experience). The assumptions are necessary if objective probabilistic techniques are to be used: writers in this genre acknowledge that the model cannot cope with a non-finite set of outcomes. This severely curtails its ability to explain decision-processes in the real world.

Let me be clear. The implication of my argument is not that positivism is somehow 'wrong'. Nor is it that the received doctrine is wrong because the assumptions from which it proceeds are 'unrealistic'. Assumptions are necessarily unrealistic, both because simplifying and 'stylised', and because any 'new' assumption ('suppose the earth is round',) contradicts 'received truth'.

The criticism is not general in this sense. It is the *nature* of the simplifying assumptions that is crucial. Can we really expect models that assume the future to be known, whether perfectly or in an objective-probabilistic fashion, to provide satisfactory explanations of human behaviour in a world in which the future is not knowable and people are not surprised when the outcome of their plans differs from their predictions?

It is because the model lacks relevance to decision-making in the real world that it is beginning more and more to restrict the contribution of the economist to the resolution of practical problems, and we need to 'break the mould' if we are to reverse this trend. The purpose is not to reject positivism, but to develop behavioural models that enable a more practically useful positivism to emerge.

This invites the question: How can we do better? It is not an easy question to answer. Intellectually satisfying models which embrace an unknowable future and are compatible with some form of positivism are not easily constructed: which undoubtedly helps explain the reluctance of economists to stray outside the neo-classical paradigms. But we are obliged to try (which is why this series is titled *beyond* rather than *in place of* positive economics). We must try to create a 'better positivism', which is not content with the *a priorism* of the more extreme proponents of the Austrian School, but also recognises the deficiencies of received positivism. The task is difficult but not impossible. It is also likely to be considered unrewarding by those for whom formal symmetry is of itself an appealing goal: we are attempting to understand human phenomena which are neither simple nor by their nature explicable by continuously reliable 'laws'. In the space available to me, I can do no more than indicate the major changes in the specification of 'the economic problem' that seem to me to be called for (these of course follow from the earlier argument), and suggest some examples of ways in which a new (or 'better') positive economics might emerge.

THE WAY AHEAD

The essential need is for a positivism that relates the 'facts' more satisfactorily to the conditions and decision-processes of a world characterised by an unknowable future. 'Learning' from historical facts and the results of past decisions cannot make the future 'knowable', since there is no permanent nexus between past, continuous present (what is happening 'now'), and the future. Indeed, it is not easily demonstrable that learning improves the quality of decision-making (since we cannot know what decisions individuals would have taken had they not 'learned', much less what the outcome of those decisions would have been). Nor is it obvious that the universe of economic phenomena is becoming more predictable. In this single lecture, I can do no more than list some of the important specific problems and suggest ways in which progress might be made. I do not claim originality for the arguments: there are many economists who would agree with some or all of them, and most will be dealt with more thoroughly in one or other of the papers to be presented here. But they may have value considered as an agenda for future development.

THE USE AND DEVELOPMENT OF MATHEMATICS AND QUANTITATIVE TECHNIQUES

This may seem a strange choice of first topic. But there is an urgent need to reconcile the mathematical and conceptual development of the subject if a more policy-relevant positivism is to evolve. Mathematics as a system of formal logic has made and should continue to make an undeniable contribution to the advancement of our understanding, and it would be stupid to deny its potential. But it is not unfair to describe the present state of the art as one in which the economic problem has come to be specified in ways that make it susceptible to mathematical formulation, rather than the mathematics being developed to deal with the important practical problems that need to be solved. The underlying reason is simple: we do not have the mathematical techniques to deal with a non-finite set of future outcomes, or with relationships between past, continuous present and future that are not subject to continuously reliable 'laws'. Professor Shackle has made the point more elegantly than I could hope to:

> The mathematicians were incisive and efficient. The formal authority and finality of their results, the swift economy with which their answers were attained, seem sometimes to deride the labours of the conceptualists. . . . The mathematicians incline to regard economics as the study of mechanism, and with mechanism we are able, sometimes in practice, always in abstract argument, to abolish the distinction between past and future, to design a system where 'ignorance' can no more affect outcomes than it can affect the operation of gravity. . . . But the rich and fruitful theory is a structure, not of nameless quantities existing only in relation to each other, but of named concepts, images, enjoying an almost personal life in our minds. That is why neither the mathematicians nor the conceptualists can be allowed to bear the palm alone.

Shackle was writing of the development of economics between the wars: since then the problem has become more severe. More and more mathematical constructs are concerned with mathematical (mechanistic) rather than with behavioural developments or sophistications: we need to persuade the mathematicians to attempt formulations more closely relevant to the economic problem as I have been describing it in this paper.

In respect of quantitative techniques, there is a similar phenomenon to be observed. The development of econometrics is a natural offshoot of the commitment to positivism. There is nothing wrong with this in principle: practically, it has tended to shift the commitment of economists away from concern with the formal properties and relevance of models (in relation to real-world decision-making) and towards sophistication in quantitative techniques.

Professor L. R. Klein, himself no mean exponent of quantitative techniques, has put the matter thus:

> [Quantitative analysis] is becoming an end in itself, and abstruse mathematical models for models' sake are substituted for reflective thought . . . Regression analysis is the new Hyperion.

He gives illustrations, such as a study of economic influences on marital separation, which concluded that the sophisticated economic model supported 'the inclusion of women as active participants in the process of marital separation'.

The illustration is no doubt extreme, but the general point is well taken. It is also worth pointing out that much of this work uses data often collected for other purposes by means that are not themselves the subject of enquiry ('secondary sources'), and treats the data as the outcome of successfully-implemented plans. But if the future is unknowable, men must make mistakes, and the historical record is a (partial and inaccurate) record of those mistakes. How can we make propositions about causal relationships based on econometric models that do not take account of the fact that the historical record is a record of disappointed expectations?

THE DECISION-PROCESS

The standard short- and long-period distinction by which time is incorporated into economics becomes inadequate as soon as it is recognised that decisions take place in time-as-a-continuum. Once this is so, decision-makers have to be seen as making present plans for implementation over different future time-periods, and those plans will be mutually interdependent. If in addition the plans are made in the light of an unknowable future, then we have to conceive of decision-makers considering and choosing between plans they believe possible of implementation in the light of their possible 'outcomes' (expected benefits and disbenefits). They will choose the plan they believe to be 'best', at the (opportunity-) cost of rejecting the next most favoured plan. Cost in its decision sense is subjective, and in an uncertain world it has no objective counterpart.

Through this process of planning and replanning, decision-makers 'learn' from the results of past plans, and this learning will influence their choice between future plans. As already explained, the future does not thus become knowable. But this is not to say that learning is irrelevant to the explanation of decision behaviour. Decisions are not taken at random, nor do decision-makers believe the future to be beyond conjecture. But equally they do not believe it to be predictable with certainty. They plan on the basis of a set of beliefs, modifiable by experience, but not explicable by devices such as objective probability. A simple illustration may help. People do not go to railway stations at times chosen randomly. They consult timetables. But they treat the timetable as a forecast, not as 'certain knowledge': they do not assume that the trains will always run at the advertised times. The possibility of error is built into their plans, and has a cost attached to it (a girl will take an earlier train to avoid the possibility of being late for her wedding, but not to avoid the possibility of being late for a visit to her mother-in-law). Learning may modify planning (e.g. the discovery that in Britain the trains do not run at advertised times on Sunday), but will not change the fundamental propositions: there is no foundation for the proposition that 'learning' must always lead to 'better' decisions, and individuals do plan their behaviour on the basis that their decisions may be mistaken.

Of course, we can use historical information to establish the probability that trains will run on time, or within different divergences from predicted times. But planning concerns *the future*, and past probabilities can give only partial information about the possibility of any train tomorrow being on time.

In sum, learning helps (we rely on the sun rising) but can never make the economic problem predictable (fog may still stop us getting to the railway station) in a sense that 'explains' how individuals make decisions. People take decisions in the expectation of error, and 'planning error' is not of itself evidence of incompetence. Individuals will incorporate it into their planning process, and not mechanistically, but as part of the ongoing process of plan-revision (learning).

An amplification of this reformulation of the economic decision-process concerns the role of competition and innovation. The neo-classical model has no satisfactory explanation of innovation (since it is developed within the assumption of a given 'state of the arts'), and competition is seen as a co-ordinating mechanism (since plans always adjust in the 'right' direction to changes e.g. in preferences or relative prices). The Austrian School, in contrast, places emphasis on the role of innovation – 'taking advantage of unforeseen opportunities'. What receives inadequate recognition is the likelihood that the innovation of one decision-maker will result in the disappointment (in terms of expected outcome) of the plans of other decision-makers. By, for example, inducing a shift in demand, innovation and competition have as their incidental objective the frustration of the plans of others.

THE LOGIC OF CHOICE AND THE EXCHANGE RELATIONSHIP

The concentration of mainstream economics on two-person transactional exchange has already been pointed out. In addition, the standard formulation distinguishes decision-makers who are 'resource-allocators' (entrepreneurs) from other decision-makers who are allowed to take decisions only in restricted contexts and about specific matters – for example as demanders or as factors of production (wage earners). This formulation is incompatible with the decision-process I am here proposing, and, I would suggest, with the reality of the decision-processes relevant to an understanding of the real world. All individuals in a position to choose between alternative plans for the future are decision-makers. At least equally important, all decision contexts, and not only two-person exchange transactions, are relevant. (Indeed, the latter are probably not a very large proportion of all significant decisions.) Particularly, the centrality of participative behaviour needs to be recognised. Men choose to participate in collaborative groups (firms, trade unions, political parties and so on), even though they frequently sacrifice freedom of future action to do so. In so choosing, they are not ceasing to maximise their own expected well-being: they are simply predicting that a plan involving membership of the chosen co-operating group will result in a better personal outcome than would direct exchange or participation in some other group. Their behaviour is still explicable in terms of choice between plans and personal opportunity-cost. But the decision context is greatly broadened.

This argument is well-recognised in some specialised branches of the literature, such as the advanced theory of the firm, in which group-participative behaviour involving non-market transactions between members of the firm is integrated with market exchange behaviour involving the products, shares, etc. of the firm. It is less satisfactorily developed elsewhere, as for example in the economics of the family or the use of rational expectations to explain trade union behaviour. What is as yet lacking is general recognition of the need for an unified and comprehensive model embracing *all* the decision-situations relevant to resource-allocation outcomes − not only market exchange, but also the decision-processes of government and constitution-making, participation in relevant social groups (firms, families, unions, political parties, pressure groups): and so on.

Such a recognition is not needed to stimulate the specialist study of particular decision-situations. But it is needed for there to be acceptance of the view that the facts and predictions relevant to a more relevant positive economics need to be more broadly conceived than they now are. Non-market decision-situations are not simply extensions of the two-person exchange model, but integral parts of a complex decision-process.

ECONOMIC 'LAWS' AND ECONOMIC EFFICIENCY

Efficiency is of course a normative concept. It is proper to introduce it here, however, since there must necessarily be a relationship between the notions of efficiency that are thought interesting, and the positive predictions that economists set out to test.

First, a comment on the nature of economic 'laws'. It is dangerous to place too much faith in the notion that positive economics is likely to produce many 'laws' which are ineluctable and timeless. This does not mean that we should abandon hope, but that we should not expect too much, and should interpret our results with great caution. Physical 'laws' are predictions which are expected to be fulfilled only in carefully specified and controlled conditions: a physicist asked to predict what would happen to the next leaf to fall from a tree in my garden would not be willing to say much more than that it would probably fall towards the ground. The subject-matter of economics is difficult because it is concerned with human behaviour: the potential for controlled experiment is very severely restricted. Further, the fact that humans exercise free will (could slaves be trusted to produce precision machinery?) and learn from experience restricts the possibilities of continuously-reliable prediction. The most significant current example is the changing influence of Keynesian policies on employment levels. Economists may disagree about monetarist and Keynesian interpretations of what has been happening. But how many would deny that the changing relationship between deficit financing and unemployment has been fundamentally influenced by learning-induced behaviour changes?

These problems become more severe if the description I have given of the real-world economic problem is persuasive. Within the current orthodoxy, one might try to save the situation by building learning into the specification of the 'laws'. But this would imply some discoverable ongoing and reliable nexus between learning and individual plan-revision. This is hardly conceivable in a world in which individuals must appraise information for themselves and relate it to a truly uncertain (that is, unknowable) future. Further, the difficulties of interpreting the results of empirical testing become more severe (or, rather, become more obvious, since they are there anyway). How to distinguish, when interpreting results, between inadequacy of data, results imputable to failed plans, statistical correlations and genuinely causal relationships? Frequently, this seems to lead to positive economics becoming a search for the 'best' correlations which are then treated as causal without much concern for their behavioural implica-tions. Of course, causality can never be 'proved'. But the 'credibility gaps' are greater in economics than in the physical sciences. Publica-tion of the falsification of predictions of articulated behavioural assumptions is relatively rare.

Second, the notion of an efficiency yardstick related to the optimum conditions of choice becomes much less helpful in the much broader choice-situation now being proposed, the more so in that all choices are subjective and do not have outcomes known with certainty. In this new context, freedom of choice cannot be concerned simply with mechan-istic problems of resource-allocation through markets. In so far as it is not treated as an end in itself, irrespective of its consequences for economic efficiency, it is as much concerned with questions of con-stitutions, trade union law and so on, as with the behaviour of markets treating other decision-situations as 'inputs'. The implication of this is the need for a major shift in emphasis from general 'efficiency' concepts towards, for example, the positive study of the consequences of institutional change, without too much concern with prescription, of which economists have no monopoly. This would not reduce their influence on policy. Currently, an important reason why their policy proposals are ignored or questioned is that their normative origins are remote from those of policy-makers. (Consider this: a policy derived from the static logic of choice will legislate against all forms of monopoly. But the value of the freedom to innovate depends upon the existence of some form of property right in the results of invention. Thus, innovation and monopoly are part of a common problem. A useful positive approach to the problem thus needs to incorporate predictions about both monopoly laws and patent laws, etc., as well as about the consequences of inhibition of choice for current consumption and economic change.)

Finally, a word about equilibrium. The mathematical modelling of the orthodox logic of choice has led economists to concern themselves increasingly with the question of whether a postulated situation is 'consistent with equilibrium' − that is, will produce an eventual outcome in which all plans are fulfilled and outcomes consistent, so that there is no further 'tendency to change'. This 'consistency with equilibrium' is commonly treated, implicitly or explicitly, as an efficiency concept. But in a truly uncertain world, in which plans are subject to continuous revision as new information emerges, the consistency of a given present set of plans with an eventual equilibrium outcome is no doubt intellectually interesting but of little practical utility. Attempts have been made to overcome this problem by programming 'learning' into the model, so that the eventual consistency situation emerges from plan-revision. But the attempts fail, as the authors themselves acknowledge, if there is no unique relationship between learning and plan-revision, and if the future is unknowable and cannot be restricted to a finite set of possibilities. Equilibrium is a fascinating intellectual toy. But it is irrelevant to the real problems of economics, and should be dropped from our vocabulary.

SOME SPECIFIC SUGGESTIONS

To conlude, I will comment on a few possibilities that seem to me potentially fruitful. The list is suggestive rather than exhaustive, and in part reflects a few interests of my own. I expect some of the suggestions to be examined more thoroughly in other papers.

PROBABILITY AND POSSIBILITY

There is room for more exhaustive consideration of the possibility of replacing objective probability, whose use in positive economics I have criticised, by Shackle's notion of bounded possibility. This sees decision-makers as choosing between a set of plans that they conceive to be possible of implementation and which may produce a desired outcome. The reformulation, which is to be found in Shackle's earlier work and will be discussed in his lecture, offers the potential for fusion of the notions that decision-makers do not believe the future to be beyond conjecture, but are also not surprised by unforeseen outcomes. It could therefore contribute to the reintegration of mathematical and conceptual approaches to the economic problem, the need for which I have earlier emphasised.

A MORE DIRECT APPROACH TO THE STUDY OF 'ECONOMIC' BEHAVIOUR

This has several facets:

The rejection of 'mechanistic' formulations of the economic problem and their substitution by comparative-behavioural ones. For example, rules for pricing-by-cost treat costs as objective − that is, as existing 'outside' the subjective judgements of decision-makers. They are irrelevant in a world of which this is not true, as has been demonstrated by their practical irrelevance to the decision-problems of nationalised industries and public enterprises. (The multi-part pricing public utility literature is a calculation of relative prices on the basis of restrictive assumptions about technology and demand. It is really an engineering-type input to the actual decision-process through time which is concerned with the planning and replanning of investment, prices, etc., through time in the face of an unpredictable future. To appreciate this point, consider what would happen to all the multi-part electricity tariffs if someone invented an effective generator small enough to be purchased and operated by individual households. The instruction to UK nationalised industries to price their products at marginal cost proved unworkable (uninterpretable?), and, practically, has been abandoned.)

An alternative and more useful approach is to attempt to predict changes in the behaviour of enterprises when institutional conditions change. Thus, nationalisation changes the decision authority, property rights, rewards and penalties, of the various 'actors' contributing to production, as well as changing the cast of actors itself. By comparing the (formal) situation before and after nationalisation, it is possible, at least conceptually, to develop hypotheses about the consequent changes in decision-processes and outcomes. The collection and interpretation of evidence will be neither easy nor tidy: but the results are potentially more policy-relevant than anything we have now.

The direct study of human behaviour. Economists are rightly suspicious of attempts to turn them into applied psychologists. But the time has come to broaden our subject from the study of the implications of 'rational' behaviour, as economists choose to define rationality, to the study of *actual* behaviour in so far as we can observe and interpret it.

Demand theory illustrates the point. It uses a concept of rational choice to demonstrate why and when more of a good will be purchased when price falls, but with some exceptions is not concerned with *why* people choose as they do, or with the fact that their predicted behaviour is one aspect of the kind of subjective planning with which this paper is concerned. In this regard, it is noteworthy that the notion of 'the' market demand curve is part of the *lingua franca* of economics. If challenged, economists will acknowledge that market demand curves are graphic presentations of forecasts, although few seem to think this worth more than a passing comment. But if the future is unknown, there are as many demand curves (forecasts) as there are individuals with an interest in the product. If demand theory were about what actually determines the demand for products, one would expect producers to make use of it in their planning. The fact that they turn elsewhere is evidence of the inadequacy of the subjective postulates and the lack of concern of 'economic rationality' with the unpredictability of outcomes.

It is interesting to observe that economists have begun trying to test the predictions of demand theory by conducting controlled experiments using rats and other species. These experiments appear to confirm the laws of demand derived from 'mainstream' economics almost too well for someone who adheres to the arguments I have made in this paper. But the preference set of the rats is severely constrained by the experimental conditions, and uncertainty is restricted to the periods of 'learning', outside of which plan predictions are not disappointed. The practically interesting results will emerge if and when these conditions are relaxed. Pavlov's experiments indicated that complete uncertainty produces madness or apathy: the interesting results will be those in which plans are sometimes fulfilled, but sometimes disappointed, and this in a non-systematic fashion.

Other papers will I hope have more to say on this subject. I will say only that economics as a behavioural science can no longer stand aloof from psychology.

Business decision-making. Linking this topic with the previous one, there is room for development of the study of the ways business decision-makers actually acquire and process information. An interesting development in this regard has evolved from the disciplines of artificial intelligence and cognitive psychology. This is the *production systems* approach. The production system provides a framework for the development of rule-based systems for modelling economic behaviour. A production system model has three elements: a data or information base, a set of production rules and an interpreter. The production rules are decision rules, indicating how the information in the data base provides the basis for decision-making. The interpreter provides the underlying control structure of economic behaviour (loosely, the firm's corporate plan). The appealing feature of this approach is that, while it is behavioural in character and can embrace the conceptualisation of uncertainty and non-market decision-processes advocated in this paper, it also lends itself to computer simulation and hence has the potential to contribute to the intellectual reintegration of the subject.

This development in turn would overlap naturally with another one: the need for a more direct concern with the way business decisions are reached. We shall be hearing something about this from someone actually involved in the process. I myself find fascinating the relation between identification of possible plans (e.g. the use of 'scenarios' to evaluate the consequence of conceived future events); and the choice between the plans which remain worth considering after the first step has been taken. This procedure is intellectually consonant with both the notion of bounded possibility and with the production systems approach. But it is not the only way the decision-problem can be approached: where better to learn more than from those who take the decisions?

In this regard, the alienation of 'business studies' using a 'case study' approach from economics as a study of 'rational' economic behaviour seems to me another limitation of our present positivism: the two should surely belong within a common intellectual construct, and that necessarily a subjective one?

THE STUDY OF COMPARATIVE ECONOMIC SYSTEMS

I have chosen this final example because it provides support for a proposition made earlier that, while the kind of 'new' positivism that I am advocating is likely to be less intellectually or empirically 'tidy' than what we have now, it has the potential to be more relevant to the world we live in.

With a few notable exceptions, the literature concerned with the comparative performance of different systems is singularly unsatisfying, commonly degenerating into a combination of description and advocacy.

It seems to me that the formulation of the economic problem here proposed has the capacity to generate many more interesting testable propositions than now emerge. The general approach I have in mind is the one already described in relation to the study of nationalised industries, and I shall not develop it further. Essentially, it calls for the systematic study of the behavioural (decision-making) consequences of specified changes in the property rights, benefits, penalties, etc. of the relevant economic 'actors' within their *total* (not just market) decision-environment. (To take one simple example, there are good grounds for hypothesising that there will be less innovation (in the sense of the emergence of new products) in the USSR than in the USA: and it should not be impossible to collect evidence bearing upon this.)

2   The Bounds of Unknowledge

G. L. S. SHACKLE

A question faces every one at almost every hour: what will the sequel be, if I do this, or if I do this? Whence can the answer to that question come, what form will it take, what force will it have, how will the questioner make use of it? The question admits of no escape, for even to sit silent and motionless is to take a course of action. What resources are at hand to help answer it? The individual has a conception of the technology of nature and of the capacities and propensities of human nature. Thus he has notions of the sort of thing that can take place. But when he sets himself to choose a course of action out of many which seem open to him, he may implicitly assume himself to be making history, on however small a scale, in some sense other than mere passive obedience to the play of all-pervasive causes. He may assume that his act of choice is in some respects an *absolute origination*, something not wholly implicit in antecedents, he may deem his thoughts to be not entirely determinate, but able to come in part *ex nihilo*. If choice can be of this kind, I shall call such an act of choice a *beginning*. It is a taking-place in some respects uncaused, yet it can help to shape its sequel. It is then an *uncaused cause*. A beginning in this sense is out of reach of foreknowledge. We cannot know in our present whether or when a beginning, a choice in part uncaused, may occur in time-to-come, or what may be its character. We cannot know these things by inspection, for there is no inspecting time-to-come. We cannot know them by inference from causal circumstances operating in the present, for the power to do this would contradict the essential nature of a beginning. Then, if choices can be beginnings in our sense, the question what will the sequel be of some specified action cannot legitimately be given only one single, solitary, self-consistent and unified answer. For the sequel will be partly the work of many people's choices-to-come whose character, if they can be beginnings, the chooser of present action cannot know. He is free to invent answers concerning the sequel in numbers unlimited by anything in their nature, in a business of invention only to be halted by his arrival at a deadline for decision. That deadline will find him with a list of answers incomplete and essentially uncompletable. Are we then saying that, for all the chooser can tell, any choice whatever of present action can have any sequel whatever? If this were so, the choosing of action would be wholly without effect, powerless and pointless. If in the chooser's thought choice is to be effective, if a choice is to be a cause, each choosable course of action must be linked with some imagined sequels, or some combination of imagined sequels, which belong to this course alone. What can effect such a discriminated linkage? The means of action, which give the chooser the power to do this, *or* to do this, or this, will be an array of material things and of human employable capacities each able to be used in any one of many different ways in endless different combinations of uses. The choosing of action will consist in the chooser's committing himself to set his array of means in motion in some exclusive way. By excluding all other ways that were open to him, the choose excludes some sequels that he could have *imagined and deemed possible*. They are excluded because materials, tools and brains that were essential to them have been denied them by the chooser's mode of inception of his enterprise, by their pre-emption for processes incompatible with those sequels. The excluded sequels may comprise some which are desired and some which are counter-desired. Choice of action is effective by *what it does not exclude*. For what does the act of choice do for the chooser? It gives to some, by denying to others, of his works of imagination a seriousness, an epistemic standing of a particular kind and quality, it gives them *possibility*, freedom from known obstruction. Imagination may be said to have two levels, two intensities. At one level, it is merely pictorial, a cloud-scape. At the other it has the power to enter the counsels of the mind, to present itself as something weighable, judgeable, pursuable. Choice of action decides which works of the chooser's imagination shall be lifted to this second level. If in the chooser's thought this freedom is complete, if possibility is perfect, this is the best that can be done to give the imagined sequels validity in their bearing on his business of choice. If, as my argument suggests, present action is at the mercy of choices-to-come which can be beginnings, the highest epistemic standing that is logically attainable by its envisaged sequels is that of perfect possibility.

We said that effective choice depends on each choosable course of action having some imagined sequels, or some combination of sequels, which belong to it exclusively (others it may share with other courses). This requirement could be satisfied in the abstract by sequels distributed over a limitless range of diversity, so that the mutual unlikeness of sequels envisaged for one-and-the-same course were subject to no constraint. But this would present the chooser with a picture of a daunting degree of complexity. Sequels envisaged for a variety of courses would perhaps be mutually interspersed. To hold lucidly in thought the selective linkage of sequels of wide-ranging mutual unlikeness with the various courses open to him would be excessively difficult. But such a conception is unreal. The sequels suggested to imagination by any one inceptive use of his resources will have at least this origin in common. They start the race from the same mark. But it is not only what, given this common start, the chooser can deem possible, but also what he desires and will by his subsequent actions seek to bring about, and what his practical conscience insists that he shall prepare his mind for, that make the sequels imagined and deemed possible for any one inceptive course of action to be in some respects kith and kin, and entitles us to think of them as a skein, the mutual unlikeness of whose members is *bounded*.

The chooser's array of means of action can be compared to the collection of chessmen which are on the board at some stage of the game. For each of them the player knows its powers in general and the scope given to those powers by its position on the board in relation to other pieces. From most states of the game the course of play can take any one of a very great number of different paths. But there are also a very great number of configurations of the chessmen which, within some specified number of moves, are unattainable from the existing configuration. The chess game provides in some respects a suggestive analogy for the predicament of the action-chooser in the general field.

We have reached the notion of a skein of sequels imagined and deemed possible for some course of action and not all of them possible for any other. Any one sequel will require for its description many statements of physical quantities, money values and human performances and utterances. This we may call a technological account. It presents the character of the sequel in all those respects which can bear on the chooser's task of deciding on one course out of many which are open to him. But comparisons of one sequel with another in the performance of this task cannot be made directly by means of such a technological description, for when two sequels are compared, one may be more desired than the other in one respect but less desired in another.

The two respects must then be relatively weighted in order to see with which sequel the balance of advantage lies. Such a procedure of assigning weights, when carried through the whole gamut of respects in which the two sequels are to be compared, provides a measure of the desiredness of each sequel as a whole. It is a product of relative valuation. When every sequel in every skein has been assigned a degree of desiredness, we can conceive each sequel to be represented by a point on an axis measuring, or ranking, degrees of desiredness or counter-desiredness. A skein of sequels will thus be represented by a set of points on this axis. Each such point represents something deemed possible on condition of an appropriate choice of action, and desired or counter-desired in greater or less degree. How can the set of such points representing one skein of sequels and thus one available course of action be compared with the set representing another skein? The solution flows from the nature of *possibility* as we are conceiving it. When each of the choosable courses of action, the different ways the chooser can envisage of setting in motion his array of resources, has been supplied by him, by way of plural rival sequels, with products of imagination exempt, in his thought, from fatal obstacles to their being realised, and when each of the choosables thus conceived has been assigned a set of points on the axis of valuation or desiredness, each imagined sequel will have been given two characteristics: some degree of desiredness or counter-desiredness, and the quality of unobstructedness in the chooser's thought. Unobstructedness is here, for us, a characteristic which can be possessed or not possessed by some creation of thought, but which we do not yet regard as varying in degree. An imagined history-to-come is, for our immediate argument, either possible or not possible. This means that we do not discriminate amongst imagined sequels on grounds of possibility: all those that are possible are *equally possible*.

Possibility means for us a character of the individual's thought, the absence from it, when he considers some imagined taking-place in time-to-come, of any obstacle that he can discern to its coming true. If he can discern no obstacle at all, possibility is *perfect*, his degree of *disbelief* in the hypothetical taking-place is zero. The two expressions here used, perfect possibility, zero disbelief, are two expressions of a degree of *epistemic standing*, that is, of the claim of the hypothesis in question to an audience in his self-counsels of decision, its claim to exert upon him without qualification or diminution such influence as its desiredness or counter-desiredness merits. When he finds upon examination that the possibility, given his present knowledge, is perfect, he is conceding the highest degree of epistemic standing, the degree which represents the upper bound of the range of assignable degrees. Can we attach any meaning to an intensifying or reinforcement of this state of thought? Suppose that the eventuality in question can be the upshot of any one of several paths of history-to-come. What bearing has this? If a building can be entered by any one of several doors, entry into it is assured by the openness of one sole door, and access is not made more real by the openness of several doors. The absence of obstacles from one route does not need, and does not allow of or afford meaning to, reinforcement by the absence of obstacles from other routes. Perfect possibility is not a matter of the piling up of 'evidence' or of suggestions, but of the existence in thought of one unobstructed path. It follows that when an available course of action is linked by the action-chooser with a skein of rival imagined sequels all deemed perfectly, and therefore equally, possible, and when these sequels are represented by a set of points on an axis of desiredness or valuation, the sequels whose points are in the interior of the range of the points as a whole have no claim to the action-chooser's attention, for they are *eclipsed* by sequels equally possible but more desired or counter-desired. This we can express otherwise by saying that since no point on the desiredness or valuation axis has any advantage of epistemic standing over any other, it follows that the best result which the *skein as a whole* can suggest is that one suggested by the most desired individual sequel, while the threat posed by the most counter-desired sequel is the threat posed by the skein as a whole, since interior sequels *offer no defence* against this worst one. Our conclusion is that the whole force and effect of the set of points belonging to the skein as a whole resides in the two extreme points. When we divide all hypotheses into possible and not-possible, it is only the valuation-extremes of the 'possible' set which count.

In the frame of thought that I have outlined, the business of choice of action is conceived to proceed in three phases. The first is imaginative, the origination of various inceptive modes of use of the chooser's array of means of action, and the conceiving, for each such mode, a skein of rival imagined sequels. The second phase is that of critical examination. The sequels which, in such time as his deadline or some exterior signal allows him, the chooser has invented for any one mode, must be *tested for possibility*. The path of each must be scanned for obstacles. Those sequels which emerge unscathed are the basis of the claim of the particular course of action or mode of inceptive use of resources to be the chosen one. The third phase is that of valuation. Each sequel imagined and deemed possible for some course of action must be assigned a representative point on an axis of desiredness—counter-desiredness. The two extreme members of any such set of points are the final specification of the course of action in question. Such pairs of *focus-points* (as I have habitually called them) may stand in any one of three kinds of relation to each other. The chooser may settle on a greatest tolerable degree of undesiredness (if his valuations are in money terms, the greatest tolerable loss) and out of those courses whose worst outcomes do not exceed this limit, choose the one whose 'desired' outcome is the best. A more general method will first exclude from consideration all those pairs of focus-points whose best outcome is less good, and whose worst outcome is worse, than those of some other available course. This will leave him with the task of deciding what degree of extra badness of its 'bad' outcome can be outweighed, for some course, by the extra goodness of its good outcome.

If thoughts can be absolute originations in some part of their character, if choices can be in some respects absolved and exempt from entire governance by cause, the content of time-to-come is not merely unknown but non-existent, and the notion of foreknowledge of human affairs is vacuous. Then the effort to gather enough data to establish an unique path of history-to-come can be renounced in favour of the discipline of possibility. We ask, not what will take place but what can take place on condition of our acting thus or thus. This is an essentially different posture of thought from that which regards unknowledge as a deficiency, a falling-short, a failure of search and study. This latter attitude leads us to say that one hypothesis of the sequel of specified action must be right *ex ante facto* and not merely *ex post facto*. If that were so, we could legitimately seek to determine and specify, perhaps numerically, the claim to rightness of any hypothesis, we could seek to put a figure on that claim, we could try to calculate its probability. The claim of an unique supposed path of history-to-come to be right is an *exclusive* claim. If one answer to the question, what will the sequel be if I do this, is right *ex ante*, and not merely *ex post*, answers which disagree with it are wrong. The more probable are some answers to the question, the less probable must some others be. Probability is *distributed* over hypotheses. By contrast, possibility is non-exclusive, is not distributive, is not limited in the number of rival, mutually exclusive ideas, answers, imagined sequels to which, in highest degree, or any stated degree, it can be accorded. The possibility, in itself, of one sequel does not, for example, by any means, in any degree, defend the chooser from acknowledging the possibility of a less-desired or counter-desired sequel of his contemplated action.

When we take possibility to be assignable to each of many rival answers or hypotheses, regardless of its being also assigned to others, we are ascribing to it an essential nature quite different from that of probability. The possibility of some hypothesis does not by its pure acceptance diminish that of others. The chooser having invented some answers to his question concerning the sequel of specified action, and having assigned them possibility, is by no means thereby precluded from inventing others and yet others, and assigning possibility to them. Any thought of 'adding together' the possibility of one answer and that of another and so on is wholly vacuous and meaningless. Possibility as I am using this term is primarily qualitative and not essentially quantitative. It represents the absence of something, the absence of discernible obstruction, and thus, of the natural product of recognised obstruction, *disbelief*. Possibility is absence of disbelief, and we can make explicit the non-additive nature of the possibility of this and of that rival hypothesis, by using as a synonym for possibility the expression zero disbelief. The adding together of zeros will not attract us.

At this point I could declare my theme complete. If I am allowed the premises or the policies of thought that I have asked for, I think the structure can stand by itself. But if, as it were, we take our stand upon it and look outwards, there is ground to be explored, the structural elements when tapped sometimes ring out a question. The last such element we put in place especially does so. To speak of *zero* disbelief prompts the question whether it may not be meaningful, and even obligatory, to consider other degrees of disbelief? Yet, in what terms, by reference to what direct sentiments, to what self-subsisting means of comparison, or to what metrical scale, can we define and locate degrees of disbelief? Disbelief is an intellection, something which has, in itself, form rather than intensity. What psychic experience can we find, that will reflect these forms as intensities? There is one emotion which directly springs from the combination of some formal kind or source of disbelief, and an actual taking-place which belies that disbelief. This is the feeling of *surprise*. The individual may be supposed to ask himself: How much or little should I be surprised if, with no relevant change in my present knowledge, such-and-such occurred? Potential surprise seems to me a practical link between formal and emotional disbelief.

We can approach the same question from a different starting-point. In my core-argument I proposed to treat the question: Is such-and-such a taking-place possible? as a Yes or No question. We had the two categories of 'possible' and 'not possible'. Could we treat these two

notions as the bounds of an interval? To do so would of course be to
step outside our core-argument. The epistemic interval so defined
would be necessary to the notion of degrees of disbelief. They must
needs be located within it. If in any sense there is a scale of disbelief or
of potential surprise, its range must be the epistemic interval. If such a
construction is permissible, how can we translate our core-argument
into its terms?

I think it natural to suppose that the power of any imagined sequel of
some course of action to arrest the chooser's attention will rest, in the
first place, on its own desiredness or counter-desiredness and on the
degree of disbelief in which the chooser holds it. Its power to arrest
attention, what I have been accustomed to call its *ascendancy*, will I
think be an increasing function of its desiredness or counter-desiredness
and a decreasing function of its potential surprise. When desiredness–
counter-desiredness is represented by some variable such as money
profit or loss, it may well be the case that, in contemplating some
enterprise–investment, a business man will assign zero potential
surprise, or zero disbelief, to a considerable range of quantities on either
side of zero for the total discounted operating profits-to-come of the
investment. Beyond the upper and lower bounds of this 'inner range'
any larger supposed profit, or larger loss, will have assigned to it some
greater than zero degree of disbelief, and this degree, it seems natural to
suppose, will be an increasing function of the excess. At some point,
then, there will be a constrained maximum of the ascendancy on the
'profit' side and another on the 'loss' side, each being a point where
increasing suppositions of profit, or of loss, are just offset by increasing
disbelief. There is, of course, no reason at all why the configurations on
the two sides should be symmetrical. Many questions present themselves in regard to this illustration of my suggested reform or refinement
of the core-argument, the suggestion of degrees of possibility in the
interior of the epistemic interval. The supposition of a continuous inner
range of hypotheses assigned zero disbelief is only appropriate to such a
context as profit–loss. Another question concerns the 'neutral'
hypothesis which, being neither desired nor counter-desired, serves as a
bench-mark from which to state the distances of other hypotheses as
expressions of their degrees of desiredness. At first sight it might seem
that the individual should be able to name or locate the neutral outcome
by a direct consultation of his desires. But except where the effect of
rival hypotheses on him is aesthetic or where they possess some other
absolute value or dis-value, he must ground his selection of a neutral
outcome on some less immediately intuitive or instinctive principle.

We might suggest that the neutral outcome is one whose realisation would make him neither better nor worse off. But on what basis does he judge how well off he is? This will depend on the entire range of outcomes that seem possible, not merely as the sequel of one particular course but as sequels of any available course. The neutral outcome ought on some principle to divide all possible sequels into two groups of equal ascendancy. I cannot doubt that the individual, envisaging some specific sequel of a contemplated action of his own, can decide, perhaps by an arcane thought-process such as constitutes the bulk of our psychic being, whether the sequel is desired or counter-desired.

The two constrained maxima of ascendancy, whose existence it seems to me reasonable to postulate very generally, may themselves be accepted as the focus-points of the extended construction. One objection which may be raised is that each of these is a point in a two-space and that they are thus not directly comparable on a single scale: they are not 'scalars'. They can, however, be reduced to scalar quantities by means of the notion of ascendancy. In a three-dimensional Cartesian frame let the west—east axis stand for desiredness—counter-desiredness, or gain and loss, with a point dividing it into two rays, the eastern for gain and the western for loss. From this same point or origin, let the south—north axis stand for degrees of disbelief, with a range extending from zero disbelief or perfect possibility at the origin to an absolute maximum for impossibility. Within the region defined by the two axes and by a line of absolute maximum disbelief parallel to the west—east axis, any point will stand for an association of some gain, or some loss, and its assigned disbelief. Let a third axis orthogonal to the plane of gain—loss—disbelief represent degrees of ascendancy. In our illustrative case, the points representing ascendancy will lie in a surface of two sheets, one for gain and one for loss. On each of these sheets, equal-ascendancy curves will enable any point with greater-than-zero disbelief to have found for it a point having equal ascendancy and zero disbelief. Thus the two constrained maxima can be substituted by points respectively of lesser gain or loss, and zero disbelief. These points will lie on the gain—loss axis and their distances from the origin will be scalar quantities. In the deepened or refined version of my argument they are the focus-points.

It will perhaps be asked whether, in putting forward a wholly unconventional and even eccentric view of the nature of choice, and grounding it in ideas unusual and even unheard of in economics, such as the notion of uncause in thought, the imaginative and originative source and nature of the choosables, and the endless proliferant creation of hypothetical sequels of choosable action, I wish to emphasise what I am calling the core-argument in its rather spare and harsh simplifications, or by contrast the deepened form which recognises levels of disbelief other than zero or absolute, and which lends itself to a number of possibly fertile manipulations. My answer is that the respective purposes are distinct. In order to gain some critical attention for ideas which at first, to 'mainstream' economic theoreticians, are naturally rebarbative, the argument is best presented in its basic and most essential lineaments, by which it must stand or fall. But we are all indoctrinated with ideals of mathematical incisive sculpture of thought, even of achieving, in however modest a degree, mathematical beauty, the surprising revelation of necessity. I am not sure that these ideals and ambitions are true for us, whose subject-matter is the ineffably mysterious, mutable and subtle nature and capacities of man. Least of all am I supposing that my theme can touch these ideals or even glimpse them. These two contrasting purposes, however, are the reason for the presentation of my theme in two editions. What, then, is that cord on which such beads as I have tried to carve are strung? It is an attempted answer to the question: What can the action-chooser, the decision-maker, *know*, and with what content can the word 'know' be used when describing his business of choice?

I have suggested, in effect, that he can tell himself where possibility reaches it limits, he can trace upon his thought map of imagined things a boundary-fence beyond which, given his resources, given his time-horizon for reaping the fruits of action, no action of his can reach. In a sense which has some degree of paradox, his knowledge is of the non-possible. It is beyond the fence that everything can be tagged with effective certainty as not belonging to the attainable. Unknowledge, for him, consists in *the plurality of rival possibles*. The bounds of the possible are bounds of unknowledge.

3   Subjectivism and Method in Economics

STEPHEN LITTLECHILD

RELATION TO THE GENERAL THEME OF SECTION F

My first duty is to relate the topic of my paper to the general theme of 'Beyond Positive Economics?' around which all the papers of Section F are organised.

The term 'positive economics' has two distinct but not unrelated meanings. As John Neville Keynes (1891) puts it, a positive science is 'a body of systematized knowledge concerning what is', thereby standing in contrast to a normative science which is 'a body of systematized knowledge discussing criteria of what ought to be'. The second meaning refers to a specific method for developing the above positive science of economics, namely, one which stresses the formulation and empirical testing of hypotheses, and which thereby stands in contrast to, for example, inductivism or *a priorism*.

In his presidential address (see Chapter 1 of this book), Professor Wiseman uses a third and broader interpretation of the term. He is concerned at what he sees as an overemphasis on empirical testing, but he is even more concerned about the kinds of models which economic theory produces for testing. In effect, he is appraising the current state of economics, with special reference to positive economics. That is the line I shall take also.

SUBJECTIVISM

Most, if not all, of the contributors to this year's Section F share a belief in the importance of subjectivism. They would probably sympathise with Hayek's famous dictum to the effect that 'every important advance in economic theory during the last hundred years was a further step in the consistent application of subjectivism' (Hayek, 1955, p. 31). My purpose in this paper is to explore some of the implications for economics of the subjectivist ideas embodied in recent writings on scientific methodology, and to suggest areas where traditional subjectivist approaches may need revision.

To explain what subjectivism is, however, is by no means an easy task. As Lachmann (1981) has pointed out, 'subjectivism has come to mean different things to thinkers of successive generations, . . . [and] the term has gradually acquired a wider and wider meaning'. It will probably be helpful to illustrate by a few examples.

1. The earliest achievement of subjectivism was the subjective theory of value: the idea that the value of an object is determined by the preferences of those who appraise it, and is not inherent in the object appraised (as implied, for example, by the labour theory of value).
2. Later writers such as Mises (1966, p. 21) interpreted subjectivism as meaning that different men pursue different ends. For economists these ends are to be taken as given, and paradoxically it is in this sense that the objectivity of economics lies.
3. Hayek (1955, p. 29) emphasised the fact that different men know different things. The market process is one of discovery, and stands in contrast to the equilibrium state characteristic of perfect information models.
4. Wiseman and the late G. F. Thirlby have argued that cost is subjective: that it refers not to a *thing* but to an *action*, that in choosing one action rather than another the chooser has to sacrifice the outcome of some other action, and that this opportunity-cost necessarily reflects the chooser's own valuation of the best alternative he had in mind. On this view, the injunction to nationalised industries to set price equal to cost is, at best, unclear. (See Buchanan and Thirlby, 1973, chaps 6–11.)
5. Most recently, Professor Shackle (1972) has extended subjectivism to incorporate the idea that different men have different expectations about the future. It is not merely that their probability distributions have different values, but that the domains over which these are defined are in principle quite distinct. Men are creative, and different men have different visions. The 'kaleidic process' which results from this fact stands in contrast to the equilibrating market process emphasised by previous subjectivist writers.

Wiseman (Chapter 1) and Loasby (Chapter 7) have emphasised the resulting learning process at the level of the individual and the firm.

What is the common thread in these examples? It seems to be an emphasis on the role of the 'human factor' in economics, and in particular upon the fact that the specific content of the human mind differs from one individual to another. In the next few sections I shall attempt to explore some further implications of this theme. I do not claim any particular originality for these ideas, only that it may be helpful to collect together the implications for and of subjectivism as noted by a diverse set of scholars.

KUHN ON SCIENTIFIC METHODOLOGY

Mises and Hayek, the major subjectivist economists of recent time, wrote extensively on methodology and their views have largely been accepted by later subjectivist economists (notably those of the Austrian School, but including also the influential writings of Robbins (1935)). During the last couple of decades, however, accepted ideas on scientific methodology have been dramatically challenged by T. S. Kuhn (1970) (and, to a lesser extent perhaps, by the related ideas of Lakatos). Now it so happens that Kuhn can be regarded as a subjectivist − indeed, one philosopher (Hilary Putnam) has described him as *too* subjectivist. It is therefore appropriate to enquire how far Kuhn's ideas are consistent with those of Mises and Hayek, and what implications they have for methodology in economics.

Central to Kunn's ideas is the notion of paradigms, that is, shared bodies of knowledge, perceptions and beliefs as to what the world is like, what the important issues are and how progress is to be made. At any time − especially in an allegedly 'immature' science such as economics − there is likely to be more than one competing paradigm. As a result, there will be disagreement as to the general 'state of the art' and as to the merit or significance of specific pieces of work.

All this is well known, and I shall illustrate in a moment. But first, it seems worthwhile to point out that *this can be seen as a further extension of subjectivism − from the people being investigated to the people doing the investigating. Just as different men have different tastes, preferences, values, knowledge, perceptions and expectations, so do different economists.* It is this extension of subjectivism which will concern us for the next few sections.

THE NEED FOR TOLERANCE OF METHOD

To illustrate this point, consider the different emphases which different economists place on the various components of a theory. *A priorists* stress the assumptions, mathematical economists stress the deductive logic and positivists stress the predictions. To some extent, of course, these preferences reflect the dictates of a methodological position. But is the position each economist adopts quite independent of his own personal tastes? Is it not quite natural for one economist to place great emphasis on achieving an intuitively reasonable basis for a theory, for another to be concerned about clarity and internal consistency, and for yet another to want to see the empirical proof of whatever assumptions and deductions are made? Surely we must conclude that a subjectivist must be tolerant of a wide variety of approaches, even though he himself may prefer one or the other.

This is not say, of course, that for a subjectivist 'anything goes' with respect to methodology (as Feyerabend argues). He will reject models which, for example, make impossible assumptions about the kind of knowledge which agents can possess, or which attribute behaviour to agents which ignores their personal aims and circumstances. He will not accept 'prediction' as the equivalent of 'explanation'. He will insist on the importance of 'understanding' the observed or postulated behaviour. And yet – he must acknowledge that a high (or low) correlation coefficient may contribute useful information merely by posing the question why it is so, and a logically clear model based on 'false' assumptions *may* conceivably enlighten us as to how the world does *not* work (cf. Mises, 1966, pp. 236–7, on the method of imaginary constructions).

Hayek (1979) has recently doubted whether the extensive discussion of scientific method has led to a great improvement in the quality of scientific work. At the same time, one could also emphasise the extent to which scientific progress has depended upon accident and error. It is increasingly difficult to be dogmatic about what methods ought to be used, and which are of no value whatsoever. Philosophers of science seem to be coming to the view that a few rules of thumb (for example, test where possible) are all one can hope for (see Putnam, 1978). Subjectivists have a reasonably clear view of the kinds of models which seem helpful, but there is room for differences of opinion here.

PREDICTIONS, LOGIC AND ASSUMPTIONS

As noted earlier, Kuhn pointed out that economists subscribing to different paradigms will view the world differently. We consider here some of the implications for particular methodological views.

Friedman (1953) and his followers argue that empirical testing of predictions is the appropriate (indeed, the only) way to discriminate between alternative hypotheses. But what constitutes an adequate test and a convincing result? People differ in their evaluation of the evidence. A case in point is the controversy over the 'concentration doctrine' – the claim that greater concentration allows greater collusion which in turn yields higher profits. A great number of empirical tests have now been carried out, yet there is little sign of agreement between the proponents and opponents (see Goldschmidt *et al.*, 1974). Each further piece of evidence is hailed as supporting or convincing by the side it favours, and as misleading or irrelevant by the other side. It would not be true to say that no progress at all is made in such debates, since frequently it is thought appropriate to withdraw from what turns out to be an oversimple ('naive') formulation of the argument. But the speed of the 'retreat' and 'advance' seem to be dictated by a variety of considerations other than the empirical evidence (notably the significance of the result for policy, and the attractiveness of other avenues or areas of research). In sum, to expect that economic hypotheses can be or will be judged purely in the light of 'the empirical evidence' on their predictions is to ignore the subjective element in the behaviour of economists.

MATHEMATICAL METHOD

One defence of mathematical economics is that it establishes more precisely the limits of our knowledge, and clarifies why certain propositions are or are not true. Critics have countered that the use of mathematics contributes no new knowledge, and is therefore unnecessary. Surely we have to recognise here that standards of rigour change over time. What in the nineteenth century was regarded as a formal proof may now be regarded as informal 'handwaving'. (To some extent this is linked with the desire for greater generality, which necessitates representing apparently different situations in similar formal language.) The opposition of some subjectivists to mathematics *per se* seems untenable. More interesting is the question how far mathematics can be used to represent and analyse the process of creating and changing expectations, which subjectivists would hold to be essential to a proper understanding of economic phenomena.

A PRIORISM

Mises argued that the only way to verify the truth of economic theory was to trace it back to its roots in human action. Certain fundamental propositions he called *a priori* true since they were fundamental to human nature, and a necessary precondition for subsequent analysis. But can there not be differences of opinion, even among subjectivists, as to the fundamental characteristics of human nature? Are we not involved here in matters of psychology, upon which even psychologists have differences of opinion? In a later section I wish to explore two aspects of this idea, but let us merely note here that, if the reservation is accepted, the *a priori* method is not an unambiguous way of resolving disputes. Even for subjectivists, logical clarity and the realism or fruitfulness of predictions may have a role to play in the choice of assumptions about human nature.

PURPOSE IN SCIENTIFIC RESEARCH

It is conventional to assume that knowledge is pursued altruistically for its own sake, yet biographies and autobiographies of scientists frequently reveal more human passions − to be first in the field, to prove a pet hypothesis or to disprove a rival's theory. Two examples in the methodology of economics are not difficult to find. Hutchison (1977, p. 59) suggested that 'Popper's prescriptions and criteria . . . were devised to counter the claims to omniscience and irrefutability of a degenerate "Marxism"'. More recently, Lachmann (1981) has suggested that Mises's views on the methodology of the social sciences 'cannot be appreciated except in the light of this circumstance', namely, that 'Mises, very much a man of the Enlightenment, regarded it as his foremost task to defend the precious inheritance we owe to the eighteenth century against all comers, but in particular against positivism which, in its various forms, threatened to engulf it for most of our century and has only recently abated.'

Here, then, is another aspect of subjectivism extended to the scientist himself. It highlights the difficulty of separating positive and normative economics, or, more precisely, the difficulty of keeping values out of positive economics. Certainly it is desirable that, as far as possible, economists should attempt to separate the two. But Myrdal's scepticism about the possibility of doing so receives support from Kuhn. The choice of a problem or a model takes place in a paradigm, which embodies a value-system. Subjectivists should be sceptical of the possibility of achieving a value-free positive economics. Instead, they should place their faith in the competitive social and scientific *process* which tends to expose value judgements that individual economists might consciously or unconsciously fail to make explicit.

THE PSYCHOLOGY OF CHOICE

Subjectivists frequently emphasise the concept of 'purposeful behaviour'. In doing so, they wish to distinguish human action from reflexive or instinctive behaviour. But is the distinction quite that clear-cut? Consider two objections.

The first objection is that the emphasis on purpose reflects a particular psychological theory of choice, associated with the *Gestalt* school. The emphasis is on learning and problem-solving, and implies a gradual convergence to 'correct' choice under appropriate conditions. One can understand that Mises and Hayek wished to emphasise such an approach in contrast to those (e.g. Marxists) who adopted a behaviourist approach, arguing that environment rather than free will determined behaviour.

Nowadays the behaviourist position is not widely held, but other theories are put forward. For example, a 'psychoanalytic' view has been advocated, in which learning and problem-solving play little role. The attractiveness of a product depends less on its filling a conscious 'need' than gratifying a subconscious instinct. The role of the imagination is emphasised, and behaviour tends to diverge unpredictably rather than to converge. As I have argued elsewhere (Littlechild, 1981), such a theory seems to be reflected in the work of G. L. S. Shackle.

My purpose here is not to argue for one approach or the other, and doubtless yet other theories have been put forward. The point is that the fundamental nature of human action is the subject of differences of opinion among psychologists – indeed, perhaps different theories are appropriate to different men, or even to the same man at different times or under different conditions.

The second and not unrelated objection is that 'instinct' broadly interpreted may have a far larger role to play in economics than has hitherto been acknowledged. Can it be argued that we do many things, not because (or not merely because) they are useful or profitable, but because it is in our nature to do so? Consider Adam Smith's famous reference to 'man's propensity to truck and barter'. Is exchange merely a mutual improvement of assets? Or is there a 'propensity' to exchange for its own sake? There is surely no doubt that competition and co-operation are part of our nature. They are not always means to an end, they may be ends in themselves — indeed, in some spheres people *pay* to compete or co-operate.

Economists have tended to see man as a purely logical animal, as an instrumentalist. In contrast, most sociologists (and a few economists, such as Pareto, Knight and Shackle) have consistently denied that this is a complete or adequate representation of human nature.

If these critics are right, what difference does it make? Does it merely mean that the profit from engaging in exchange, competition or co-operation need be that much less because of the pleasure which such activities provide? Or does it not suggest a rather different emphasis in our analysis of, for example, the gains from trade, the role of competition policy and taxation, the formation of firms and other groups, the formation of corporate policy, and so on. Even more broadly, should we see the economic structure of a society merely as a means of furthering the maximisation of wealth, or does it perhaps reflect the instinctive and less purposeful tastes of its members? Finally, if economics is defined as the study of *purposeful* human action, is the study of the instinctive element in market phenomena to be ceded to some other discipline such as sociology?

GROUP BEHAVIOUR

Firms and trade unions have become increasingly important in all modern economies, yet the leading subjectivist writers provide virtually no analysis of group activities. Mises and Hayek, for example, hardly mention 'the firm' as distinct from 'the entrepreneur' — though admittedly the same could be said of almost all economists until the last few decades.

In recent years there have been important advances in the economic theory of groups. One version particularly congenial to subjectivists is that of Wiseman (forthcoming), building upon earlier contributions by Coase, Buchanan and Tullock, Olson and many others. In this version, people decide to form or leave groups, just as they make other kinds of decisions. They also need to decide on group objectives and the means to achieve these. Group decision-making is thus given a 'choice-theoretic' foundation. It enables us better to understand how groups can exist to serve the conscious objectives of their members, and how, in a precise sense, groups can have objectives of their own as explicitly determined by their members.

Yet, once again, this is a somewhat instrumentalist view. Is this all there is to a group? Cannot groups take on a life of their own, independent of their members? Do not some members of a group come to value the health and survival of the group as an end in itself, beyond their own financial or personal interest in it? Can the feeling of pride in belonging to a group (such as Britain, or Marks and Spencers, or Aston Villa Football Club) be explained if the group is regarded merely as the means by which its members achieve their own objectives?

There is a tendency in these approaches to see the group purely as the creation of its members, and to play down, or even ignore, the feedback from the group *to* the members. Perhaps subjectivists should be more concerned with the nature and sources of the values and ideas held by group members (and, indeed, by non-members).

This brings us to the important topic of the relationship between the individual and society.

METHODOLOGICAL INDIVIDUALISM

Subjectivism is invariably associated with methodological individualism — that is, with the proposition that societies and social phenomena are to be explained in terms of the actions of their members, and that societies do not have an existence or personality independent of their members. But is strict methodological individualism a necessary implication of subjectivism?

Consider a writer who declares 'that the individual is a mere abstraction, that human beings can neither be known nor know themselves except as members of a society, and that society — not society in general, but a particular society — is therefore the determinant reality and the only proper starting-point for the study of mankind'. On the face of it this is hardly the language of methodological individualism — yet the author is J. Enoch Powell (1978), whom most would have classified as a subjectivist, and, in political terms at least, as an eminent champion of individualism. It is therefore worth devoting considerable space to Powell's point of view.

He first refers to 'the concept of society as created by the contractual and conditional coming together of individual human beings, the primordial atoms of mankind, to form a society'. This is the concept envisaged, for example, in the American Declaration of Independence.

Only in such a world can there be such things as 'natural rights' or 'human rights' vested in individuals. For those of us who do not inhabit that fantastic theoretical world the rights of an individual are part of the description of a particular society and of the relationships in that society between its members, dependent upon a network of shared opinions, beliefs and myths which regulates and determines their thoughts and actions.

Powell continues with a beautiful metaphor that illustrates perfectly the point made earlier about the nature of man. Their business, he says, 'is to talk about our society, our country, our nation, to praise it and to blame it, because it is in our nature to do that thing, as it is in the nature of a flock of birds to call to one another as they fly through the half light of morning to their feeding-grounds'.

But human nature is both instinctive *and* rational.

The language in which *we* do so [i.e. talk about our society] will be in form rational, proceeding from premises to conclusions, seeking to reason about good and evil, about collective survival or collective dissolution. For although human individuals are no more conceivable or intelligible apart from their society than individual bees apart from the swarm or individual baboons apart from the herd, we are men and not bees, human and not simian. Whatever human analogies or premonitions there may be in the rest of nature, man is unique and set apart from it by the fact that the individual is self-conscious, conscious of himself as having his own beginning and end and as being unrepeatable. Indeed, self-consciousness is the ultimate reality about the individual, inseparable from the power of thought and speech, the Word 'which lighteth every man that cometh into the world'.

It is because men are thus that human societies have a quite different sort of life-story from non-human societies. They vary and change with violent and bewildering unpredictability, never still, but caught up in endless self-examination, experiment, collision and debate, neither wholly rational nor wholly irrational.

Is this not a similar view to that of G. L. S. Shackle, the most radical subjectivist of our time? Can we then deny that subjectivism is consistent with the view that 'society is the only proper starting-point for the study of mankind'? What seems to be required is not so much a rejection of methodological individualism, as a radically subjectivist reinterpretation of that concept. Such an exercise will probably reveal much more common ground between economists and sociologists than is at present apparent.

THE FUTURE DIRECTION OF ECONOMIC THEORY

Let us finally return to the ideas of T. S. Kuhn. Largely as a result of Kuhn's work, philosophers have gradually abandoned the 'treasure chest' or 'crossword puzzle' view of science, whereby knowledge is gradually accumulated, in favour of the view that existing knowledge continually becomes redundant, as existing theories are superseded by new ones (see Putnam, 1978). The path along which any theory develops is unlikely to be a smooth one, nor is it wholly determined by the properties of the physical world and the nature of society. It will reflect, possibly to an important degree, the perceptions, preferences and values of scientists, and indeed their professional and personal likes and dislikes.

The implications of this change of view are far-reaching. As Kuhn (1970, pp. 170–1) points out, although science evolves, it does not evolve *towards* anything. This may at first seem disturbing, but 'if we can learn to substitute evolution-from-what-we-do-know for evolution-toward-what-we-wish-to-know, a number of vexing problems may vanish in the process'.

All this is as true of economics as of the natural sciences. The future of economic theory is susceptible to direction by economists themselves. Via their perceptions and values, they are free to create the very phenomena they analyse – provided that they can persuade fellow economists and other interested parties of the plausibility and attractiveness of their point of view.

Let us conclude by noting a parallel of Kuhn's thought within the toolbox of economics itself. The concept of general equilibrium is currently central to economics. The neo-classicals think of the economy as approximately in equilibrium, the Austrians of the economy as tending to equilibrium (albeit a moving one). But for G. L. S. Shackle the relevance of the whole concept is in question. Every act of choice embodies the chooser's creative imagination of the future. The market therefore follows a 'kaleidic' process, with moments of order interspersed with disintegration into a new pattern. The economy is changing and developing, but in no sense does it have a single goal.

In accepting a radically subjectivist point of view, economists are liberated from the stranglehold of general equilibrium. By the same token, however, they are able and obliged to find room in economic theory for the charismatic leaders – for Ford and Carnegie, Luther King and Churchill – men who had a vision and sought to remake the world accordingly.

REFERENCES

Buchanan, J. M. and G. F. Thirlby (1973) *LSE Essays on Cost* (London: LSE/Weidenfeld and Nicolson).

Friedman, M. (1953) 'The Methodology of Positive Economics', in *Essays in Positive Economics* (University of Chicago Press).

Goldschmidt, H. J. *et al.* (eds) (1974) *Industrial Concentration: The New Learning* (Boston: Little, Brown).

Hayek, F. A. (1955) *The Counter-Revolution of Science* (Glencoe: Free Press/London: Collier Macmillan).

Hayek, F. A. (1979) *Foreword* to Murray N. Rothbard, *Individualism and the Philosophy of the Social Sciences* (San Francisco: Cato Institute).

Hutchison, T. W. (1977) *Knowledge and Ignorance in Economics* (Oxford: Basil Blackwell).

Keynes, J. N. (1891) *The Scope and Method of Political Economy* (London: Macmillan) (as quoted in Friedman, 1953).

Kuhn, T. S. (1970) *The Structure of Scientific Revolutions* 2nd edn (University of Chicago Press).

Lachmann, L. M. (1981) 'Ludwig von Mises and The Extension of Subjectivism', in I. M. Kirzner (ed.), *The Contributions of Ludwig von Mises to Economics* (forthcoming proceedings of a conference held in New York, September).

Littlechild, S. C. (1981) 'Advertising, Brand Loyalty and Habit' in *Analysis of Consumer Policy* (Philadelphia: Wharton Applied Research Center) pp. 107–24. Reprinted in revised form as 'Controls on Advertising. An Examination of Some Economic Arguments,' *Journal of Advertising*, 1 (1982).

Loasby, B. J. (1976) *Choice, Complexity and Ignorance* (Cambridge University Press).

Mises, L. von (1966) *Human Action* (Yale University Press, 1949), 3rd edn (Chicago: Henry Regnery Col).

Powell, J. Enoch (1978) Address to the Institute of Directors, Annual Convention, London, 28 February.

Putnam, H. (1978) 'The Philosophy of Science', ch. 20 in Bryan Magee (ed.), *Men of Ideas* (London: British Broadcasting Corporation).

Robbins, L. (1935) *An Essay on the Nature and Significance of Economic Science*, 2nd edn (London: Macmillan).

Shackle, G. L. S. (1972) *Epistemics and Economics* (Cambridge University Press).

Wiseman, J. (forthcoming) 'The Economic Theory of Group Behaviour', in *Festschrift for Professor Biucchi*.

4   Towards the Progress of Economic Knowledge

HOMA KATOUZIAN

THE PROBLEM

It is not the first time that economic science finds itself in difficulty. It was in difficulty when interventionist theories and policies of the sixteenth and seventeenth centuries seemed to have outlived their usefulness; when the physiocrats proved their case against intervention only by assuming that industry was unproductive; when Adam Smith corrected that mistake but left a legacy of unresolved problems; when Ricardo tried but failed to produce a clear and logically faultless theory of value and distribution; when J. S. Mill attempted to draw socialist rabbits out of purely Liberal silk hats; when Marx tried to prove the inevitability of the proletarian revolution through the science of political economy; when Marshall saw nearly all the basic faults of neo-classical economics but did not make them sufficiently explicit; when Keynes argued his case against hoarding so well as to undermine the significance of long-term accumulation.

Nor is it the first time that the approach, methods and techniques of economics have been put to the test by their critics. Ideological conflicts apart, think of the disagreements between naturalists and scholastics, the arguments between orthodox and radical classical economists, the debates between the German and British historical schools and the early neo-classicals, or the differences between so-called *a priorists* and their critics in the inter-war period. Indeed, the annals of these perennial arguments contain − in an open or occult fashion − nearly every basic aspect of current methodological discussions, such as those on fact versus value, or abstraction as opposed to application or dynamics in contrast to statics, or description as compared to prescription.[1] There must be many reasons why these arguments have so far failed to settle some of the more basic issues permanently, and one of them must be the fact that there has been a tendency to put too much emphasis on logic and ideology and too little on methodology, and the sociology of the economics profession. In any case, these debates and arguments have tended to be better in showing what is wrong than suggesting ways of putting it right.

The fact, however, that the critics are often asked to suggest *alternatives* to replace the existing orthodoxies is not as reasonable as it may sound, first, because if a theory is either incorrect or irrelevant then there could be no intellectual justification for holding on to it, and, secondly, because such alternatives are themselves subject to *discovery*, and discovery requires effort and commitment. Furthermore, the demand for a ready-made alternative is itself an effective barrier against breaking new ground and discovering alternative frameworks. The most convenient but least fruitful position in both science and society is to blame everything on the inevitable, and fulfil one's own prophecy by thus making it 'inevitable'. If one continues to ignore the critics, dismiss (often with contempt) *alternative approaches* and make little or no effort to go beyond existing frameworks, then the vicious circle of 'inevitability' will be likely to go on until it is broken by ideas and events which are outside the social and/or professional domain of our discipline.

Yet, there *is* a sense in which the demand for alternatives is just and reasonable, and that is when the critic is asked, not to offer a ready-made blueprint, but to suggest *attitudes, approaches and methods* which, in his judgement, will help realise the discovery of alternatives. The issue then is, not *what* the critics can readily provide, but *how* they think it can be achieved.

WHAT IS *NOT* WRONG WITH ECONOMICS

Now, the claim that − in discussing the chronic maladies of economic science − there has been too much emphasis on the purely logical and ideological aspects of the problem requires a brief explanation. Take the case of positive economics. Whatever we may think of logical positivism, the faults and shortcomings of positive economics cannot be blamed on that philosophy of science, if only because, both in theory and in practice, there is little correspondence between it and the methodology of orthodox economics: some very important economic theories are inherently untestable, other theories which *are* testable are

still retained even when they are contradicted by reason or reality, and
– in any case – a considerable amount of current publications consist
of either purely inductive (or 'empirical'), or purely deductive (or
'mathematical') generalisations, which are, therefore, immune to
external (rational or empirical) criticism, as opposed to *internal*
(logical or technological) consistency and accuracy. Some positive
economists even believe that a distinction between descriptive and
normative statements is all that is needed for 'scientific' discovery.
Others believe that scientific knowledge is a stock of *false* hypotheses
which somehow 'work'. Still others freely use the terminology of
Thomas Kuhn's radically different theory of scientific change – the
favourites being 'paradigm', 'crisis' and 'revolution'.[2]

The same goes for the near impossibility of conducting controlled
experiments which is sometimes thought to be the root of the problem.
As it happens, some successful physical sciences, notably astronomy,
do not depend on laboratory tests, and, in general, it is doubtful if the
relative success of a natural science can be measured by its ability to
apply experimental methods. Perhaps the availability of this technical
facility could have been helpful to the development of economics, but
it would be misleading to think that without such a panacea one cannot
place economic knowledge on more certain grounds, or increase the
pace of its progress. The *ceteris paribus* clause by itself is not a great
problem; more often, it is the use to which it is put which makes the
results too narrow in scope or of little relevance in application.

Suppose, for example, that we somehow simulated an experimental
world, consisting of two countries which were different only in their
relative endowments of two homogeneous inputs. Suppose further that
– in the absence of domestic and foreign distortion, restriction and
intervention – each country specialised in the production of the commodity which used more of its abundant input, and exported it to the
other. What would such a successful laboratory test of a well-known
theory of international trade add to our knowledge of the patterns and
problems of international trade? What would it tell us about the
origins and causes of the turn in the wheel of fortune, say, between
Japan and the countries of Western Europe and North America. How
would it help us to explain or bring to some kind of conclusion the
perennial 'conferences' and 'dialogues' between rich and poor countries, the only tangible consequence of which has been to institu-
tionalise the conference and the dialogue themselves, and create a few
more posts in the international civil service?

But, in any case, to *blame* the backwardness of economics on the difficulty of controlled experimentation would be almost as grotesque as if a physicist began to complain of having to study mute and unconscious objects, incapable of interaction and communication, and unable to respond to interviews and questionnaires, or keep records of their own development. That is, the near impossibility of controlled experimentation in economics is characteristic of the very nature of its subject-matter, which therefore affords it other facilities and methods of investigation not open to all sciences. In general, what is wrong with economics should be sought, not in what it cannot do, but in what it does, and in not doing what it *can* do.

It would be difficult to deny the role of ideology in influencing economic ideas, decisions and events. Yet, whether we think of ideology as conscious lies or unconscious prejudices in favour of one's own social class, or that of one's paymasters; or as a *conception du monde* which is bound up by the stage of (moral or material) development; or as an intellectual framework which explains or justifies particular social and economic systems – whatever concept of ideology we may have in mind, ideological intrusions cannot be exclusive to economics or the social sciences alone, nor can they explain the relative success of different scientific disciplines, or that of various theories within the same ideological framework. A Liberal, Marxian, Conservative or Institutionalist economic theory may be correct, mistaken or simply irrelevant with regard to the problem to which it is addressed. Indeed, there have been many economists of *various* schools of thought and ideological persuasions who have succeeded in throwing considerable light on the problem which they have set themselves to resolve. Karl Marx, whose authority is frequently invoked in the (often not so accurate) applications of concepts of ideology to social and economic knowledge, recognised both the science and the ideology in Darwinism; and, moreover, he accepted and praised the science, but rejected the ideology in spite of Darwin's own sympathy for it.

Suppose, for example, that Keynes had consciously set himself the task of saving no less than the capitalist system itself. The question is this: if the ideological outlook and motivation would predetermine the success or failure, truth or otherwise of the results, why then did Keynes succeed where many other economists – and among them some of the committed well-wishers of capitalism – did not. The answer is that – unlike many intellectuals of *all* ideological persuasions – he was not a prisoner of closed intellectual frameworks; because he was both willing and able to think outside such frameworks, and break them, if need be, in order to solve the problem;

because he himself was involved in real social and political processes, without, however, turning into Mr Hyde each time he entered a common room or a lecture theatre; because, in other words, he was a scientist in the most distinctive sense of the term which emerges from the history of science itself: that is, a man who − whatever his predilections and prejudices − searches for solutions to real problems, if necessary, by breaking the established frameworks and attempting to construct new ones.[3]

For obvious reasons, value judgements and ideology are important to both theory and practice. The argument here is that they cannot necessarily predetermine the truth or falsehood of the knowledge which they generate.

WHAT *IS* WRONG WITH ECONOMICS

SOME BASIC ISSUES

What is wrong with economics is simple but elusive. It often appears in logical and ideological guises, and it is frequently discussed in terms of abstraction versus description, theory versus observation, or mathematical economics versus applied econometrics. Yet, no critic would argue that a science without a substantial body of theoretical knowledge is worthy of the name, and few orthodox economists − certainly none that would call himself a positive economist − would claim that empirical knowledge is of no use for the development of economic science. It is true that statisticians and econometricians sometimes complain about the unrealism of mathematical models, or that mathematical economists occasionally give the impression that they are not too impressed with the standards of rigour and precision in applied economics. Such differences are, however, more in the nature of family disputes, reflecting personal and professional rivalries rather than serious intellectual disagreements.

Economic theory would necessarily involve abstraction, and abstraction is a valid scientific process so long as the subject of inquiry and the resulting theory have a *counterpart* in the world of reality. To give but a textbook example, while one can easily think of a concrete counterpart to the simple consumption function, it is difficult to envisage a corresponding reality to life-cycle hypotheses of consumer expenditure. In the words of Alfred Marshall:

If one shuts one's eyes to realities, one may construct an edifice of pure crystal by imagination . . . Such playful excursions are often suggestive in unexpected ways: they afford good training to the mind; and seem to be productive of good, so long as their purpose is clearly understood.[4]

It would be too restrictive in social and economic science to demand of every theoretical proposition that it be empirically testable. The problem about a large and expanding body of economic theory is that it is either inherently immune to all possible criticism or of no relevance to *any* real economic problem, or both.[5]

It might look as if this problem would be solved at a stroke if only economists concentrated their efforts on measurements, estimations, empirical tests, etc. But this is no more than an illusion. It is a grave mistake to believe that the mere collection or manipulation of data could result in veritable 'general laws' or theories, or that so-called 'direct observation' avoids selective abstraction or subjective preconception. And regarding the latter possibility, Marshall's words are still as good as any other:

> Experience . . . teaches that the most reckless and treacherous of all theorists is he who professes to let facts and figures speak for themselves, who keeps in the background the part that he has played, perhaps unconsciously, in selecting and grouping them, and in suggesting the argument *post hoc ergo propter hoc*.[6]

This was said when few published data were available, when economic statistics was still undeveloped, when econometrics was nonexistent, and when electronic computers had not yet been invented. The development of both economic technology and electronic machinery has helped widen the scope, and added to the rigour and precision of applied economics; but at the same time, it has made it easy for the manipulation of abstract numbers (in a demonstration of some basic technical know-how − of multiple regression, for example, together with the r^2, the standard errors and the Durbin−Watson test) to replace serious and painstaking studies of economic problems. There are, in particular, three important and related points which seem to be in danger of being overlooked by modern applied economics: one, that a *number* − and especially one which is found in an official publication − is still a highly *abstract* datum; two, that *qualitative* evidence is just as important as quantitative data; and three, that the social and economic context of the subject of inquiry is of crucial significance both to the choice of assumptions, models and techniques of investigation, and to the interpretation of the results; and that therefore much care and caution is needed before a single model is mechanistically applied to 'the British data', 'the American data', 'the African data' or 'the international data'. And if this looks like a tall order, then that itself is a comment on the state of economic science.

To give a simple example, some quantitative studies of manufacturing output and productivity have tended to suggest that the industrial capital–output ratio is unusually high in developing countries, and this has occasionally led to unlikely explanations of the phenomenon. Whereas, a closer knowledge of the firms and/or the countries might have shown that − because of manpower or spare-part shortages, or because of overoptimistic forecasts of domestic or foreign demand − the firms have been running substantially below capacity, so that the ratio of their full-capacity capital costs to the value of their current output would turn out to be high.

It is fashionable for economists to compare their subject and its methods to those of the natural sciences, or to what is sometimes called 'the scientific method'. This has led to a tendency for *emulating*, rather than adapting and developing, various forms and techniques used in the natural sciences, without much success; in fact, it has tended to encourage the mystification of simple ideas, and the application of theoretical and statistical techniques in ways which often do not bear much real fruit. Whereas, if the natural sciences are significantly more developed than the social sciences, it is not so much because they can use 'the' scientific method (whatever that may mean); but because they have developed scientific methods and techniques appropriate to their own tasks. As a matter of fact, natural sciences themselves use a variety of methods and techniques, though this does not mean that each and every one of them has developed a set of such methods exclusively for itself: it means that each *set* of methods tends to have an integrity and identity of its own.

This is what we generally lack in economics, because, rather than using sources, methods and techniques which are most obviously suggested by the problems themselves, we would tend to emulate − or 'ape', as Popper would put it − those which have been developed in other scientific disciplines; rather than speaking to men, or studying human society, its history and its institutions, we are depressed about being unable to experiment with them; rather than considering the significance of social and political systems for the economic phenomena, problems and events which are manifested within them, we behave as if they are wholly irrelevant; rather than studying the role of governments and their impact on economic decisions and behaviour, we either assume them away, or regard them − both in Britain and in Timbuctoo − as impartial arbiters of the social good.

Apart from that, we tend to identify theoretical analysis almost exclusively with mathematical symbols or (at least) diagramatic pictures, and think of empirical analysis only in terms of numbers and their manipulation. This involves us in two eventful mistakes: one, that theoretical and empirical approaches which do use these forms and techniques are necessarily 'scientific', positive or whatever; and two, that those which do not are necessarily 'unscientific', at best 'descriptive', normative or some other type of 'categorical untouchable'. The degree of scientific backwardness which these attitudes betray is only partially reflected in their complete substitution of means for ends.

Another consequence of these attitudes is the tendency for the *mere* availability of certain techniques to determine the choice of problems. It is sometimes said that it would be extremely tedious for the author or teacher, and almost unintelligible for the reader or student, if some of the more rarefied economic models were to be expressed in words, or even in terms of simpler mathematical or geometrical techniques. That would be a plausible argument on the condition, (a) that the model itself is not a simple idea in a technically tedious guise, and (b) that it is of some relevance to the understanding, if not solution, of a real economic problem. Let the most advanced mathematical or econometric techniques be used for the solution of a real economic problem if they are the most appropriate means for the purpose; but do not allow techniques alone to select the problem, or determine the intellectual and practical value of its results.

The whole of the foregoing argument may be summarised in a few words, namely that methodological universalism is not a cause of progress, but a symptom of backwardness both in science and in society.

UNIVERSALISM IN SUBSTANCE

Universalism is a common affliction of our time, although its origins are in the nineteenth century, when man began to play God, and science was turned into a religion. It is the view that confuses − both in science and in society − *generality* with *totality*, *comparability* with *homogeneity, correspondence* with *identity, conscious action and interaction* with *mechanical motion and reaction.* It sees the oneness but ignores the otherness of phenomena; it observes the uniqueness of the human species but overlooks the uniqueness of the human individual; it recognises the common economic problems of all societies, but discounts their specific forms and qualities in different times and places. That is how we discover 'feudalism' in tribal African or despotic Asian societies; or confuse Third World bureaucrats and shop-keepers for 'bourgeois', 'capitalist' or 'entrepreneurial' classes; or compare the 'risk-sharing' of share-cropping peasants with that of 'modern corporations'; or speak of 'money' and monetary institutions as if they would have the same significance here, there and everywhere; or use mathematical models developed for space engineering so as to determine the growth path, and its stability, of wholly imaginary economies; or declare that Britain would end up in the same politico-economic position as Chile, solely because the share of the state in the national income is the same in both countries.[7]

The argument against universalism can easily be confused with what is known as historical relativism: the view that, in spite of superficial similarities, each stage of (social or intellectual) progress is unique to itself and different from earlier and later stages. In economics, this would mean that, for example, what was true of the British economy under Queen Victoria was not true of the German economy under Bismarck – a view that was extensively debated between the adherents of the German Historical School and both classical and neo-classical economists. Marshall, Sidgewick, John Neville Keynes, Schumpeter, Mises, Hayek, Robbins and – in more recent times – Blaug have all either rejected the so-called relativist view or sought a more or less genuine compromise with it.[8] Both historical relativism and its opposite are in fact metaphysical problems in the sense that the debate between them cannot be resolved with reference to the internal logical analysis or the external factual evidence.

The case against universalism, however, is one that is thoroughly scientific and totally independent of the truth or falsehood of historical relativism: *every scientific theory is general; therefore, no scientific theory can be universal.* Take, for example, Galileo's celebrated law of falling bodies which states that *in all possible situations where there is a given force of gravity,* the rate of acceleration of a body falling freely in *vacuum* will be 9.81 metres per second. It follows that when there is no force of gravity nothing would 'fall'; where the force of gravity is different from that which has been assumed, the rate of acceleration will be different; and even where the given force of gravity prevails, the rate of acceleration would be different outside vacuum. Hence, the law is a general scientific theory by virtue of its not being a universal description or, what is effectively the same, a tautological statement.[9] In fact, the tacit belief in universalism is even more astonishing in economics, especially now that every textbook of macroeconomics rejects Say's Law on the argument that it is true only in a barter economy, and ridicules the old quantity theory of money for being no more than a tautology, because it is 'true' in all situations, or, in other words, because its truth is necessary rather than contingent.[10]

It looks as if the young Marx was attacking precisely this concept of universalism − a brilliant insight which, in some of his later writings, he occasionally allowed himself to forget − when he wrote to Arnold Ruge:

> Up to now, the philosophers have had the solution of all riddle lying in their lectern, and the stupid uninitiated world had only to open its jaws to let the roast partridges of absolute science fly into its mouth. . . . But if the designing of the future and the proclamation of ready-made solutions for all time is not our affair, then we realise all the more clearly what we have to accomplish in the present. I am therefore not in favour of setting up any dogmatic flags. On the contrary, we must try to help the *dogmatics* to clarify to themselves the meaning of their own positions . . . [emphasis in the original][11]

Universalism stands on two legs: one, homogeneity, the other, mechanicism. It homogenises factors, entities and categories, individuals, institutions and societies, well beyond the usual assumptions of homogeneous inputs, outputs and the like: it is not only their technical characteristics, but also their social qualities that are homogenised: 'money' is money now as it was two centuries ago', in Britain as in the Congo; labour is labour, or 'man-powers', whether supplied by slaves, by traditional peasants, or by workers on wage contracts; 'higher education' is a matter of numbers and percentages, taken and compared from India, Korea, Madagascar, France or Canada; 'the' scientific method is what it says, both in physics and in economics. Once the substance is, in this sense, homogeneous, the approach and method is bound to be mechanistic. It was this mechanicism in approach, and the associated universalist conception of the results that Keynes was attacking when he wrote:

> The object of our analyse is, not to provide a machine, a method of blind manipulation, which will furnish an infallible answer, but to

provide ourselves with an organised and orderly method of thinking out particular problems. . . . This is the nature of economic thinking. Any other way of applying our formal principles of thought (without which, however, we shall be lost in the wood) will lead us into error.

And he went on to add:

Too large a proportion of recent 'mathematical' economics are mere concoctions . . . which allow the author to lose sight of the complexities and interdependencies of the real worl in a maze of pretentious and unhelpful symbols . . . I do not myself attach much value to manipulations of this kind . . . they involve just as much tacit assumption as to what variables are taken as independent as does ordinary discussion, whilst I doubt if they carry us further than ordinary discourse.[12]

This was written long before the so-called 'mathematical revolution'; and it is equally applicable to some contemporary works in applied economics. In fact, we are now well past the stage when, as Keynes put it, excessive formalism did not add much to ordinary discourse; we have reached the stage when it threatens to discredit reasonable hypotheses by stretching them beyond their limits. The situation may be likened to one in which the barrel of a gun is heavily overloaded in the hope of increasing its fire-power. This was foreseen by Marshall who wrote, in his typical style of dealing with controversial questions:

. . . when a pure mathematician uses economic hypotheses . . . his concern is to show the potentialities of mathematical methods on the supposition that material appropriate to their use had been supplied by economic study. He takes no technical responsibility for the material, and is often unaware *how inadequate the material is to bear the strains of his powerful machinery* [emphasis added][13]

He might have said the same of some contemporary empirical studies which come out of computers almost as soon as the data are copied out from official publications.

A WAY FORWARD

To sum up, although logical and ideological issues are of theoretical as well as practical importance, they do not constitute the most urgent problems of modern economics, partly because they have been given a lop-sided emphasis in the history of the subject, partly because logical criteria — whatever they might be — are treated as ideal rules rather than practical guidelines, and partly because there could be both progressive and degenerative scientific tendencies within each and every ideological framework. In fact, the most urgent and immediate problems of economics arise from a methodological outlook which — by sacrificing substance for form, reality for appearance — homogenises economic categories and phenomena, mechanicises the associated problems, and universalises the results of their study. This is the diagnosis, and it already implies its prescription. It would therefore look as if the present discussion should be concluded at this point.

There are two further points, however, which arise from the question 'How is the prescription itself — the move away from formalistic universalism towards scientific realism, from puzzle-solving to problem-solving — to be achieved in practice?' We should certainly not expect a sudden resurrection, not even a *danse macabre*. But there could be a *process* whereby the level of scientific knowledge in economics is raised, and it will involve two types of adjustment — one intellectual, the other social and professional — which are closely related to each other.

The intellectual adjustment will simply require a more substantial, a wider as well as deeper knowledge of society in the past and at present. Such a social and economic knowledge will become a part of the (conscious and unconscious) reservoir of the economist's direct and indirect *experience*, and it will inevitably add to the sophistication of his theoretical models, his empirical studies, and his policy prescriptions; it will also increase the depth and the rigour of his appraisals and arguments. It might be helpful, however, to spell out and clarify the more important implications of this process of intellectual adjustment:

First, it should be repeated and re-emphasised that the idea is not to replace analytical depth or empirical precision by 'descriptive general knowledge', but to make it possible to construct rigorous as well as relevant theoretical models, and to use statistical and other quantitative techniques more effectively. Nor does it mean that economists should try to specialise in several disciplines of social science: most economists are familiar with mathematical and statistical methods at some level, but — perhaps except for a few — they cannot be said to have *specialised* in these subjects as well as in economics.

Secondly, the emphasis on historical knowledge should not be confused with historicism. Historicism is the method of constructing general 'laws' or theories by supposedly direct generalisations from historical data. It is another lingering illusion of the nineteenth century which economists have done well to reject. Yet, a confusion of historicist methods with *historical knowledge* has led to two important mistakes: one, to downgrade or even ignore the immeasurable uses of history – economic, social and political; regional, national and international – for a well-founded and progressive science of political economy; two, to generalise from *quantitative* historical data – think of Phillips Curve, or the 'theory' of linear and proportional consumption function – as if 'direct' generalisations from simple and abstract fragments of history are any less historicist than those from wholesome and concrete historical events.

It so happens that not only abstract numbers but even many theoretical hypotheses have their roots in historical or contemporary *experience*. A substantial amount of current research in applied economics, at any rate, consists of quantitative extractions and abstractions from social and historical events, and this is particularly true of empirical studies which use time-series or cross-section data. What are these data but abstract symbols of past and 'present' events? Therefore, it is not as if economists do not use social and historical knowledge, only that they do so in an extremely narrow and limited fashion. We have yet to realise the significance of *time*, not merely as a theoretical parameter or statistical datum, but as *history* itself.

Thirdly, the acquisition of some social and historical knowledge by economists will not be too exacting in time or effort, although – just like mathematics and statistics – it would vary from one eonomist to another depending on personal preference and professional specialisation. They would not end up by writing on history or sociology any more than they now contribute to mathematical and statistical theory, but their familiarity with social and historical processes would significantly raise the substantial (as opposed to formal) quality of their teaching and research.

It might be utopian to hope, or illiberal to demand, that large numbers of economists would, or should, pay much attention to recommendations of this kind, although one would certainly hope that – even in this dim, authoritarian age of paradigms and programmes – those who claim to subscribe to knowledge and science would occasionally respond to open and rational discourse by means of explicit argument rather than implicit rejection. But what is simpler, more important as well as less drastic to hope and demand is that some such proposal is implemented in a revision of the curricula, syllabi and references of undergraduate courses in economics. It is surely not unreasonable to expect those who regret the impossibility of economic experiments to have the courage of their own conviction in this respect.

It is at this point that our brief discussion of the necessary *intellectual* adjustment for an improvement in the methods and results of economic science reveals its links with the required *professional* adjustment. For far too long the simple truth has been overlooked that − in spite of all the ceremonials concerning the sanctity of intellectual freedom, and other constitutional niceties of university life − the majority of professional academics would rather promote their own 'career structure' than risk the wrath or displeasure of their senior colleagues, within both their departments and their discipline. And, for reasons that would take too long to discuss, it would be unrealistic, perhaps even unfair, to expect them to act in a radically different manner. How many economists would spend time on the study of historical, social and institutional events, ideas and processes, if, for reasons other than the relative intellectual merit of their work, they received little or no recognition for it; how many of them would − in the time that it takes to set up and solve purely logical puzzles, or push different sets of numbers through the computer − take pains to study a single economic *problem*, if the resulting paper ran a much higher risk of rejection by the learned journals; how many of them would begin to interest their students in the subject itself − and not merely in the relative price of their certificates in the labour market − by introducing them to the history and traditions of economic theories and methods, or by placing contemporary problems in their social and historical contexts, as long as an unspoken law regarded such sins as being no less original than a bite at the forbidden fruit, punishable, if not by a Fall, then perhaps by a Promethean chain − with or without eagles?[14]

Kafkaism apart, we owe it to society to take positive steps, at least in making the contents of the undergraduate courses somewhat less rigid in scope, method and approach. It is, after all, not only professionally anonymous critics like this speaker − even in spite of his elevation by this learned Association to the privilege of addressing its meeting − but also some of the knights, peers and presidents of the economics profession who have been complaining of 'the irrelevance of equilibrium economics', or saying 'down with the economist as such'.[15] Would it be too impertinent to ask for *their* support in humble efforts to push this science beyond the arid, no-rent frontiers of so-called positive economics, towards the progress of economic knowledge?

NOTES AND REFERENCES

1. See further, Guy Routh, *The Origin of Economic Ideas* (London: Macmillan, 1975) chap. 1, and H. Katouzian, *Ideology and Method in Economics* (London: Macmillan, and New York: New York University Press, 1980) chap. 2.
2. For a more elaborate discussion of these points, see Katouzian, *Ideology and Method*, chaps 3, 4 and 7.
3. See further, Elizabeth Johnson, 'John Maynard Keynes: Scientist or Politician?' in Joan Robinson (ed.), *After Keynes* (Oxford: Basil Blackwell, 1973) pp. 12–25, R. F. Harrod, *The Life of John Maynard Keynes* (London: Macmillan, 1952); Katouzian, *Ideology and Method*, chap. 6, and 'The Hallmarks of Scholasticism and Science', forthcoming in Richard Whitley *et al.* (eds), *The Yearbook of the Sociology of Sciences* (Dordrecht, Holland: Reidel, 1982).
4. Alfred Marshall, *Principles of Economics* (London. Macmillan, 1961) Appendix D, p. 645.
5. See further, Katouzian, *Ideology and Method*, chap. 7.
6. See R. L. Smyth (ed.), *Essays in Economic Method* (London: Duckworth, 1962) p. 44.
7. For some of these references see *Ideology and Method*, especially chap. 8.
8. See Smyth, *Essays*; J. M. Keynes, *The Scope and Method of Political Economy* (London: Macmillan, 1891); J. A. Schumpeter, *Economic Doctrine and Method* (first German edition, 1912) (London: Oxford University Press, 1954); L. von Mises, *Epistemological Problems of Economics* (1933) (New York: Van Nostrand, 1960); L. C. R. Robbins, *An Essay on the Nature and Significance of Economic Science* (London: Macmillan, 1933); F. A. Hayek, *The Counter-Revolution of Science* (Evanston, Ill.: Free Press, 1952); M. Blaug, *Economic Theory in Retrospect* (Cambridge University Press, 1979). See further, T. W. Hutchison *The Significance and Basic Postulates of Economic Theory* (1938) (New York: Kelly, 1965), whose argument, not for historical relativism, but against the universalism of Liberal economics is one of the earliest of its kind.
9. Galileo's law has been deliberately expressed in post-Newtonian terms – i.e. with *explicit* reference to the force of gravity, etc. – in order to emphasise the conditions which limit the scope of its application.
10. See further, *Ideology and Method*, chap. 7.
11. See Robert C. Tucker (ed.), *The Marx – Engels Reader* (New York: W. W. Norton, 1978) p. 13.
12. See *The General Theory of Employment Interest and Money* (London: Macmillan, 1961) pp. 297–8.
13. *Principles*, Appendix D, p. 645.
14. See further, *Ideology and Method*, chap. 5.
15. See N. Kaldor, 'The Irrelevance of Equilibrium Economics', *Economic Journal* (December 1972); and E. H. Phelps Brown, 'The Underdevelopment of Economics', *Economic Journal* (March 1972).

5 Subjectivism, Falsification, and Positive Economics

JEREMY SHEARMUR

INTRODUCTION

Since the time of Adam Smith, economists have often paused to reflect on the methodology of economics, or to consider the general character of either the social or the natural sciences. These reflections have also *sometimes* had a connection with their work as economists. As someone with a particular interest in these matters, and in their history, I would like to be able to think that such reflections had played a major role in the development of economics. But here, as elsewhere, Adam Smith is someone from whom we can learn. For while, in his brilliant essay on the history of astronomy,[1] Smith produced some very interesting ideas on the philosophy of science – ideas which have led some people to regard him as a precursor either of Popper or of Kuhn – it is highly debatable whether these ideas had any influence on his work as an economist.

Nonetheless, there are times when methodological issues come to the fore, and when work produced by economists does seem directly influenced by ideas about methodology that are held in a fairly self-conscious manner. Some people, following Thomas Kuhn,[2] would see in this a sign that the normal procedures of economics, as a mature science, have broken down. They would view such periods as a kind of messy interregnum, following which, under the benign rule of a single new orthodoxy, economists will be able to leave such matters alone, and get back to their normal task of detailed piecemeal work. Others, perhaps following Lakatos,[3] would wish to view the history of economics somewhat differently: as normally consisting of competition between different 'research programmes', each characterised by its own particular philosophical and methodological beliefs, but between which assessments are ultimately to be made on the basis of empirical success alone.

In my view, both Kuhn and Lakatos are unduly pessimistic as to the possibility of our being able to learn, and to make progress, in the realm of methodology and in the discussion of programmatic ideas. And while the history of economics has so far exemplified more closely Kuhn's and Lakatos's views than mine, I believe that we could do better, especially if we were to pay attention to the history of disputes about methodology. For then, not only might we avoid merely repeating what has been said in the past — and make progress in the discussion of methodology — but methodological discussions might actually make a contribution to the progress of economics itself.

There is at present a considerable degree of self-conscious concern about methodological issues, and about what general programmes of research the economist should follow. One focus of attention has been the revival of interest in Marxian and neo-Ricardian approaches to economics. But there is also a revival of interest in those various doctrines which are often now known as 'subjectivism' — as is witnessed by the general theme of the lectures in this session. But what *is* really at issue between 'subjectivism' and the inherited, more orthodox, position? If we are to hope for genuine progress, we must unearth, and try to resolve, those points at issue as best we can. For the purposes of this paper, I will take the more orthodox position to be broadly empiricist in character, and to be *more or less* in accord with the ideas of Milton Friedman in his 'The Methodology of Positive Economics'.[4] I will therefore look at some of the points at issue between Friedman's views and 'subjectivism'.

EXPLANATION, PREDICTION AND 'MATERIAL REQUIREMENTS'

One focus of disagreement between Friedman and the subjectivists relates to those criteria that a theory has to meet if it is to be any good. The character of the disagreement can well be brought out if we look briefly at what is often referred to as the 'Popper–Hempel' model of deductive explanation.[5]

This view, developed by Popper in the 1930s,[6] and much written about and discussed thereafter,[7] amounts to the idea that an adequate explanation consists of the logical deduction of a statement of what we want to explain from statements of universal laws and statements of initial or boundary conditions, where these statements themselves satisfy certain requirements (of which I will say something shortly). At its simplest, therefore, we would explain that Henry is black by deducing a statement to this effect from the initial condition 'Henry is a raven' and the universal law 'All ravens are black'. This universal law may, of course, itself be susceptible to further deductive explanation, in terms of more fundamental universal laws and statements of initial conditions; but this fact would not undermine our original explanation. However, if the 'universal law' in question is discovered not to be true, then it wouldn't be acceptable as part of an explanation.

As I mentioned, our statements of universal laws and of initial conditions themselves have to meet certain requirements, and it is with these that I will be particularly concerned. Popper and Hempel both firmly emphasised that these statements should be independently testable — testable in respect of other cases — and that they should pass these tests. Indeed, they emphasised testability in contrast to what are sometimes called 'material requirements' on explanation; for example, the demand that our explanatory premises comply with some particular kind of metaphysical theory — or general theory about the world — that is held to be true on *a priori* grounds (such as were, at one time, some of the theories of the physicist and philosopher Descartes, say, the idea that the physical world cannot be intrinsically indeterministic in character). Moreover, these requirements may include demands such as that the premises of our explanations be intuitively obvious, or perhaps even self-evidently true — demands not unknown in the history of economics.

For our present purposes, it is not important whether the ideas of Popper or of Hempel are in all respects adequate as a theory of explanation.[8] What matters for us is their insistence on the sufficiency of the non-material requirement of empirical testability. This stands, in fact, as almost the mark of the empiricist, and it is a disagreement about precisely this that, I suggest, is one of the main points at issue between Friedman (and, more generally, the empiricist tradition in economics) and the subjectivists.[9] For while Friedman emphasises as crucial the ability of an economic theory to generate testable predictions, the subjectivists make common cause with those who have emphasised that the social sciences are distinct in character from the natural sciences, and that the social scientist, because he is dealing with meaningful human actions, has available to him a kind of knowledge that is not available to his colleague in the natural sciences. There is, thus, a tradition, in the methodology of social science, that stresses the importance of our personal acquaintance with meaningful behaviour 'from the inside',[10] as it were; and that stresses, also, the relevance of items of 'common-sense' knowledge in the construction of economic theory. As a result, it sees compatibility with such knowledge as playing the role of a material constraint on the acceptability of theories and explanations in economics.

Before discussing this, however, there is one further issue which must be touched on briefly. It relates to the now almost infamous issue of the realism of the economist's assumptions. Friedman argued that economic theories should be appraised just in terms of their ability to furnish us with correct predictions, and not in terms of what he called the realism of their assumptions. But in his paper, 'The Methodology of Positive Economics', Friedman frequently clothed the term 'assumptions' in quotation marks which, however, he did not explain; and he also in certain respects qualified, or even withdrew, in the latter sections of his paper, what had seemed to many to be the main point for which he was arguing. So what did Friedman want to assert when he said that economic theories should not be appraised in terms of the realism of their assumptions? I would suggest that Friedman might reasonably be taken to be arguing for either one of two rather different positions.

The first of these – which goes back at least to John Stuart Mill's 1836 essay 'On the Definition of Political Economy' – amounts to the idea that the economist works with ideal types; with what are, when applied to any particular concrete situation, false oversimplifications.[11] Examples here might include, concerning human motivation, the idea of 'economic man', or of the profit-maximising businessman. A proponent of this position would claim that one would be making a mistake if one thought such ideal types could be appropriately tested against the behaviour of particular individuals, or particular businessmen, or even against what might prove to be the motives of the average businessman. However, it would be claimed, they must nonetheless bear *some* relation to the motivation and behaviour of actual economic agents or businessmen; and they would be explained and defended on the grounds that they represent legitimate oversimplifications, made since we are interested not in the particular individual, but in the overall patterns that are generated as the consequence of the behaviour of individuals.

The second position which Friedman might be taken as advocating is the analogue, in the social sciences, of what, in the methodology of the natural sciences, is sometimes called 'instrumentalism' or 'conventionalism'.[12] These views amount to the idea that theories are merely devices which we construct for the convenient ordering of data and the making of predictions. For the proponent of one or other of these views, it would be a misunderstanding to think that the entities to which a scientist might refer when offering an explanation of something – say, in the natural sciences, the plethora of quarks and other unlikely-sounding subatomic particles about which one might be regaled in other sections of the British Association – are supposed to have any real existence at all.

This view is certainly arguable in regard to the physical sciences. For it may indeed be the case that certain physical theories cannot be given a realistic interpretation. Some people have also argued – less plausibly, I think – that *all* our knowledge is limited to appearances, behind which it is impossible for us to penetrate, and therefore that all physical theories must have an instrumental or conventional character.[13] But in the case of the social sciences such a view seems to me very odd. For we *can* know what lies behind the successful predictions of some economic theory – it is, in one way or another, the all-too-real behaviour of actual individuals, or actual businessmen, acting in the various different situations in which they find themselves. Instrumentalism, in the social sciences, would therefore seem to me to be an unsatisfactory theory. And if someone produces an economic theory that has led to a number of spectacularly successful predictions, I think that it is very reasonable to ask: *why* does it work? a question that an instrumentalist must rule out as unanswerable.

But must our answers to such questions consist only of statements, made at one or another level of abstraction, about the actions of individuals and their consequences?

Instrumentalists often formulate their theories in an 'as if' manner; for example, 'businessmen behave as if they maximise their profits'. But an 'as if' formulation does not necessarily signal instrumentalism. Friedman himself here provides an example.[14] For at one point he explains the idea that businessmen behave as if they maximise profits in terms of the selective effects of the market in which they are operating; that is, in terms of what could be called a selective filter mechanism[15] (he suggests that conditions may have been such as to eliminate any businessmen who did not behave in this way). But in this case, I suggest, what one has actually got here is a realistic theory concerning certain properties of a selective filter mechanism that is claimed to exist, and about which we can reasonably ask for more information.

I will have more to say concerning this type of theory – to be found also in the work of writers such as Alchian and Gary Becker[16] – in the final section of this paper.

Here, however, I would like to sum up these remarks about the realism of assumptions: while instrumentalism is a highly unsatisfactory position to take up in the social sciences, something like Mill's view, of working with false oversimplifications, or with ideal types, is very much part of the mainstream of economic thought.

But there is, I believe, a point at issue here between subjectivism and the mainstream of economic thought. For many subjectivists have criticised other economists for customarily making assumptions of a false and illegitimately oversimplifying character, claiming that this has led to inadequacies in their theories. In part, what is at issue here is simply that one group of economic theorists prefer models of a different type to those that are used by other economists – an issue that is presumably either to be decided empirically, or which will lead us back to our first issue of the criteria for assessing theories. But there is at least also an element of dissatisfaction with certain kinds of oversimplifying abstraction as such – an issue which I will discuss later.

TESTABILITY IN ECONOMICS

Now, however, I would like to turn back to our first dispute between the subjectivists on the one side, and Friedman and other empiricists on the other: to the issue of empirical testability in economics.

This dispute has, quite obviously, been going on for years; and, in many respects, the ideas of contemporary subjectivists on this topic amount to a restatement of themes to be found in the work of Mises, Hayek and the early Robbins in the 1930s. At that time, those ideas came in for a certain amount of direct criticism; but this criticism itself depended to a considerable extent on the presupposition of the correctness of certain forms of positivism (for example, operationalism) that have themselves since been recognised to be clearly untenable.[17] The major line of criticism was, however, indirect. It consisted of the offering of a competing vision of economics; of economics as being, roughly, comparable to a natural science, with pride of place being given to testability. And as this alternative developed, it has tended to identify itself, albeit somewhat loosely, with the views of Karl Popper, who has been adopted as a kind of patron saint of empirical science.[18] As a result, it is not surprising to find certain recent proponents of subjectivism developing, or making use of,[19] criticisms of the idea of testability or of falsifiability that have been directed against Popper's work. For, they doubtless consider, if one could undermine the ideas of testability, falsifiability and successful prediction as criteria by which the success of economic theories is to be judged, this would leave the field more open for their ideas.

A few years ago, such an approach might have seemed merely eccentric. But today, subjectivists can call on criticisms of the ideas of testability and of falsification that have been developed within the philosophy of science,[20] and by proponents of other non-empiricist approaches to methodology – such as that of Hollis and Nell in their *Rational Economic Man*.[21] Two such criticisms have had great currency, and seem to have made a considerable impression.

The first of these criticisms could be called the argument from the theory-impregnation or the value-impregnation of test data. The empirical testing of theories, it is alleged, depends upon our being able to have access to 'data' that are simply 'given', and which merely reflect what the world is like. But, it is claimed, such data are never in fact available to us – for so-called data are the result of our approaching the world from a certain point of view, and must be described in terms which are essentially theoretical in character. It is further suggested that, in the social sciences, the descriptive terms that we use for our data will also reflect various value judgements. There is, it is therefore claimed, no such thing as the data that the empiricist tradition requires.[22]

I would admit these points about the role of theories, values and points of view in the constitution of data; and I would also agree that they are indeed telling against those rather naive forms of empiricism that pretend that theories can be generated simply by the correlation of supposedly neutral data. But I would contend that this whole line of criticism is way off the mark if it is advanced against the views of Karl Popper and those empiricists genuinely guided by his work. For a central theme of Popper's ideas about testability and objectivity is that these are not things that are simply given, but that they depend on our *active* efforts, and on our *choosing* to adopt certain specific procedures for the handling of our theories. For Popper, the scientific status of a theory depends precisely on its proponents being able to indicate what would be a genuine test of it, and, indeed, in their choosing to hold the theory in such a way that it *is* open to correction and criticism on the basis of something that is *relatively* autonomous of it.[23] This, however, will not always be simply there to hand, and it will be one of the prime tasks of the proponent of a theory to try to develop ways in which his theory can genuinely be tested.

But in what will this activity consist, and how could it possibly overcome the kinds of problems to which I have referred? These problems might, in fact, come in one of two forms. First, we might be faced by two theorists who, while claiming in some way to be addressing the same problem, nevertheless seem to be talking past one another, because they insist on characterising anything that one might regard as empirical data within the terminology of their different theories, each claiming that it supports them, and refutes the other view. Here, from Popper's perspective, the relevant task will be for each group genuinely to try to understand the theories of their opponents, and the problems to which they are directed, and to work with their opponents to try to agree on what would be a relevant test. This might involve both groups trying to evolve some elements of a new theoretical terminology, which is neutral relative to the two theories in question, and with the use of which genuine comparisons and tests can be made. Or it may merely involve one group working within the theoretical terminology of the others, and working out with them − on their own ground, as it were − what would be a relevant test of the theory. (What is clear enough, from Popper's perspective, is that there is little point in undertaking 'tests' concerning which there is not already general agreement as to their relevance for the choice between theories.)

This, however, brings us to the second form of our problem: namely, how are tests even possible, if one doesn't leave the 'closed circle' of a single theory? For if our data is couched in the theoretical terminology of the theory under test, can it not but reinforce the theory?[24] Some writers seem to see, in this, an insuperable problem for empiricism. But the answer to it is, I think, surprisingly simple. One just asks the proponent of the theory to specify how certain entities or objects, to which the theory refers, are supposed to behave − for example, to offer us some quantitative or even qualitative hypothesis about them. We then ask him how we can *independently* identify the objects in question − and we then see if they in fact behave in accordance with his specification. That is to say, we then simply run a test, and corroborate or refute the theory in question.

This answer, however, might be thought objectionable on a number of grounds. First, I might seem to have spoken too lightly about our ability to enter into the theoretical ideas of those who take a perspective different from our own – or at least to do so in a critical spirit. For, all too often, the only way in is claimed to be through a kind of conversion experience, or Kuhnian *Gestalt* switch, after which, it is claimed, there is no real possibility of turning back to compare your new ideas with some other theory, or even with empirical evidence representing a world thought of as existing independently of your theory. But while this description indeed fits the attitude of the devotees of some theories, it seems to me to be of a rather special character: namely, to be a form of senile decay of a theoretical position. For it is a viewpoint which could hardly have been upheld at the time of the inception of the theory in question. For then, it would have been necessary for the inventor of the theory to understand just how his new ideas added up to a solution to *pre-existing* problems if he were to be able to value the theory himself, or if he were to try to convince others of its merits. Of course, claims that are put forward in this context may not be correct; and people may come to adopt a new theory for the silliest of reasons. But that the theory must in *some* way be seen as resolving pre-existing problems is, I think, a condition of its intelligibility, and the question of whether it provides a *good* solution to those problems provides a check on its acceptability in terms of something independent of itself. Accordingly, I would suggest that, in order to appraise a theory that is being taken by its proponents as being self-justifyingly self-contained one can well concentrate on the problems to which it was *originally* claimed to be relevant. And it is for this reason, also, that I think that a concern with the history of ideas is important in the evaluation of current theories.

Aside from the issue of theoretical or value-impregnation of our data, however, there is a second problem regarding testability; one that has been extensively discussed in recent years in the philosophy of science. It relates to what is sometimes known as the 'Duhem-Quine' argument,[25] and also to certain points that have been made in the work of Thomas Kuhn. It has been discussed, at great length, as a problem for Popper's views, in the writings of Imre Lakatos and, through him, it has influenced certain writers on the methodology of economics – notably, Spiro Latsis.[26]

But what is the problem? Very simply, it results from the fact that in trying to test a theory, we are not just testing one theory, but a whole bundle of theories and statements of initial conditions. Thus, if our predictions don't come out right, then, if our formal reasoning has been correct, all we are entitled to conclude is that *one* (or more) of our assumptions is incorrect: the test doesn't tell us which. And so there might seem to be the possibility of modifying one of our subsidiary assumptions, so as to explain why our prediction wasn't right – and of our continuing to adopt this strategy, in the face of further predictive failures, in such a way that our theory itself is never brought into question. If this should sound familiar to economists, the reason is that it is, in effect, another way of putting certain of the problems raised by one of our old favourites: the problems of the *ceteris paribus* clause.[27]

But how serious a problem is this for Popper's idea of falsifiability, and hence for the idea of testability? Somewhat unfashionably, I don't think that there is as great a problem here as some have supposed. First of all, this was a problem with which Popper himself was concerned in his *Logic of Scientific Discovery*, and to which he there offered a solution.[28] What he there said was that it is indeed possible to avoid any falsification, if you choose to do so. But, he suggested, it was typically by adopting certain strategies that people avoided the possibility of their theoretical ideas being adversely affected by what appeared *prima facie* to be refutations of them: for example, they would make *ad hoc* reinterpretations of the evidence; or they would restrict the scope of their theories (while professing to have done no such thing); or they would turn their theories from being empirical in character into maxims that are rendered true by convention.

Popper emphasised that, for theories to be falsifiable, it is necessary that their proponents adopt certain methodological rules – the effects of which are to close off the possibility of saving a theory from refutation by the means to which I have just referred, and which suggest, instead, that we should adopt the strategy of holding our theory in its boldest possible form.

There is a danger, however, that this remedy may seem to have gone too far. For there are obviously cases in which it is, indeed, some subsidiary assumption that is at fault, and which stands in need of modification. Popper allowed for this, too. He suggested that it was quite in order to make such modifications, provided that we did not diminish the content of our total theoretical system in so doing. While I am not sure if this idea of content can be given a precise technical explication, the common-sense idea is clear enough: modifications are in order provided that we don't diminish the scope of what we are saying, and save ourselves from empirical criticisms by saying less and less.[29]

It might be maintained, however, that if Popper can get round this problem in the way that I have described in the previous paragraph, then he is in fact back to square one. For Imre Lakatos, at one point in his writings, seemed to suggest that it was *always* possible for us to avoid a *prima facie* refutation of a theory in a content-increasing way, and he offered the model of the discovery of Neptune as a case in point.[30] Here, an unexpected disconfirmation of the prediction of the path of the planet Uranus, on the basis of currently accepted know-ledge about initial conditions, led, not to the refutation of Newtonian theory, but to the postulation and subsequent discovery of a hitherto unknown planet, responsible for the disturbance in question. Lakatos seemed to indicate that such an option was always open to us.[31] But it seems to me that it is not. For Lakatos's example is highly untypical, in that the changes in initial conditions involved in it have very few relevant consequences outside the original problem-situation. But our more typical situation is such that, if we make a change to the initial conditions assumed in one part of our knowledge, this will have ramifications in other parts of our knowledge (i.e. on those hitherto unproblematically accepted explanations that themselves make use of these same items of knowledge). Any modification that is introduced, in these cases, would therefore not only have to deal with the prob-lematic test result, but also have to 'save the appearances' with respect to the other areas of our knowledge that would be affected by the change. And this, it seems to me, introduces a constraint on the ease with which we can make such changes in such a way that Popper's solu-tion to the problem remains intact.

Of course, this solution to the problem does not tell the economist what he should do if his theory appears to be falsified; it merely suggests that there are some procedures that he shouldn't adopt when trying to cope with the problem, and also offers some general sugges-tions about the kinds of properties that it is desirable that his new theoretical system should possess.

To sum up: I don't think that these two arguments against Popper's views, and against the idea of testability, are as powerful as their pro-ponents believe, and I certainly don't think that they serve as grounds for dismissing the importance of testability as a principal desideratum in the selection of our theories.

There are, however, three rather more mundane problems that may, perhaps, limit the power of testability as the principle criterion of theory choice in economics.

First, we often work not merely with ideas that abstract radically from reality, but with oversimplifications that we know actually to be false. But then we can well expect that some of the consequences that we draw from them will not be correct, either. As a result, if our theory does badly in a test, we may not know whether to judge it inadequate, or merely to put its failure down to the fact that it is not quite true (which we knew anyway). This difficulty might, however, be mitigated by making our tests ones in which we compare the relative performance of two theories.[32]

Second, there is the problem that, in economics, we seem reasonably happy to work with a variety of situational models, rather than striving for substantive universal theories. I don't think that there is anything wrong with this as such (such models will typically consist of generalised statements of initial conditions, which obviously may vary from situation to situation); but it may, nonetheless, serve to undermine the notion of testability, by undermining the role of boldness and of high content, on which, according to Popper, testability depends. For, on finding that a model doesn't work in some area, we may merely develop another, additional model for use in that area alone, so that the landscape eventually becomes dotted with a proliferation of such models. The result may be that what initially appeared to be tests of our theory turn out merely to be an investigation of the areas in which it can successfully be used to make predictions, and this seems to lead us back to a kind of instrumentalism or conventionalism (of, for example, the sort espoused by Machlup[33]).

Third, there is the more practical point, often voiced by economists, that in testing their theories and models, they have typically to make do with data that have been gathered by other people for other purposes – and which may therefore be of doubtful relevance to their work.

I would see these problems as posing difficulties for the idea of testability in economics, but I do not think that it is sunk. Indeed it would seem to me that if it goes down, then so does all economics, for there is surely more than one possible explanation that could be offered for any phenomenon, even *given* some general point of view that an anti-empiricist wishes to urge on us, such as Marxism or an 'Austrian' approach, and we'd need to test between these different possibilities. Here, again, Descartes furnishes us with an interesting model. For while he hoped that fundamental truths about the physical world could be established through purely philosophical argument, it was still an empirical matter to discover how these fitted together so as to explain any particular occurrence in the physical world.[34] But while I do not think that testability is sunk, it certainly seems that, in economics, it can do with any help that it can get. It is therefore important to see what the subjectivist (and other) traditions can offer us in the way of material criteria to be satisfied by our explanations.

THREE CONTRIBUTIONS FROM SUBJECTIVISM

I turn, now, to three contributions that subjectivism has offered the economist as material criteria in his choice of theories.

First, there is an idea that is not distinctive to subjectivism — it is also an element in some strands of classical economics — but which is to be found in the writings of some of the notable spokesmen of the subjectivist tradition, such as the early Robbins and Hayek.[35] It is, essentially, that economic knowledge should be obtained by deductive reasoning from common-sense knowledge — either from simple maxims concerning human motivation, or from common-sense empirical knowledge. But while such an approach may be of heuristic value, and while such knowledge may be a useful repository of ideas that can be used in the criticism of other theories, it seems to me unsuitable for the purposes for which Robbins and Hayek have wished to use it. For the economist will typically need to work with premisses that are more explicit than are the ideas we are familiar with from common sense. (An obvious example is the economist's treatment of the individual's preference for goods.) But there will be a number of *different* premisses that the economist might adopt, each of which would be compatible with our 'common-sense' knowledge, but each of which might lead to different consequences in the economist's theoretical work. One or other of these premisses must be selected by the economist; but which, and on what basis is he to make his choice? The approach of Hayek and of Robbins does not seem able to help us here, as each of these premisses is compatible with our common-sense knowledge. Common sense alone cannot, I think, help us in this choice; and *this* element of the subjectivist tradition seems to me, in consequence, of limited value, especially if it is regarded as an alternative to empirical testability.

Second, there is the tradition of 'methodological individualism'. This, in my opinion, properly speaking goes back to the work of Carl Menger who developed a form of individualism in his *Principles* and who, in his *Untersuchungen*,[36] insisted that the organic patterns that the theorists of the historical schools of law and of economics discerned in the development of legal and economic institutions were to be understood as the result of the actions of individuals, taking place in social situations, and their unintended consequences.[37] Subsequent writers in this tradition, such as Mises and Hayek, have emphasised the importance, for the social sciences, of the fact that human action takes place on the basis of our subjective beliefs about the world and about the objects in it and the value that they possess, rather than on the basis of a direct orientation towards properties that they may actually possess or may be described as possessing by the physical sciences.[38] These writers also made something of a common cause with spokesmen of that largely independent tradition which, in Britain, is often referred to under the name of *Verstehen*.[39]

Third, there is what I earlier referred to as a certain kind of realism. By this, I mean an insistence on the illegitimacy of certain kinds of oversimplifying assumption that are customarily made by economists − especially that of perfect knowledge − and of the disregard of the importance of expectations and their uncertain character. Some of those who regard themselves as 'subjectivists' are primarily interested in advocating a measure of psychological or behavioural realism concerning the premisses of economic explanations, and suggest that these are appropriately to be established or tested directly, by empirical means. *These* subjectivists may show little sympathy with those criticisms of empiricism with which this paper has so far been largely concerned, and there is a continuity between their work and that of the historical and institutional schools, which often prided themselves on their 'empiricism'.

There is, I think, a very great deal that can be said for the interest, and importance, both of methodological individualism and of this kind of 'realism', and about the suggestiveness of some of the work to which it has led. But I will not discuss the merits of these approaches here, and will, instead, play devil's advocate, and raise a problem about their implications for economics.

The problem is that these ideas seem to have a destructive − and, indeed, almost a self-destructive − aspect to them. For by directing our attention to individual trees, and the particular, distinctive features that they possess, they lead us away from any overall theoretical knowledge of the economic wood. And it is with this − the overall problems of the economy and the patterns that result from the actions of individuals in their various situations − that the economist is primarily concerned. First, methodological individualism has been taken, by some, to imply the illegitimacy of any theory in which causal interrelationships are postulated as holding between aggregates.[40] It is, I think, true enough that economic aggregates do not possess, in themselves, causal properties (other than as concepts grasped by individuals). But a theory which speaks in such terms may nonetheless give us a picture of a particular relationship at just that level of simplification in which we are interested. A philosophical objection is often made here, where what in fact is called for is a claim that a theory which does not oversimplify as much, or in the manner in question, would be a better one. The latter claim would be open to empirical assessment, whereas the philosophical objection would serve to rule out entire areas of the economy as objects of theoretical understanding.[41]

Second, insistence on the ignorance, the imperfect knowledge or the incorrectness of the expectations of economic agents may lead to much the same problems. For once again, while the objection to such assumptions is correct enough, and some interesting ideas have been developed by those who reject it, there is a danger that the consequence of this objection will be merely to rule out a lot of theories, and to offer us nothing in their place. In particular, there is the danger that we will be left with premises that will be too weak for anything of importance to follow from them, so that, as economists, we will have nothing to say on such issues as the likely welfare consequences of a free market system; on issues of economic policy or the theory of economic development; or as to whether we can or cannot reasonably hope for the efficient utilisation of resources, or a low rate of unemployment, given the prevalence of a free market (a point which should be of particular concern to those spokesmen of subjectivism who have so favoured market mechanisms, as opposed to governmental action).

Third, there is the danger that the demand for 'empirical realism' with regard to the motivation of economic agents will lead us in the direction of excessively detailed work and to a proliferation of models for particular problem areas – or even individuals – with the result that all we ultimately end up being able to do is to reconstruct retrospectively what has already taken place.

Some of these tendencies seem to me already to be present in the work of Hayek – in his writings on economics and knowledge, and in his attack on the idea of equilibrium and on the postulation of relationships between aggregates.[42] And they have come to fruition in the work of Ludwig Lachmann and Professor Shackle, the tendency of both of whose work has been described as 'nihilistic' even by some who sympathise with it and find it stimulating.

There would thus seem to be a real danger that the adoption of the criteria that are offered by the subjectivist tradition *may* have a destructive effect, and rule out just about any theory that is oriented towards some of the most important problems in economics. But at the same time, there is much that seems both sound and interesting in this tradition: its philosophical ideas, as developed by Hayek, Weber and Popper;[43] Hayek's vision of competition as a discovery procedure;

the LSE approach to costs; Shackle's and Lachmann's emphasis on expectations; Wiseman's very natural attempts to combine subjectivism with concerns more common in the behavioural and institutional schools . . . and much more.

What are we to conclude?

I would like to offer two suggestions.

First, for the working economist, a somewhat sober comment. The subjectivist tradition, as it stands at present, seems to me to represent a fertile source of substantive ideas, and also to include some useful suggestions as to criteria to be used in the selection of theories. The working economist would, I think, do well to keep abreast of developments here. But he should also, I think, bear in mind that *some* of the appealing suggestions to be found in this tradition may serve as a will-o'-the-wisp, leading us away from theories of much power and towards ideas that, while grounded in common sense, or in empirical studies of human behaviour, and 'realistic' in character, would debar us from making any real contribution to many major problems in economics.

THE 'NATURAL SELECTION' MODEL AS A NATURAL COMPLEMENT TO SUBJECTIVISM

In this final section of my paper, I would like to offer a second and more speculative suggestion. The subjectivist approach stands in need of something to complement it, so as to mitigate the 'nihilism' into which it threatens to lead us, and to enable us to recognise the effects of institutional and other systematic constraints on the actions of individuals. A promising candidate here, I suggest, is the Alchian, Friedman, Becker 'natural selection' approach.

To explain: the subjectivist tradition is correct in its emphasis on individual action, and thus on the relevance of the material criteria discussed in the previous section. At the same time, it largely ignores the way in which the behaviour of individuals is shaped, selectively, by the reactions of other people, and by the situations in which individuals act. It therefore stands in need of something to complement it. This the 'natural selection' approach can do, because it is concerned precisely with the selective effects of situations, and because the way in which it treats of these is completely compatible with the view of individual action canvassed by the subjectivist tradition. Nozick is correct to say that talk of selective filter mechanisms is incompatible with methodological individualism. But such mechanisms bear no resemblance to the 'group minds' or 'Spirits of the Age' which individualist writers have properly taught us to spurn, and they may themselves be understandable, in their turn, as being the product of the actions of individuals in various social situations. The descriptions of individual action to which we would be led by the material criteria discussed in the previous section would contribute the basis of individual behaviour which is then subject to the selective effects of filter mechanisms. The nihilistic tendencies of the subjectivist tradition may, I think, be overcome by this same approach. For the concern of the economic theorist will be with the *products* of the interaction between individual behaviour and filter systems, and with their consequences. And here, as Alchian, Friedman and Becker have sought to suggest, we *may* be able to rehabilitate certain oversimplified, and highly contentful, statements concerning human behaviour, of which use can then be made in economic theory, by seeing them as describing the *products* of individual action in the subjectivists' sense, and the selective action of filter systems.

There seems to me, however, to be no particular reason why the kind of conduct which happens to be the product of such filter systems must be that of profit maximisation; and I would wish explicitly to sever the natural selection approach from its customary use as an apology for the 'classic' theory of the firm. Instead, I would see this approach as guiding us to a concern with the individual's detailed subjective motivation and specific aims, after the fashion of the behaviouralists, when there is little selective pressure upon him. Where there are particular local or institutional constraints, we would be guided to the customary concerns of the institutional and historical schools. And we may also be able to generate a basis for more ordinary theoretical economics (much as Alchian and Becker have suggested that their views serve to underpin some of the assumptions of orthodox economic theory). But this basis would have built into it a sensitivity both for those issues that have concerned the subjectivists and for those that have hitherto been largely the concern only of institutionalist and Marxist writers, and of members of 'historical' schools of economics. Finally, we may also develop theories that relate not just to the selective effects of filter systems, but also to the way in which individuals learn and modify their behaviour within them, after the spirit of Adam Smith's remark that 'good management, can never be universally established but in consequence of that free and universal competition which forces everybody to have recourse to it for the sake of self defence'.[44]

I am well aware that, as it stands, this is merely a vague suggestion, requiring much detailed elaboration. To start with, we must get round those criticisms that have been advanced against the older experiments in the direction of 'natural selection' approaches to economic theory.[45] In addition, those of you acquainted with subjectivist writings of the 'modern Austrian' variety might think my suggested partnership of subjectivism, and a 'natural selection' approach doomed to failure, as one of the hardest critics of Gary Becker's excursions in the direction of 'natural selection' models was Israel Kirzner,[46] a leading spokesman of the revival of 'Austrian' subjectivism. Nonetheless, it seems to me that these ideas should be explored in tandem with the subjectivist tradition. For not only does subjectivism stand in urgent need of a theory dealing with the impact on individuals (and on their aims, motives and actions) of the systematic pressures exercised by the circumstances in which they act. It also seems to me that many features of a 'natural selection' approach form a natural complement to subjectivism. Here we have a form of 'holism' that should not offend the subjectivists' philosophical susceptibilities; moreover, the selection approach rests on a view of the economy as a process, an idea closely related to ideas strongly emphasised in recent 'subjectivist' work;[47] there is, in addition, room in this approach for that emphasis on the importance of institutional factors that has recently concerned, for example, Wiseman; and finally there is a natural affinity with Hayek's long-established concern for all kinds of selective mechanisms. Similarly, I think that at least some of the criticisms of the natural selection approach – as made, for example, by Winter – may be met more easily from a subjectivist than from a more orthodox neoclassical background.

Whether this suggestion of mine will amount to anything, however, is not for me to say. It obviously stands in need of much elaboration before it can be easily evaluated; and that task of evaluation I must leave to the selective processes and filter systems that operate in the community of economists. Though just what kinds of epistemological properties these, and the institutions of the world of economics, select for is itself an interesting question – but a topic for a paper on another occasion.[48]

NOTES AND REFERENCES

I would like to thank Larry Briskman for criticism and discussion, and for invaluable suggestions as to how this paper could be transformed from an informal talk into something more suitable for publication.

1. Adam Smith, 'The Principles which Lead and Direct Philosophical Enquiries; as Illustrated by the History of Astronomy'; see, for example, Adam Smith, *Essays on Philosophical Subjects* (Oxford: Clarendon Press, 1980).
2. T. S. Kuhn, *The Structure of Scientific Revolutions* (Chicago University Press, 1962, 1970).
3. See I. Lakatos, *The Methodology of Scientific Research Programmes*, and *Mathematics, Science and Epistemology* (Cambridge University Press, 1978).
4. M. Friedman, 'The Methodology of Positive Economics' in his *Essays in Positive Economics* (Chicago University Press, 1963). For criticism, see the references in note 25 on p. 110 of M. Blaug, *The Methodology of Economics* (Cambridge University Press, 1980). On p. 127 of this book, Blaug identifies the views of Friedman (and Machlup) as 'the current mainstream'.
5. See K. R. Popper, 'The Bucket and the Searchlight' in his *Objective Knowledge* (Oxford: Clarendon Press, 1972).
6. In his *Logik der Forschung*; English translation, *The Logic of Scientific Discovery* (London: Hutchinson, 1959).
7. See, notably, Carl Hempel, *Aspects of Scientific Explanation* (Glencoe: The Free Press, 1965).
8. For criticism, see E. Sosa (ed.), *Causation and Conditionals* (Oxford University Press, 1975), and R. Harré, *Principles of Scientific Thinking* (London: Macmillan, 1970) especially chap. 1.
9. As Jack Wiseman was to suggest in the discussion of my paper, my formulation here may be somewhat misleading, as it is only *some* of those who refer to themselves as 'subjectivists' who oppose empirical testability. Others − as I mention later in the paper − take the issue of the realism of psychological, sociological or institutional assumptions as being crucial, and those who take this view may be staunch empiricists.
10. I here have in mind both those who uphold the importance of introspective knowledge and those, like Peter Winch, who stress the importance of internal relations between ideas and concepts in the understanding of human behaviour.
11. J. S. Mill, 'On the Definition of Political Economy'; see, for example, his *Essays on Some Unsettled Questions in Political Economy*. If this interpretative suggestion is correct, Samuelson should have called the 'F-Twist' the 'M-Twist'. See F. Wong, 'The "F-Twist" and the Methodology of Paul Samuelson', *American Economic Review* 63 (1973) 312–25.
12. I do not wish to suggest that, in all respects, these views are identical. For a brief but very hostile exposition of instrumentalism, see K. R. Popper, 'Three Views Concerning Human Knowledge' in his *Conjectures and Refutations* (London: Routledge & Kegan Paul, 1963) and, on conventionalism, Pierre Duhem, *The Aim and Structure of Physical Theory* (Princeton University Press, 1954); and W. V. O. Quine, 'Two Dogmas of Empiricism', in his *From a Logical Point of View* (Harvard University Press, 1953).
13. There is also a more interesting argument for conventionalism, which suggests that the selection of theories must depend on the use of simplicity

requirements which, as they are not empirical in character, have the result that our knowledge is in part conventional. Cp. W. Newton-Smith, 'The Underdetermination of Theory by Data', *The Aristotelian Society Supp. Volume* LII (1978) 71–91.

14. Friedman, 'The Methodology of Positive Economics', Section III.
15. See, for this idea, and for the suggestion that it poses a problem for methodological individualism, R. Nozick, *Anarchy, State and Utopia* (Oxford: Blackwell, 1974) p. 22.
16. See A. A. Alchian, 'Uncertainty, Evolution and Economic Theory', now in his *Economic Forces at Work* (Indianapolis: Liberty Press, 1977) and G. Becker, 'Irrational Behaviour and Economic Theory', *Journal of Political Economy* 70 (1962) 1–13; see also M. Blaug, *The Methodology of Economics*, pp. 116–19 and S. G. Winter, 'Economic "Natural Selection" and the Theory of the Firm', *Yale Economic Essays* (1962) 225–72.
17. See Machlup's discussions of radical empiricism and operationalism in his *Methodology of Economics and Other Social Sciences* (London: Academic Press, 1978), and also F. Suppe (ed.), *The Structure of Scientific Theories* (University of Illinois Press, 1977), in which Suppe's introductions give an excellent guided tour through the relevant material in the philosophy of science.
18. The most recent statement of this is Blaug's excellent *Methodology of Economics*, though, as he points out, there is reason to believe that economists do not always practise the Popperian empiricism that they preach.
19. See, for example, M. J. Rizzo, 'Praxeology and Econometrics: A Critique of Positivist Economics', in L. M. Spadaro (ed.), *New Directions in Austrian Economics* (Kansas: Sheed, Andrews and McMeel, 1978). Rizzo's essay is to my mind vitiated by his failure to appreciate the significance of Popper's replacing of a criterion of meaning by one of demarcation.
20. For example, in the writings of Lakatos, Kuhn and Feyerabend.
21. M. Hollis and E. J. Nell, *Rational Economic Man* (Cambridge University Press, 1975), which is cited by Rizzo. Other sources of such criticism are B. Hindess, *Philosophy and Methodology in the Social Sciences* (Brighton: Harvester, 1977), and K. Williams, 'Facing Reality: A Critique of Karl Popper's Empiricism', *Economy and Society* 4 (1975).
22. For arguments in this vein, see the first part of the discussion of Popper in Hindess's *Philosophy and Methodology in the Social Sciences*, and S. Lukes, 'The Underdetermination of Theory by Data', *The Aristotelian Society Supp. Volume* LII (1978) 93–107, where a meal is made of the role of values, in this context, in the social sciences.
23. For a qualification of this emphasis on active choice, see my 'Epistemology Socialized?', forthcoming in *ETC*.
24. This suggestion seems to me to be implicit in the work of Kuhn and of Feyerabend, and to be explicit in the work of some of those who have emphasised the role of values in social science.
25. For a collection of relevant papers, see S. Harding (ed.), *Can Theories be Refuted?* (Dordrecht: Reidel, 1976).
26. See Lakatos's works as cited in note 3 above, and S. J. Latsis, 'Situational Determinism in Economics', *British Journal for the Philosophy of Science*

23 (1972) 207–45, and S. J. Latsis (ed.), *Method and Appraisal in Economics* (Cambridge University Press, 1976).

27. See also K. R. Popper, 'Replies to my Critics', note 75 on pp. 1186–7 of P. A. Schilpp (ed.), *The Philosophy of Karl Popper* (La Salle, Illinois: Open Court, 1974).

28. See his discussion there of 'conventionalist strategies' in sections 6 and 20ff.

29. See *The Logic of Scientific Discovery*, section 20.

30. See I. Lakatos, 'Falsification and the Methodology of Scientific Research Programmes', section 2(a); for example in his *Methodology of Scientific Research Programmes*.

31. Just what Lakatos is arguing here is not completely clear. He was either wishing to suggest that we can always avoid falsifications through 'conventionalist stratagems', a view with which Popper is in agreement, and for which problem he suggested a remedy, or that we can always avoid refutations in a manner that is 'content-increasing'. This, if it were true, would indeed constitute an argument against Popper's views, but I do not think that it is true, for reasons that I advance in the text.

32. It is possible that we may get some assistance here from statistical techniques developed to tell us which of two theories is giving us a better fit to our data; but David Miller, 'The Accuracy of Predictions', *Synthese* 30 (1975) 159–91 raises very general problems about the comparative empirical appraisal of false theories.

33. See F. Machlup, *The Methodology of Economics and Other Social Sciences*, and my review in *Giornale degli Economisti e Annali di Economia* (November–December, 1980) 817–18.

34. See A. I. Sabra, *Theories of Light from Descartes to Newton* (London: Oldbourne, 1977) chap. 1.

35. See L. Robbins, *The Nature and Significance of Economic Science* (London: Macmillan, 1935) chap. 4, and F. A. Hayek, 'The Pretence of Knowledge', now in his *New Studies* (London: Routledge & Kegan Paul, 1978), where, on p. 25, he describes his own account of unemployment as relying on 'facts of everyday experience' and 'the logical correctness of the conclusions drawn from them'.

36. See C. Menger, *Untersuchungen über die Methode der Sozialwissenschaften . . .*, English translation by F. J. Nock, *Problems of Economics and Sociology* (University of Illinois Press, 1963).

37. I have discussed these matters in more detail in my 'Hayek, Menger and "Methodological Individualism"' and 'The Future of Methodological Individualism', delivered, respectively, to meetings of the Carl Menger Society and the Seminar for Austro–German Philosophy, and in my 'The Austrian Connection: Carl Menger and the Thought of F. A. von Hayek', forthcoming in W. Grassl and B. Smith (eds), *Austrian Philosophy and Austrian Politics* (Munich: Philosophia Verlag).

38. See F. A. von Hayek, *The Counter-Revolution of Science* and L. von Mises, *Epistemological Problems of Economics*, both of which have just been reissued by Liberty Press.

39. There are, however, interconnections, notably in the cases of Weber and Schutz.

40. See, for example, F. A. von Hayek, *The Tiger by the Tail* (London: Institute of Economic Affairs, 1972).

41. Unless, that is, some other way of understanding these phenomena is offered – as it is, for example, in Hayek's notion of 'understanding of the principle' – see his *Studies in Philosophy, Politics and Economics* (London: Routledge & Kegan Paul, 1967), and his 'The Pretence of Knowledge' in his *New Studies*.

42. See, for example, his *Individualism and Economic Order* (London: Routledge & Kegan Paul, 1948).

43. Popper's methodological individualism, itself in part a product of the influence of the Austrian tradition – see, in this context, my contribution to 'Making Sense of History', *Inquiry* 22 (1980) 459–89 and R. Cubeddu, 'L'influenza del "marginalismo" sulla filosofia politica di Popper', *Il Penserio Politico* (1981) – serves as a material requirement on explanation in the social sciences.

44. See Adam Smith, *The Wealth of Nations*, Book i, chap. xi, part 1.

45. See, for example, S. G. Winter, 'Economic "Natural Selection" and the Theory of the Firm'.

46. I. Kirzner, 'Rational Action and Economic Theory', *Journal of Political Economy* 70 (1962) 380–5. Note, however, that Kirzner's objections largely concern Becker's use of the idea of irrational behaviour, while, in the ideas that I am advancing here, we are concerned with behaviour which is rational, but possibility based on incorrect information or unrealistic expectations.

47. See, for example, G. O'Driscoll's study of Hayek, *Economics as a Co-ordination Problem* (Kansas: Sheed, Andrews and McMeel, 1977).

48. On the idea of institutional arrangements as having, in this way, epistemological consequences, see my 'The Religious Sect as a Cognitive System', *Annual Review of the Social Sciences of Religion* 4 (1980) 149–63, and my 'Epistemology Socialized?'.

6 The Revival of Subjectivism in Economics

A. W. COATS

INTRODUCTION

Generally speaking, historians are loath to report on current or very recent movements, and the very sound reasons for this disinclination will soon become clear to readers of this chapter. In examining the nature of and reasons for the revival of subjectivism in economics the obvious strategy is to begin by defining the subject and then proceed to trace its origins, development and pre-revival decline; but unfortunately this is much easier said than done. Quite apart from the problem of definition, which will be considered later, the origins of subjectivism in economics go back at least as far as the medieval Scholastics, perhaps even to the Greeks, and its subsequent history has been complex as well as protracted. As it is obviously impossible to cover all this ground in the time allotted, an arbitrary choice of starting-point is unavoidable.

Nevertheless, notwithstanding the difficulties involved, the subject is eminently worth tackling. This is a splendid time for historians of economic ideas, for during the so-called 'crisis' in economics of the past decade or so there have been repeated appeals to history as a practical guide to those who have lost their bearings in the welter of current controversy.[1] Even where this is not the case, the historian can find ample justification for his specialism by exposing the pretensions of those controversialists who seek impressive intellectual pedigrees to enhance the respectability of their current notions or nostrums. The subjectivists are no exception in this respect, for they are fond of quoting an assertion by their leading living representative, F. A. Hayek, that:

> it is probably no exaggeration to say that every important advance in economic theory during the last hundred years was a further step in the consistent application of subjectivism.[2]

It is doubtful that many present-day economists would endorse Hayek's contention uncritically, yet it forms a convenient starting-point for this enquiry, for at least two reasons. The first is that Hayek was alluding to one major landmark in the history of subjectivist economics, the so-called 'marginal revolution' of the 1870s, an essential ingredient of which was the reaction against the 'objective' or cost-of-production theory of value that had been prevalent prior to that time. As any decent history of economics text contains an account of this episode it need not be examined further here.[3] The second reason for citing Hayek's claim is that the recent revival of subjectivism extends far beyond value theory − a branch of economics now somewhat undervalued, if the expression is admissble − and this latest phase owes much to Hayek himself and his former teacher, Ludwig von Mises. But at this point the problem of definition can no longer be avoided.

WHAT IS SUBJECTIVIST ECONOMICS?

The crucial difficulty is to identify the outer periphery or limits of subjectivist economics, and to determine the precise relationship between the territory as a whole and the core doctrines of Austrian or neo-Austrian economics, which constitute the most readily identifiable components of the current revival. While these doctrines are primarily attributable to Hayek, Mises and their disciples, their origins are directly traceable to the school's nineteenth-century master, Carl Menger. There were in fact significant disagreements between Menger and his leading associates and followers, Eugen von Bohm Bäwerk and Friedrich von Wieser, as indeed there are among current neo-Austrians; but this is not the main source of definitional difficulties. It is significant that the latest review of the field, by Alex Shand, seems to have been originally entitled *Austrian Economics: A Survey*, whereas by the time it was published it had become *Subjectivist Economics: The New Austrian School*.[4] If this implies that the two categories are co-extensive, such an interpretation is clearly incompatible with the views of several contributors to this symposium, including its founding father, Professor Wiseman. But if, on the other hand, they are not, then exactly how are they connected: how far do they overlap?

In confessing my inability to provide satisfactory answers to these questions I am, at least, in distinguished company.[5] The issue is, however, of practical as well as academic importance from both the Austrian and the general subjectivist standpoints. If subjectivism is identified with Austrian or neo-Austrian ideas, it necessarily carries with it a penumbra of intellectual connotations, not all of which will be welcomed by all subjectivists. Under the influence of Hayek and Mises, Austrian economics has become associated with a comprehensive and mutually reinforcing combination of elements, including epistemology, methodology, theory, policy recommendations and political ideology. As represented by the more skilful and dedicated neo-Austrian expositors, these ideas appear to possess a logical coherence and systematic character such that those who find parts of the message appealing are liable to be seduced into acceptance of the entire intellectual creed, or *Weltanschauung*. By contrast, the non-Austrian (or even anti-Austrian) subjectivists possess no such central allegiance or collective identity; and if their views are taken to be typical then subjectivism does not constitute a school or movement capable of effectively mounting a challenge to the reigning orthodoxy.

Reference works in the history of philosophy do not appear to recognise subjectivism as a distinct doctrine or stream of thought, and it was therefore interesting to find Shand's citation from Anthony Quinton's *Fontana Dictionary of Modern Thought*:

In a general way, subjectivism is defined as any theory which takes private experience to be the sole foundation of factual knowledge, even if it admits that objective knowledge can be derived from this subjective base.[6]

This is, of course, vague, no doubt intentionally so, on the central epistemological question of the relationship between private experience – which is necessarily subjective – and the type of objective (public, or inter-subjective) knowledge required by any discipline claiming scientific status; and this issue has figured prominently in subjectivist writings. An examination of recent neo-Austrian literature reveals considerable, even fundamental, disagreement on the matter. To some neo-Austrians Mises's outspoken and explicit *a priorism* seems to be a distinct embarrassment, and as T. W. Hutchison has shown in a powerful recent paper,[7] Hayek has radically altered his epistemological views since the early 1930s. At that time he whole-heartedly endorsed Mises's position, emphasising the fundamental differences between the social and the natural sciences, whereas more recently he has moved much closer to Karl Popper, a leading advocate of objective knowledge, acknowledging that the differences between the natural and the social sciences have been 'greatly narrowed'. In his Nobel lecture, Hayek conceded that despite their difficulties the social sciences could 'achieve predictions which can be falsified and which therefore are of empirical significance', and he congratulated Popper on the formulation of the demarcation principle, 'by which we can distinguish between what we may accept as scientific and what not'.[8] These views are very far from the radical subjectivism endorsed by such neo-Austrians as Ludwig Lachmann;[9] and while they fall well short of the naturalistic predictivism espoused by some logical positivists and operationalists in the 1930s, they bear no close resemblance to Mises's position.

This is an issue of considerable importance to subjectivists in general and to neo-Austrians in particular, since most of the latter profess some allegiance to Mises. If the time-honoured Austrian doctrine of methodological dualism is abandoned or severely whittled away, so that the differences between the natural and social sciences appear merely as matters of degree (e.g. complexity) rather than differences of kind, then the basis for a subjectivist separatist movement is seriously undermined. Certain beneficial consequences would, of course, follow from such an interpretation, since it would facilitate a reconciliation between subjectivists and the many mainstream or orthodox economists who have become disenchanted with the exaggerated claims of the 'positive' or 'positivistic' economists, who were in the vanguard of the post-war so-called mathematical and quantitative/economic 'revolution'. However, such a reconciliation may not be entirely welcome to some of the active neo-Austrians who have been so successfully conducting a scholarly and professional struggle for recognition during the past decade or so.

This is not the place to discuss this campaign in detail, which has included the inauguration of undergraduate and graduate programmes in Austrian economics; the holding of special instructional seminars designed to spread the doctrine and to enlist proselytes; the organisation of numerous scholarly conferences; the launching of scholarly journals and publication series, including reprints of Austrian economic classics;

and the founding of a *Newsletter*.[10] Of course these are the customary paraphernalia of modern academic life, and the fruits of this movement have already proved to be of genuine scholarly value.[11] Nor is there necessarily anything sinister in the fact that these activities have been so strikingly varied and vigorous partly, if not largely, because they have been generously subsidised by individuals and groups favourably disposed not only to Austrian economics but also to a wide range of other 'libertarian' causes, including the defence of private enterprise and attacks on government intervention in economic affairs. As with the earlier Mises–Hayek dominated phase of modern Austrian economics, the current neo-Austrian movement possesses epistemological, methodological, theoretical, policy and ideological features, although the last two aspects are much less prominent in the recent scholarly writings than the first three. Moreover, despite the expositors' efforts, these elements are by no means incorporated into a comprehensive and unified whole. Indeed, the prevailing methodological tolerance to which Professor Littlechild referred in his paper might well be regarded by hostile critics as evidence of fundamental confusion and inconsistency.[12]

There is, of course, some justification for the contention that special efforts were required in order to secure scholarly *lebensraum* for proponents of Austrian economics at a time when the major scholarly journals and leading research-funding agencies were dominated by a professional establishment or elite prejudiced against them. Nevertheless, it is probably fair to say that no other among the many contending schools and dissident splinter groups in contemporary economics enjoys such substantial outside resources. And this is directly relevant to the present occasion, when it is important not to exaggerate the significance of the neo-Austrian component in the subjectivist revival simply because it is the most visible and coherent part of that movement.

Any brief attempt to specify the precise differences between contemporary neo-Austrians and other proponents of subjectivist economics is liable to be misleading, given the current diversity of opinions among both groups. In view of his influence, it is tempting to cite Mises as the exemplar of modern Austrianism, especially as he so often expressed himself in clear, forthright and unambiguous terms. Nevertheless, despite their collective loyalty, which sometimes amounts to adulation, few of the younger neo-Austrians would endorse Mises's views *in toto*. Apart from his *a priorism*, referred to earlier, he rejected all attempts at quantification in economics, denying the existence of any constants, and arguing that as all economic statistics refer exclusively to past, non-repeatable historical cases, they therefore provide no basis for reliable predictions of future trends.[13] These contentions are, of course, in marked contrast to the moderate subjectivism expressed in Professor Wiseman's paper, where he acknowledges that 'the development of econometrics is a natural offshoot of the commitment to positivism' and denies any intention of destroying or rejecting 'positive' economics.[14] Without going into the question whether positivism (which Mises and Lachmann explicitly reject) is compatible with subjectivism, which may be largely a semantic issue, it seems clear that few of the younger neo-Austrians wish to cut themselves off entirely from the main stream of the profession. Rather, like many 'orthodox' economists, they complain that disproportionate efforts and resources have been devoted in recent years to econometrics, mathematical modelling and excessively sophisticated static theorising. Unlike earlier Austrians, such as Mises and Hayek, who were profoundly suspicious of or antagonistic to macroeconomics because it was associated with philosophical 'holism' and collectivist thinking, some neo-Austrians are seeking ways of establishing the connections between macroeconomic aggregates and the underlying microeconomic entities in accordance with the long-established Austrian belief in the principle of methodological individualism.[15] Unfortunately it is too early to say whether this approach is likely to yield fruitful results.

Another significant difference between what might be termed Mises-type Austrians and other subjectivists is their attitude towards psychology. Without necessarily espousing an extreme form of methodological dualism, all subjectivists recognise that the social scientist is necessarily concerned with two distinct levels of 'reality' — the external world of observable phenomena (which also concerns the natural scientist), and the 'inner' world of human motives, purposes and interests (which does not). The precise relationship between economics and psychology has long been a bone of contention. Austrians such as Mises and Lachmann have categorically denied that psychology has any role whatsoever in economics, and they seek to dissociate subjectivism from any so-called 'psychological school' of economists.[16] According to Lachmann the social scientist *'explains* social phenomena by reducing them to acts of the mind',[17] a form of reductionism far too extreme for many subjectivists; but he also maintains that *'Not the psychological causes of human decisions, but their logical consequences form the subject-matter of the analytical social sciences.*'[18] This entails no commitment to any specific psychological doxtrine, least of all behaviourism, which epitomises the objectivist fallacy of assuming that human action can be comprehended by studying it exclusively from the outside. Like Mises, he contends that the economist is not concerned with detailed explanations or predictions of human behaviour but with general patterns – with the logic of choice or the general theory of action, for example as set out in Mises's major treatise *Human Action.*[19] This is in complete contrast to Professor Wiseman's paper, which boldly appeals for 'a direct study of human behaviour' and concludes that 'economics as a behavioural science can no longer stand aloof from psychology'.[20] Further examples of contemporary subjectivist efforts to take account of psychology in economics, for example in studying the behaviour of firms and consumers, are provided in Professor Loasby's and Mr Earl's papers in this symposium.[21]

One of the most frequent criticisms of the logic-of-choice approach to economics adopted by some positivist and behaviourist economists is that it is too abstract, general and lacking in empirical content. As Herbert Simon observed more than a decade ago,

> economics has been moving steadily into areas where the power of the 'classical' model has never been demonstrated and where its adequacy must be considered anew . . . Classical economics was highly successful in handling small-maze problems without depending on psychology. Labour relations, imperfect competition, uncertainty, and long-run dynamics encase the decision-maker in a much larger maze than those considered in classical short-run static theory. In these areas the economist and the psychologist have numerous common interests in cognitive theory that they have not shared previously.[22]

Most neo-Austrians share the general dissatisfaction with theories that assume stable tastes and preferences, perfect information and predictable mechanistic or probabilistic relations between past, present and future. But unlike some contemporary subjectivists,[23] they do not favour empirical studies designed to reveal the precise links between learning and experience, or the nature of decision-making in organisations or groups. Indeed, in Kirzner's case, which may be untypical yet possibly indicative of a general Austrian tendency, so strong is the emphasis on the diversity of human tastes and abilities, and the unpredictability and indeterminacy of individuals' preferences, explanations and knowledge, that it becomes difficult to see how any empirical science is attainable in practice.[24]

It would be pointless to try to compile a complete inventory of the differences between the neo-Austrians and other subjectivists partly because the distinction between them is blurred, and partly because their intellectual interests do not exactly coincide. Thus, as might be expected, notwithstanding the differences within their ranks, the neo-Austrians naturally tend to reflect the breadth, coherence and systematic quality of the Austrian tradition in economics, whereas other subjectivists usually focus attention on specific problem areas, and consequently remain silent on a number of issues that figure prominently in Austrian writings. These issues include, for example, the concept of a 'spontaneous order' in economic affairs; the difference between 'causal genetic' and 'functional' analysis; the crucial role of the market process; and the inequities and inefficiencies resulting from government interference in economic and social affairs. At the same time, they emphasise the dangers and limitations of equilibrium economics, especially when it is interpreted mechanistically; the problem of uncertainty and information; and the role of time in economic affairs. Some of these problems are, of course, fully acknowledged by many other economists, a fact that further complicates the task of classifying various individuals and groups.

THE REVIVAL OF SUBJECTIVIST ECONOMICS: PROVISIONAL EXPLANATIONS

Although there were premonitory rumblings in the two preceding decades, the revival of subjectivism was not conspicuous until the 1970s. Given the proximity of these events and the definitional difficulties involved, any attempt to explain this movement is bound to be tentative and incomplete. No attempt will be made here to differentiate between neo-Austrian and other species of subjectivism; but any worthwhile account must include developments in at least four distinct but interrelated spheres:

(a) 'autonomous' developments in the subjectivist movement itself – including the emergence of a contingent of neo-Austrians, and the increased recognition of behavioural elements in microeconomic activity;

(b) developments in economics as a whole, especially the break-down (or at least manifest inadequacy) of the dominant professional consensus (i.e. Keynesian, neo-classical or positivist). This, of course, provided opportunities for a variety of existing dissident and heterodox groups, in addition to the subjectivists;

(c) developments in other intellectual disciplines, which reacted back on economics − e.g. in the history and philosophy of science; in other cognate social sciences; and even in the natural sciences, to which social scientists have customarily looked for their ideal of 'scientific method'; and, finally,

(d) developments outside the academic world − e.g. in economic policy; in the performance of the economy (the so-called 'crisis of capitalism,'); and in the public reputation of the economics profession.

Any such schematic arrangement is necessarily arbitrary, for there was a combination of interacting influences at work, not all of which can be considered in the space available. The following account is therefore selective, and will need to be supplemented and corrected by subsequent research.

Under (a), the most intriguing historical problem is: why did the subjectivist revival of the early and mid-1930s − in the works of Mises, Hayek, the Swedes, the so-called 'LSE cost' theorists,[25] and even Keynes himself − prove so transitory? Why were these innovations so completely submerged in the high tide of Keynesian economics, the mathematical/quantitative 'revolution', and positivism (both in Friedman's 'positive' economics in particular and positivist philosophy in general)? An explanation in terms of purely intellectual, scholarly and scientific factors is obviously inadequate, for there were also more directly practical (i.e. applied and policy-relevant) professional, political and ideological influences. Economists turned from microeconomics, where the subjective aspects of individual actions are more obviously pertinent, to macroeconomics, which seemed at once more exciting and more relevant to contemporary problems. For example, Hayek's attempt to explain the early 1930s depression attracted support only briefly, and his passive approach to policy-making seemed entirely inappropriate to the emergency. By contrast, Keynesian ideas and the concomitant activist policy recommendations gave professional economists unprecedented opportunities to participate in public and private decision-making during and after the Second World War. And it was not until serious misgivings arose concerning the adequacy of the Keynesian theoretical apparatus that a number of subjectivists – mainly a handful of distinguished elder Austrians – were again able to secure a hearing.[26] Microeconomics gradually re-emerged as an intellectually challenging field, rather than merely a subordinate part of the curriculum. Recent research has rediscovered and developed earlier pioneering efforts to incorporate uncertainty, expectations and imperfect knowledge into economic theories. So prominent has been the neo-Austrian movement in this connection that there is some danger of overstating the influence of Menger, Mises and Hayek. T. W. Hutchison has provided a valuable corrective in his essay on 'The Keynesian Revolution, Uncertainty, and Deductive General Theory', which draws on a penetrating paper he published as far back as 1937.[27] Indeed, the virtual neglect of Keynes's own writings (with the honourable exception of G. L. S. Shackle)[28] on this topic in the era of Keynesian hegemony is a striking phenomenon.

One lesson subjectivists may learn from this experience is that if they wish their movement to continue and flourish, let alone effect a counter-revolution, they must not rest content with attacks on the ruling orthodoxy and the pursuit of interesting theoretical problems, as the neo-Austrians seem inclined to do. They must also demonstrate the practical relevance of their ideas not only in the policy realm, but also as a means of enhancing their exponents' career prospects within the economics profession.[29]

(b) The second category of developments favouring the subjectivist revival – i.e. those in other branches and approaches to economics – are complex, but familiar to readers of the professional journals. They can be summed up as a reaction, perhaps inevitable, against the excessive claims made on behalf of Keynesian, mathematical and quantitative economics, and the break up of the so-called neo-classical synthesis. There was a growing sense that the returns in terms of new theoretical insights and new empirical relationships were comparatively meagre, given the enormous investment of intellectual and financial resources.[30] Other grounds for dissatisfaction included: the neglect of microeconomics and monetary economics; the inadequacy of the microeconomic foundations of macroeconomics; the failure of repeated, often overambitious, efforts to formulate meaningful and relevant large-scale growth models; the economists' limited success in dealing with the problems of underdeveloped countries – the list is not exhaustive, but it is surely sufficient to establish the general point.

When it came, whether justified or not, the reaction played into the hands of other dissident and heterodox groups as well as the subjectivists — including the institutionalists, Marxists and radical economists, many of whom would have endorsed the subjectivists' criticisms of orthodox or mainstream economics.[31] There has been, in effect, more agreement about *What's Wrong with Economics?*,[32] to cite the title of Benjamin Ward's provocative book, than about appropriate remedies.

(c) The third category of developments favourable to the revival of subjectivism — i.e. those within academic disciplines other than economics — is so large and imprecise that it would take a confident polymath to cover them adequately. As previous papers in this symposium have shown, subjectivists do not feel constrained by the conventional boundaries of economics. They readily incorporate into their analysis elements from any source — e.g. psychology, anthropology, sociology, organisation and decision theory, political science — which help to shed light on economic problems. To attempt to examine these linkages systematically would be an impossible task. But as subjectivist economics is usually, though not invariably, anti-positivist, or at least sceptical of the cruder positivist approach to the social sciences, it is appropriate to note certain compatible trends in the philosophy of science during the past two decades, for example in the works of Michael Polanyi, Norbert Hanson, Stephen Toulmin, Thomas Kuhn, Imre Lakatos and Paul Feyerabend.[33] In this context Karl Popper's role is crucial, for his influence has been virtually all-pervading among British social scientists in the early post-war decades.

Popper strenuously resisted the tendency to take account of psychological and sociological factors in the development of scientific knowledge, a tendency of great interest to historians of economics. He also consistently opposed subjectivist epistemologies — writing an influential essay on 'Epistemology Without a Knowing Subject', in which he insisted that 'scientific knowledge belongs . . . to the world of objective theories, objective problems, and objective arguments'.[34] This was in direct contrast to those continental philosophies that influenced authors such as Menger, Marx, Weber, Mises, Hayek[35] and Fritz Machlup. It is, of course, essential to recognise the difference between the *sources* of knowledge, which may include introspection, and the *nature* of scientific knowledge, which must be either 'objective' in some sense, or at least 'inter-subjective'. If the latter position is adopted the problem arises: whose judgement is to count? Who are the competent authorities? These questions pose significant issues in the sociology of science — such as the sources and criteria of scientific authority; the organisation and control of knowledge; and the role of scientific elites — issues that have become more obvious to economists and social scientists generally as a by-product of developments in the natural sciences.[36] Kuhn, for example, may not be a subjectivist, as Professor Littlechild has argued; but his work certainly encouraged a more comprehensive and sensitive appreciation of the nature of scientific development and the processes of testing or validating knowledge within the scientific community.[37] This more flexible, historical and humanistic approach discredited earlier, more rigidly naturalistic and mechanistic views of the growth of scientific knowledge, with their concomitant emphasis on the steady accumulation of new 'truths' and their 'naive falsificationist' conception of empirical testing.[38]

(d) Finally, it must be acknowledged that the revival of subjectivism is at least partly attributable to circumstances outside the academic world, for the development of economics has seldom for long been effectively insulated from societal pressures and inducements.

During the post-war period there has been an unprecedented expansion in the employment of economists in non-academic organisations — in government, business and international agencies; and many leading members of the profession have played a prominent part in public discussion of economic affairs and in key policy-making positions. This was a highly satisfactory state of affairs during the first two post-war decades, when economists seemed to be making constructive contributions to the achievement of such goals as the maintenance of full employment, the promotion of economic growth and the extension of international economic co-operation. But when, in the late 1960s and early 1970s, economic policy-making no longer appeared successful and events seemed out of control, there was inevitably a public reaction which contributed directly to the so-called 'crisis' in the discipline, for this was essentially a crisis of professional self-confidence.[39]

This is not the place to assign blame for this state of affairs. The reasons for recent policy failures are complex, and can be explained in a variety of ways. The economists' influence has frequently been exaggerated, both by the economists themselves and by their critics. Admittedly some economists have oversold their product, claiming more than they could deliver, while others have colluded with party politicians seeking re-election or anxious to stay in office.[40] Nevertheless economists have not been primarily responsible for the general tendency to politicise economic affairs or for the consequential public disillusionment at the politicians' failure to fulfil their electoral promises. There has, indeed, been a growing concern about professional ethics, and a novel feature of the situation has been the severe criticism of the academic training of new recruits to the profession by non-academic economists employed in business and government.

Against this background it is easy to see why the combination of public and professional dissatisfaction with the discipline has given aid and comfort to a variety of academic critics of the prevailing economic orthodoxy. Perhaps the best example of a subjectivist reaction is Lachmann's comment that subjectivism appeals to all those who feel that our age has somehow 'gone wrong'[41] − to those who find science, technology and modern materialism distasteful; and who favour individual freedom over large-scale organisation. In other words, the revival of subjectivism is, itself, a product of the age.

NOTES AND REFERENCES

1. Cf. my survey article 'The Current "Crisis" in Economics in Historical Perspective', *Nebraska Journal of Economics and Business* 16 (Summer 1977) and references cited therein. Also the recent special issue of *The Public Interest* (1980) entitled 'The Crisis in Economic Theory', with contributions from a dozen well-known authors. It includes an article on 'The "Austrian" Perspective' by Israel M. Kirzner, a leading neo-Austrian.
2. *The Counter-Revolution of Science* (Glencoe, Ill.; Free Press, 1955) p. 38.
3. For a comprehensive survey of the subject see R. D. Collison Black, A. W. Coats, Crauford D. W. Goodwin, *The Marginal Revolution in Economics. Interpretation and Evaluation* (Durham, N.C.: Duke University Press, 1973) especially the essay 'To What Extent was the Austrian School Marginalist?' by Erich Streissler.
4. Alex Shand, *Subjectivist Economics. The New Austrian School* (Exeter, Devon: Pica Press, 1980) with a comment by G. L. S. Shackle. For other useful surveys see Edwin G. Dolan (ed.), *The Foundations of Modern Austrian Economics* (Kansas City: Sheed and Ward, 1976); Louis M. Spadaro (ed.), *New Directions in Austrian Economics* (Kansas City: Sheed, Andrews and McMeel, 1978).
5. See, for example, Professor Littlechild's paper in this symposium: also the various meanings of subjectivism referred to in the unpublished paper by Ludwig M. Lachmann, 'Ludwig von Mises and the Extension of Subjectivism', delivered at the New York University Conference in honour of Ludwig von Mises, September 1981. According to the *Austrian Economics Newsletter* there is a division between a 'nihilistic' species of subjectivism associated with Keynes (1937 version) and Shackle, and a more mechanistic strain of Ricardianism in recent Austrian literature.
6. Shand, *Subjectivist Economics*, p. 12.
7. 'Austrians on The Philosophy and Method of Economics − (since Menger)' in his *The Politics and Philosophy of Economics. Marxists, Keynesians and Austrians* (Oxford: Basil Blackwell, 1981). For a different,

less penetrating account of Hayek's shifts of position see Norman P. Barry's *Hayek's Social and Economic Philosophy* (London: Macmillan, 1979) chap. 2.

8. The quotations are from Hayek's *Studies in Philosophy, Politics and Economics* (London: Routledge & Kegan Paul, 1967) p. viii (this volume is dedicated to Karl R. Popper): also his Nobel Lecture, 'The Pretence of Knowledge', in his *New Studies in Philosophy, Politics, Economics and the History of Ideas* (London: Routledge & Kegan Paul, 1978) pp. 33, 31.

9. See, for example, his collection of essays *Capital, Expectations, and the Market Process. Essays on the Theory of the Market Economy*, ed. Walter E. Grinder (Kansas City: Sheed, Andrews and McMeel, 1977). Also his article 'From Mises to Shackle: An Essay', *Journal of Economic Literature* 14 (March 1976) 54–62.

10. The neo-Austrian revival has been led from New York University, where Mises conducted an influential seminar until 1969. Two of his students, Israel Kirzner and Murray Rothbard, have been prominent, together with a member of the older generation, Ludwig Lachmann. The resumption of the seminar, in 1975, followed the 'crisis' in orthodox economics and may have been influenced by the centenary of the marginal revolution and renewed interest in Menger's works. See, for example, J. R. Hicks and W. Weber (eds), *Carl Menger and the Austrian School of Economics* (Oxford University Press, 1973). In addition to the *Austrian Economics Newsletter*, from 1977, a new periodical *The Journal of Libertarian Studies* has also appeared. These activities have been supported by the Center for Libertarian Studies, the Liberty Fund, the Institute for Humane Studies, the Cato Institute, the Economic Institute for Research and Education, the Schultz and Koch Foundations.

11. See, for example, the volumes in the Studies in Economics Series referred to above, in notes 4 and 9. Also papers have been given and symposia organised at meetings of the American, Southern and Atlantic Economic Associations, and no doubt others too.

12. Littlechild, Chapter 3 in this book. For additional examples of disagreements among neo-Austrians about such fundamental matters as the predictability of human preferences, expectations and knowledge, testing and falsifiability, and *Wertfreiheit*, see Hutchison, 'Austrians on the Philosophy and Method of Economics'. There are not only basic differences between such leading neo-Austrians as Kirzner and Rothbard, but others can be cited as in fundamental disagreement with Hayek's later views. For example, Mario J. Rizzo in Spadaro, *New Directions*, pp. 42–4; Lachmann in *Capital, Expectations*, pp. 88–9.

13. See, for example, Rothbard's quotations from Mises in Dolan, *Foundations of Modern Austrian Economics*, pp. 33–5. The principal sources are his *Theory and History* (New Haven: Yale University Press, 1957) pp. 10–11, and *Human Action. A Treatise in Economics* (New Haven: Yale University Press, 1949) pp. 55–6, 345.

14. Wiseman, Chapter 1, pp. 18, 15.

15. For example, Roger W. Garrison, 'Austrian Macroeconomics: A Diagrammatical Exposition' in Spadaro, *New Directions*, pp. 167–204. The author begins, significantly, by apologising for having focused on aggregates

rather than processes, as prescribed by Austrian methodology. For a more conventional Austrian reaction, see Lachmann, 'Toward a Critique of Macroeconomics' in Dolan, *Foundations of Modern Austrian Economics*, pp. 152–9. Hayek's *Counterrevolution of Science*, contains an extended attack on 'holism'.

16. Cf. Rothbard, in Dolan, *Foundations of Modern Austrian Economics*, pp. 30–2; Lachmann, *Capital, Expectations*, pp. 52, 53; Mises, *Human Action*, pp. 12, 125, 483–5. The term 'psychological school' has been applied both to the late nineteenth-century Austrians and to a group of early twentieth-century American economists. For an account of this phase of the debate see A. W. Coats, 'Economics and Psychology: the Death and Resurrection of a Research Programme', in S. J. Latsis (ed.), *Method and Appraisal in Economics* (Cambridge University Press, 1976) pp. 43–64.

17. Lachmann, *Capital, Expectations*, p. 170 (italics in original). This is an explicit statement of a view that is implicit in many subjectivist writings. It poses obvious problems for the methodology of science. For example, Lachmann (ibid., pp. 57–8) virtually excludes the possibility of verification.

18. Lachmann, ibid., p. 173 (italics in original). However, according to Kirzner, 'Economics has to make the world intelligible in terms of human *motives*'. Cf. Dolan, *Foundations of Modern Austrian Economics*, p. 45 (italics added).

19. Mises, *Human Action*, pp. 12, 483–5.

20. Wiseman, Chapter 1, p. 25.

21. Loasby, Chapter 7; Earl, Chapter 10.

22. 'Theories of Decision-making in Economics and Behavioural Science', *The American Economic Review* 49 (1963) 709, 711. For more general comments and references on this point see Coats 'Economics and Psychology', pp. 57–8.

23. Cf. by contrast Earl's comment on the need 'to engage in fieldwork which investigates consumer perceptions'. Chapter 10, p. 189. The subjectivists' willingness to cross conventionally accepted subject boundaries, as noted by Earl, is another reason why it is difficult to define the scope of subjectivist economics.

24. Kirzner, in Dolan, *Foundations of Modern Austrian Economics*, p. 42.

25. See J. M. Buchanan and G. F. Thirlby, *LSE Essay on Cost* (London: Weidenfeld and Nicolson, 1973); also J. M. Buchanan, *Cost and Choice* (Chicago: Markham Publishing Co., 1969); and Jack Wiseman, 'Costs and Decisions', in *Contemporary Economic Analysis*, vol. 2, David Currie and Will Peters, eds (London: Croom Helm, 1980).

26. Although there seems to have been little or no significant innovation within Austrian economics during the early post-war years, later subjectivists were able to draw upon important developments taking place outside economics during that period.

27. Included in his volume *On Revolutions and Progress in Economic Knowledge* (Cambridge University Press, 1978) chap. 7. On p. 211 he quotes, with approval, Herbert Simon's view that 'If economics is to deal with uncertainty, it will have to understand how human beings in fact behave in face of uncertainty, and by what limits of information and computability they are bound. . . . This requires a basic shift in scientific style from an

emphasis on subjective reasoning within a tight system of axioms to an emphasis on detailed empirical exploration of complete algorithms of thought.'

28. For example his *Uncertainty in Economics and other Reflections* (Cambridge University Press, 1955); and *The Years of High Theory. Invention and Tradition in Economic Thought 1926–1939* (Cambridge University Press, 1967): 'A recognition and insistence on the role of *uncertainty* are what the *Treatise* lacks and the *General Theory* has' (p. 184, italics in original).

29. For penetrating, if somewhat cynical, insights into the professional dimensions of this process see Harry Johnson's 'The Keynesian Revolution and the Monetarist Counter-Revolution', reprinted in Elizabeth S. Johnson and Harry G. Johnson, *The Shadow of Keynes. Understanding Keynes, Cambridge and Keynesian Economics* (University of Chicago Press, 1978) pp. 183–202.

30. See, for example, the Presidential Addresses by F. H. Hahn, 'Some Adjustment Problems', *Econometrica* 38 (January 1970) 1–17; and W. Leontief, 'Theoretical Assumptions and Nonobserved Facts', *American Economic Review* 61 (March 1971) pp. 1–7.

31. I have benefited from reading an unpublished paper by Warren Samuels, 'Austrian and Institutional Economics: Some Common Elements'.

32. Benjamin Ward, *What's Wrong with Economics?* (London: Macmillan, 1972).

33. To list all the relevant works of these well-known authors would take up too much space. Moreover, it might obscure the parallels between technical works in the history and philosophy of science and the broader, more radical contemporary reaction against objectivist approaches to science and society. For penetrating insights into this wider phenomenological movement see Roger Pool, *Towards Deep Subjectivity* (London: Allen Lane, 1972). 'Without taking the fact of subjectivity into account . . . without integrating the ideological factors of the subjective revolt into its analysis, objectivity's considerations are less than objective and its conclusions are no conclusions at all', p. 43.

34. See Popper's essay in *Philosophy Today*, ed. Jerry H. Gill (New York: Macmillan, 1968) p. 228; also his *Objective Knowledge* (Oxford University Press, 1972).

35. For evidence of the recent shifts in Hayek's views see above, pp. 89–90 and note 7.

36. On the sociology of science, for example, Joseph Ben-David, *The Scientist's role in Society: A Comparative Study* (Englewood Cliffs: Prentice Hall, 1971); and Warren O. Hagstrom, *The Scientific Community* (New York: Basic Books, 1965). For a brilliant study of the interrelationships between subjectivity and the organisation of science see Michael Polanyi, *Personal Knowledge. Towards a Post-Critical Philosophy* (University of Chicago Press, 1958).

37. Thomas S. Kuhn, *The Structure of Scientific Revolutions*, 2nd edn (University of Chicago Press, 1970); also *The Essential Tension. Selected Studies in Scientific Tradition and Change* (University of Chicago Press, 1977) especially chaps 7, 9, 11, 13.

38. The concepts of 'naive' versus 'sophisticated' falsificationism are especially associated with Imre Lakatos's 'Falsification and the Methodology of Scientific Research Programmes' in *Criticism and the Growth of Knowledge*, ed. I. Lakatos and A. Musgrave (Cambridge University Press, 1974) pp. 91–196. For a valuable brief introduction to the issues see A. F. Chalmers, *What is This Thing Called Science? An Assessment of the Nature and Status of Science and its Methods* (Milton Keynes: Open University Press, 1978) especially chaps 4–6; and, with special reference to economics, Mark Blaug, *The Methodology of Economics or How Economists Explain* (Cambridge University Press, 1980) chap. 4.
39. Cf. the sources cited in note 1, above.
40. See, for example, the severely critical analysis by T. W. Hutchison, in his *Economics and Economic Policy in Britain 1946–66* (London: Allen and Unwin, 1968) and *Knowledge and Ignorance in Economics* (Oxford: Basil Blackwell, 1977) Appendix.
41. Lachmann, *Capital, Expectations*, p. 181.

7 Knowledge, Learning and Enterprise

BRIAN LOASBY

Although there is no intention, here or elsewhere in this volume, to develop an extended critique of conventional microeconomic analysis, it is appropriate to begin by indicating the problems which seem to provide the opportunity for a new approach. These problems are associated with the concepts of equilibrium and production.

EQUILIBRIUM AND KNOWLEDGE

The equilibrium of an economy is normally defined in terms of a set of prices and quantities (or, in growth models, rates of change in these variables) which, in the absence of any outside disturbance, would persist indefinitely. G. B. Richardson (1960) has drawn attention to the dependence of such equilibria on assumptions about the knowledge and expectations of economic agents, and emphasised the inadequacy of perfect competition as a plausible justification for the kind of assumptions which are needed. More recently, Professor Hahn (1973) has proposed a definition of equilibrium in terms, not of prices and quantities, but of *theory* and *policy*. An agent's *theory* is a procedure for deriving predictions (which may take the form of a probability distribution) from information; his *policy* is a procedure for deriving decisions from predictions. An appropriate example would be the use of a specific econometric model to forecast demand each month, together with a production-scheduling technique which generates output plans from the forecasts thus produced. A less formal example is a theory which predicts that it is safe to cross the road at a controlled crossing when a green light is showing to pedestrians, and a policy to cross only under such conditions.

Rational decisions appear to require both theory and policy. Indeed, it is difficult to see how policy can exist without theory, though the converse is often true: cosmological theories, for example, are not usually associated with decisions. Professor Hahn offers the following definition (1973, p. 25): 'an economy is in equilibrium when it generates messages which do not cause agents to change the theories which they hold or the policies which they pursue'. But although he introduces notions of knowledge and decision into his definitions, Professor Hahn follows conventional practice by confining his attention to the conditions which will sustain equilibrium; he explicitly renounces any attempt to cope with learning. Thus his further analysis is of no direct help to us here; his concepts, however, will serve as a reference point for our discussion. What should be noted immediately is that equilibrium, so defined, does not necessarily depend on the truth of a theory: someone who (in this country) will never have honey in the house because honey attracts bears is unlikely to receive any messages from his environment which will cause him to change either his theory or his policy.

Professor Hahn's definition of equilibrium is an unconscious paraphrase of that advanced over forty years ago by Professor Hayek (1937, p. 41). Professor Hayek, however, was addressing himself precisely to the problem of the acquisition and use of knowledge in an economy. Interest in processes of adjustment through a sequence of human decisions which improve knowledge is characteristic of the Austrian School of economists, and has been effectively developed by Professor Kirzner in his *Competition and Entrepreneurship* (1973). A market in which prices and quantities are out of equilibrium offers profit opportunities to entrepreneurs; they formulate plans to buy and sell particular quantities at particular prices on the basis of their expectations. These plans are then tested in the market, and the results may confirm plans and expectations or cause them to be modified.

The economy thus, it is claimed, moves towards an equilibrium of both plans and prices, through a market process that seems to parallel the sequence of conjecture and exposure to refutation which is at the heart of Sir Karl Popper's (1972) theory of scientific progress. Now Sir Karl has written extensively about the difficulties involved in deciding whether a conjecture has been effectively refuted, and what should be done if it is. Professor Kirzner, however, discusses no such difficulties. Knowledge, in his original model, lies waiting to be discovered; an entrepreneur simply recognises a change in preferences or technology which has already happened. (In a recent (1981) paper, Professor Kirzner has allowed uncertainty into his analysis; but he does not consider this problem.) As he defines it, Professor Kirzner's model is therefore of limited applicability; this can be seen by contemplating some of the implications of production.

PRODUCTION AND ORGANISATION

Austrians and conventional microequilibrium theorists both start with the analysis of exchange. Production is then introduced as a special case of exchange – the exchange of inputs for outputs – by adding technology to preferences and resource endowments, either (for conventional theorists) as the basic data from which an equilibrium configuration of prices and quantities is to be derived, or (for Professor Kirzner) as the set of knowledge which is open to entrepreneurial perception. In a formal sense, production functions are closely analogous to preference functions, converting inputs into outputs just as the latter convert commodities into utilities.

But this simple theoretical extension entails a formidable increase in the knowledge attributed to economic agents. Not only is the requirement that technologies be available, and known to be available, a good deal more demanding than the requirement that consumers should know their own preferences; these preferences must now cover not just those commodities which currently exist but those which might be brought into existence. Although many potential objects of exchange may have no place in the equilibrium solution, yet they exist independently of that solution; but commodities which result only from production have to be included in the equilibrium production set in order to come into existence at all. Even Professor Kirzner's entrepreneurs will need to be extremely alert in order to perceive production technologies and consumer preferences for goods which can be brought into existence only by their own decisions.

The opportunity may arise only from a combination of perceptions. Consider, for example, the opportunity created by juxtaposing the realisation that fluorine compounds might well prove effective anaesthetics and the recognition that all existing inhalant anaesthetics had significant disadvantages. These two perceptions occurred in different divisions of ICI; but it was some time before they were combined to stimulate the search which led to the introduction of a superior and profitable new anaesthetic. They also occurred, separately, to a number of people outside the company, but these perceptions were never combined into a productive opportunity (Bradbury *et al.*, 1972). Nor is such a search bound to succeed, even in inventing a product with the desired properties; a profitable outcome will require active management, and in many instances, numerous further instances of creative imagination. To confine entrepreneurship, as Professor Kirzner does, to the exploitation of ready-made opportunities, and thereby to exclude the problems of management in complex organisations, is to impose severe potential restrictions on the applicability of his theory.

Since the time of Adam Smith, production has been associated in economic theory with the division of labour; and the division of labour produces most of its benefits through differentiation, which enhances specific skills but narrows the range of competence. Thus individual firms cannot have effective access to the known set of technologies within the economy, but are favourably placed to initiate, or to adopt, improvements within certain specific technologies. Nor can they possibly be well informed about all actual or potential products but they may be quick to perceive, or to create, opportunities in particular markets. A firm, like an individual, possesses specialised knowledge, and pays for it by limitations on its flexibility.

Similar conclusions follow from the analysis, pioneered by Professor Coase (1937), of the firm as an alternative to the market, avoiding some of the information- and transaction-costs of using the market by substituting administrative arrangements for the internal allocation of resources. Within the firm, the advantages of division of labour are sought through organisational design. The specialisation of function thus prescribed may also be thought of as a means of accommodating the constraints of bounded rationality, which have provided a foundation for Professor Simon's (1976) analysis of organisational behaviour. But these constraints will affect behaviour as well as structure. Members of an organisation will thus give selective attention to phenomena, both internal and external, and will learn from their own particular patterns of experience. Their theories and their plans will be influenced by their own situation and their own history.

INTERPRETATIVE FRAMEWORKS AND THE METHODS OF SCIENCE

Whether, or in what condition, such theories and plans might be roughly consistent, is, in the broadest sense, the question underlying the analysis of general equilibrium theorists and of the Austrians. However, neither come very close to the issues which have been raised in the last few pages. The Austrians, it is suggested, are right to think in terms of processes, but avoid many of the difficulties by considering only how individuals interact through the market, and by assuming, in effect, that such individuals acquire knowledge by perceiving the truth. The purpose of this paper is to explain, and to begin to apply, a method of analysing human understanding and human action – the theories that people hold and the policies that they pursue – which, although unfamiliar to most economists, seems particularly appropriate to the problems of knowledge, learning and enterprise. The method was proposed by an American psychologist, George Kelly, and this is now well known in the analysis of personality (to which it was originally directed) and in studies of consumer behaviour. Those familiar with the work of Lakatos (1970) will recognise many similar ideas, expressed in a different language; but there is no space here to consider the attractive notion of a firm's 'research programme'.

Kelly's fundamental proposal is to analyse human beings as scientists: that is, as people whose *'ultimate aim is to predict and control'* (1963, p. 5). This, we may note, is the obverse of Sir Karl Popper's conception of scientific method as a carefully designed version of human trial and error: people learn (imperfectly and inefficiently) from their mistakes; science attempts to discover mistakes quickly and efficiently. A detailed comparison between the two views might be very rewarding; but in this paper we shall attempt no more than a few passing observations.

The selection of data, and its interpretation in the light of both theory and experience – the latter either natural or contrived – are central issues for anyone seeking to predict and control, whether as professional scientists or as human being. Why this is so emerges from the confrontation between the limits of human rationality and the interconnectedness of all phenomena, as Kelly explains. 'The universe that we presume exists . . . is integral. By that we mean it functions as a single unit with all its imaginable parts having an exact relationship to each other' (1963, p. 6). That, of course, is a general equilibrium concept, with the scope of the equilibrium far wider than has been essayed by any economist. Kelly can afford such a wide conception because he is not concerned to offer any general equilibrium solution. In fact, he argues that since anything like a total comprehension of this interdependent system is far beyond our powers, every discipline must necessarily take a partial view, and, recognising that the view is partial, should be wary of making claims outside the realm thus (roughly) defined.

> Man looks at his world through transparent patterns or templets which he creates and then attempts to fit over the realities of which the world is composed. The fit is not always very good . . . Even a poor fit is more helpful to him than nothing at all. (1963, pp. 8–9)

Notice that these patterns, or theories, are created; they are neither perceived, nor derived in any simple way from the phenomena to which they are subsequently applied. Such a concept of theory-creation, and a similar explanation in terms of the desire to impose order on the unimaginable complexity of phenomena, is developed in Adam Smith's remarkable, though little known, early 'History of Astronomy' (1979), and is the key to Professor Shackle's account of the development of economic thought in *The Years of High Theory* (1967); Professor Skinner of Glasgow has examined Smith's ideas and their modern counterparts in a recent article (1979). Sir Karl Popper's rejection of induction as logically impossible has led him to emphasise the importance of imaginative conjecture in providing theories worth testing: however, he is primarily – though far from exclusively – concerned with the ways in which such conjectures may be exposed to possible refutation, whereas Smith, Shackle and Kelly all emphasise the defensive use of theories to accommodate experience. Sir Karl has persistently attacked such defensive uses as an impediment to the progress of knowledge; but they do appear to give a kind of security, even though it may be false. Moreover, as Kelly argues, it is necessary to close off some avenues of enquiry, if necessary by a theoretical fudge, in order to improve our understanding at all.

> We limit the *realm* and try to ignore, for the time being, the intransigent facts just outside the borders of that *realm* . . . For the time being we shall have to content ourselves with a series of miniature systems, each with its own realm or limited range of convenience . . . (1963, p. 10).

That such a strategy should gain even modest success requires that almost all interdependencies are of no significance almost all the time. In Professor Simon's (1969) phraseology, the universe is decomposable into a hierarchy of systems which for the most part interact only weakly. Kelly assumes this to be true within the human time-scale; Professor

Simon argues that complex systems are unlikely to evolve or to survive, unless they are nearly decomposable. But near decomposability is not identical with complete decomposability; and if the latter is assumed, as it has to be in order to construct miniature systems, then the theory embodied in these systems must be, to some extent, false. Two consequences should be noted. Not only are these systems unreliable beyond a limited range of application; they are liable to unsuspected collapse wherever the assumption of decomposability is falsified. Past performance is no guarantee of future success, either for a theory or for a firm which uses it. This inevitable fallibility is a good reason for possessing alternative structures of interpretation, even if they appear less immediately useful.

Kelly's analysis is intended to apply both to the discipline of psychology and to the behaviour of people trying to make sense of their situation. Since psychologists are, one presumes, people trying to make sense of the world, it should indeed apply to both − and to economists and managers also. But, as has been observed, any usable pattern must be incomplete and distorted − at least at the boundaries, where it necessarily denies connections which we believe to exist, and to matter; and it therefore follows that whatever pattern we happen to be using has no claim to exclusivity. 'The same event may be construed simultaneously and profitably within various disciplinary systems' (1963, p. 10). Alternative constructions may be profitable, not because they lead to similar conclusions, but because they do not. 'It is not a matter of indifference which of a set of alternative constructions one chooses to impose upon his world' (1963, p. 15) . . . 'often the facts assume their particular shapes only in the light of a certain theory' (1963, p. 26).

Like Kelly, I wish to use this argument at two levels. The underlying justification for this paper is the belief that by looking at firms in a different way from those employed either in the prevalent kinds of equilibrium theory or in Austrian theories, we can discover different interpretations which offer something additional to anything that the prevalent interpretations can provide. These prevalent interpretations, as was true of psychology when Kelly wrote, are based on theories of situational determinism and an experimental method of external observation. Economists and psychologists alike had reacted against introspection, and denied the relevance of personal testimony. Behaviour was all that mattered; knowledge and motivation, if used at all, appeared as conscious fictions. But the preference for behaviourism is a subjective preference, and even if it were − as it may be − the best single principle of selection, it must, like any other principle, have a limited range of convenience. An approach which leaves room for human initiative, human experimentation and human interpretation, as do several modern theories of scientific development, seems worth exploring.

That is the argument for using alternative methods of analysis. But the view of firms as organisations being explored here uses this argument for alternative frameworks as its core. Managers, like scientists, or any other person who wishes to predict and control, must impose some pattern on events. No single pattern can claim any exclusive rights, yet different patterns may lead to different interpretations, and possibly to different decisions. It is part of the 'perfect knowledge' assumption which is never more than slightly attenuated in standard theories that all firms would have the same perception of any given situation; by abandoning that assumption one can gain some understanding of the behaviour of firms.

EVENTS AND FRAMEWORKS

The focus of Kelly's analysis is the interaction between events and the frameworks which are used to interpret them. These events are of two kinds. First, there are those which impinge on a passive observer. 'The universe is continually changing with respect to itself. Within our universe something is always going on. In fact, that is the way the universe exists; it exists by happening' (Kelly, 1963, p. 7). Thus the passage of time generates a stream of events to be interpreted by the use of whatever patterns people use. 'Experience is made up of the successive construing of events. It is not constituted merely by the events themselves' (p. 73). It is the recipient of the data who converts it into information; and this conversion may involve the use of existing theory to make fresh predictions, or a revision of theory to accommodate recalcitrant data. Since the events which are observed depend upon the time period, and a variety of patterns may be used, the lessons of experience are not common to all, even within a single industry. Different events (at different times, or in different places) and different interpretations are each capable of producing different conclusions about both theory and policy. It is of course possible that a variety of events and a variety of patterns should all lead to similar conclusions. Indeed, if this never happened, human behaviour would no doubt be much less coherent than it is. But there are no logical reasons for assuming that this will be generally true, and some fairly persuasive evidence that it is not. Our data rarely meets the requirements of sampling theory, and our interpretative frameworks are incomplete.

The passage of time gives us a chance to check the serviceability of the patterns which we use by testing them against subsequent events, either by the rigorous method of making explicit predictions before-hand, or by the more dangerous – but still quite often effective – method of seeing whether the new events can be accommodated within the currently-accepted framework. By either route, there is a presumption that the serviceability of a person's constructs will tend to improve over time, provided that the nature of the phenomena being observed is changing more slowly than he is able or willing to revise his interpretative framework – in particular that neglected interdependencies do not become significant – and furthermore that he does not seek to apply his interpretations to phenomena of a different kind. Both qualifications will be taken up later.

The second class of events are, at least in part, internal to the analysis. People do not simply observe and interpret; they also act. Agents have policies as well as theories. What happens in the universe is partly the result of human action, based on interpretations, and providing material for fresh interpretations – not only by the originating actors. The outcome of one set of entrepreneurial decisions provides opportunities for other entrepreneurs. Thus interpretations and decisions produce an interactive (but not closed) system which evolves over time. Whether this system moves towards some sort of equilibrium is an open question. That it should reach a static equilibrium is incompatible with the conception of the universe employed here. This is not to deny that static equilibrium concepts may sometimes offer a useful scheme of interpretation, provided one remembers that, like any other scheme, it is incomplete.

ORGANISATION AND INTERPRETATION

Let us now begin to apply these ideas to the firm as an organisation. A firm is composed of a group of people who all, in varying ways and to varying extents, interpret what they observe and take decisions according to their interpretation. We will follow convention by concentrating on those people who are usually called managers, though we should not forget that much of what follows applies also to those usually called workers.

If a new firm is created, and staffed by people who are unfamiliar with the line of business which the firm has chosen to enter, its managers are likely to be ill-equipped with constructs which will help them to understand what is happening and to take good decisions; but, provided that the firm does not collapse as a result of their inexperience, they will learn from events and their own mistakes, and will eventually acquire a set of frameworks which proves serviceable for that line of business. Indeed, the danger of collapse before the minimum amount of learning has been achieved is so generally recognised that it is unusual to staff a new organisation with people who have no knowledge of the business area; even those with such experience will probably need to modify their constructs to accommodate the somewhat different circumstances of the new firm.

It is even more certain that before things can run fairly smoothly, there will be a need for the alignment of the constructs used by different members of the firm. Even within a particular kind of business, different constructs may be employed, and people moving between organisations – be they two universities, two government departments, two consultancy firms or two manufacturing firms – will usually find some differences in the way things are done, and will have to spend time learning how the system into which they have entered works. Thus, even if there were no need to learn about the technology or the market, there would still be the need to learn about the working style of other members of the organisation.

While the learning process continues it consumes managerial resources; indeed, in the early stages it may consume a great many, and long hours and frequent meetings may be the price even of survival; but as people gradually learn to develop and to use interpretative frameworks which not only seem to offer a satisfactory fit to the data but are reasonably compatible with the systems used by other people within the organisation, so the effort required diminishes. Resources are thus released, and may be used to increase the throughput of the organisation, if necessary by bringing in additional people, who will also need to learn and to be assimilated, at some cost both to old and new members of the organisation.

In this process of learning, organisational design plays an important part, in two major ways. First, it determines the flow of events which will come to the attention of each manager, and thus the material which his developing constructs will have to fit. This sets limits to the interpretative possibilities, but, by the arguments advanced earlier, does not fix them. Second, by defining the extent, and the limits, of responsibility, it prescribes what the constructs must accomplish, and what they need not — the kinds of policy models which the theories are required to serve. As Kelly observes (1963, pp. 9–10), 'when one limits the realm of facts, it is possible to develop a detailed system without worrying about the inconsistencies in the system which certain peripheral facts would reveal'. What inconsistencies would matter depends on how the periphery is defined; constructs which would suit a functional manager may be quite inadequate for a product manager. The policy requirements, and thus the theoretical requirements, are very different. Indeed, the redrawing of organisational boundaries is usually intended to invalidate old constructs which were thought to be leading to decisions that are now judged to be undesirable when assessed from some higher viewpoint. Restructuring is intended to improve policy through the use of more appropriate theories.

A successful organisational design is one that generates a stream of events for each manager which enables him to develop quickly an effective set of constructs. Effectiveness is here assessed by the decisions which result from the use of these constructs: they must be consistent both with the world outside, and with those decisions taken by other members of the organisation. Consistency between decisions does not necessarily require similar constructs. For good organisational design not only brings some kinds of people together; it also keeps other kinds of people apart. Partial insulation may allow the development of simpler constructs within each field of interest, making management more effective within those limits. The art of organisational design requires the creation of such insulating barriers where they will facilitate good and low-cost local decision-making, while maintaining a sufficient commonality of framework to ensure (if assurance is indeed possible) that the outcomes of local decisions are not disastrous — for example, that products designed to replace the existing range are not totally outside the manufacturing competence of the existing equipment and workforce.

The speed of learning depends on what it is desired to learn. As Burns and Stalker (1961) taught us twenty years ago, in a very stable environment a mechanistic system of management, in which functions are narrowly defined, is very effective in developing the skills for dealing with that environment. Simple interpretative frameworks with very narrow ranges of convenience may be perfectly adequate. But its effectiveness depends on that environment remaining stable; and the great danger is of a failure to recognise how limited is the range of convenience of the simplified frameworks to which everyone has become accustomed. The structure reflects an assumption that neither theory nor policy will require more than minor amendment; no innovations are called for. Professor Hahn's self-imposed restriction of theory to the examination of equilibrium conditions may likewise lead to a specification which is quite incapable of adjusting to unforeseen events. At the other extreme, an organic system, providing for interaction anywhere within the organisation, slows down learning by providing only small samples of each kind of phenomenon and requires the development of many different patterns to fit different situations (or, improbably, some elaborate pattern which fits them all). The release of managerial resources from such a system is not likely to be rapid; on the other hand, those resources which are released are likely to have a far wider range of use than the resources released by a mechanistic system − not least because managers are likely to realise that new circumstances may require the creation of new schemes of interpretation.

GROWTH AND ADJUSTMENT

This apparent trade-off between the rate at which spare managerial resources are generated and their applicability suggests that the most rapid growth of firms may occur by simple expansion within an existing field, with additional output being supplied to existing customers, or to new customers with similar characteristics. Of course, if the total market is not expanding, or expanding only slowly, such growth must be at the expense of other firms, which might be expected to have similar potential for growth (though we should be careful not to assume that all will have similar ambitions). Thus one might expect to find fairly bitter battles in such circumstances, with little scope for avoiding direct confrontation by way of diversification. Control over customers or sources of supply might suggest itself as a competitive tactic.

There will also clearly be differences between firms with different patterns of experience (and experience, remember, depends both on events and their interpretation) in the rate at which resources are released and in their applicability. Even within the same industry, different firms may develop different capabilities; between industries there are liable to be wide differences. Nor is the release of resources an irreversible process. A drastic change in the environment of a firm (for example, through the development of new technology or a new source of competition) may impose a need for relearning how to conduct its own business — a need which has proved beyond the powers of some organisations which were only too well adapted to their familiar circumstances. Too strong an assumption of convergence towards a state approximating to equilibrium is dangerous both for the theorist and for the manager.

Adjustment to new circumstances is not often easy. For what is required is often more than the revision of some local constructs in response to environmental change. Local constructs must be mutually compatible, at least to the extent that they impinge upon each other; and revisions in response to external events may disrupt that compatibility. The difficulty of adjustment may well be aggravated by the need to revise also the inter-relations between local constructs, so that some need to be more closely interlocked than before. As Kelly remarks (1963, p. 9), 'in seeking improvement [a person] is repeatedly halted by the damage to the system that apparently will result from the alteration of a subordinate construct'. We can all see how difficult it is for well-trained economists to give up a particular theoretical approach; but the difficulty is not peculiar to our discipline. Such a threat to a person's thought-system helps to explain why some people continue to make the same mistakes; any adequate response seems to them to require an adjustment of their ways of thinking which threatens their way of life — even, in the last resort, their personality. Kelly's professional interest in developing his theory was in fact to provide a better interpretative framework for the analysis of personality disorders.

Of course, this problem of maintaining one's personality applies directly to managers as to anyone else (to practitioners of an academic discipline, for example). But there is in addition the requirement to maintain some kind of working system for the organisation; and it may seem impossible to maintain that system if those adjustments are made which would permit more effective handling of particular problems. Thus learning, at a personal or an organisation level, may be impossible. For example, both management and union representatives in some firms may simply be incapable of changing their approach to industrial relations, despite the repeated failure of their current methods, because a more effective method would require so radical a change in their conceptions of the 'opposition' as to threaten their whole interpretation of the economic and social system. Chandler (1962) has explained how Du Pont's attempts to come to terms with the needs of a diversified business were agonisingly protracted by the company's devotion to the accepted practices of good management; and Burns and Stalker (1961) have shown how a deep-rooted belief in certain fundamental notions of orderliness frustrated the attempts of some Scottish firms to break into a new and technically-progressive industry. The history of British Rail, of British Leyland and its predecessors, the fate of AEI and BSA, are just a few instances of the appalling difficulty experienced by people and by organisations in abandoning well-confirmed theories and policies which have been carried by events far beyond the limits of their applicability. Some principles an organisation must have, if it is to remain an organisation; some principles of behaviour a person must cling to, whatever the evidence, if he is to remain a person. Some changes are simply not possible, even if the alternative is death.

GROWTH AND THE THEORY OF THE FIRM

The kind of analysis which has just been outlined may be used to add some detail to Penrose's (1959) treatment of the growth of firms. Penrose, like Coase (though she does not refer to him), regards the firm as an administrative framework which serves as an alternative to the market for the purposes of resource allocation: it is 'an autonomous administrative planning unit, the activities of which are interrelated and are coordinated by policies which are framed in the light of their effect on the enterprise as a whole' (Penrose, 1959, pp. 15–16). A feasible plan for the firm requires compatibility – not, we may repeat, identity – of interpretative frameworks between the component elements of the organisation.

These plans are derived jointly from its expectations – 'the way in which it interprets its environment' (p. 41) – and from its appraisal of its own internal resources. Its expectations, in the language of Professor Hahn, are generated by the theory which it holds; and among its own internal resources Penrose lays especial emphasis on managerial services, which we can now interpret as a well-validated set of constructs for selecting and interpreting data and for making effective and timely decisions. Perceived resources and expectations are brought together in the firm's ' "productive opportunity", which comprises all of the productive possibilities that its "entrepreneurs" see and can take advantage of' (p. 31); and this productive opportunity, as Penrose makes clear, exists in the imaginations of entrepreneurs, not in the world outside. (The resemblance to Professor Shackle's ideas should need no emphasis.) The more imaginative the entrepreneur, the greater the productive opportunity.

Penrose pays very little attention to the relationship between perception and reality. She does not choose, like Professor Kirzner, to restrict entrepreneurs to the perception − selective and incomplete − of opportunities which already exist, as consequences of changes in preferences or technology which have already taken place. Instead she contents herself with observing that if the productive opportunities are a mirage, then the firm's plans will not be successful, and disclaiming any interest in such firms. Her theory is explicitly designed for success-ful firms; but might it not be helpful to have a theory which can help to explain the difference between success and failure?

Though success is not guaranteed, it does not necessarily depend on the choice of one particular course of action. The firm's own action may change its environment − a point also made by Kelly about individual actions (1963, p. 8). Both authors provide much more scope for originative choice than do the behaviourist traditions of situational determinism in psychology and economics. This analytical recognition of alternative possible futures adds to the significance of entre-preneurial versatility, which not only widens the range of perception but augments creativity. Within Kelly's system, versatility requires either constructs with a very wide range of convenience, or, more likely, a range of constructs with different foci of application. It certainly implies the capacity, and willingness, to adapt constructs as circumstances change.

The application of Kelly's mode of analysis to Penrose's theory rein-forces the latter's argument for the heterogeneity of firms. Hetero-geneity has important theoretical uses. It provides a basis for an assumption which Professor Kirzner needs but does not explain: the assumption that a few entrepreneurs will perceive an opportunity which is hidden from everyone else. As Richardson (1960, p. 57) has pointed out, 'a general profit opportunity, which is both known to everyone and equally capable of being exploited by everyone, is, in an important sense, a profit opportunity for no one in particular'. If every individual has his own pattern of experience, mediated by his own interpretative framework, then each may have a slightly different per-ception; thus relatively few will recognise any particular change in the environment. (For the great majority, it will not be within their own environment that the change occurs.) If the profitable exploitation of that change requires the use of a pool of resources within an adminis-trative framework, then some of those who see the possibilities will feel unable to take advantage of them. Barriers to the entry of most firms may be necessary to give confidence to the remainder. Such barriers may thus, contrary to the presumptions of static theory, contribute to economic welfare.

COMPETITION

In welfare economics, any departure from the conditions of perfect competition is still likely to be condemned as a violation of Pareto optimality. Strictly speaking, of course, both Pareto optimality and perfect competition are valid only for equilibrium, and are not appropriate for the analysis of adjustment processes. Something close to perfect competition might perhaps be appropriate for adjustment, if we could somehow avoid the paralysing criticism of Richardson, and if we could assume that we all knew where to search for the equilibrium configuration: in Kelly's terms, we would be certain that there was no need to stray beyond the range of convenience of a single, commonly-shared set of constructs. But this is to assume a far greater degree of knowledge than we can hope to possess. Within an economy, just as within academia, we need a variety of interpretative frameworks; indeed we need them within an industry as we need them within an academic discipline. Possibilities of intellectual and of economic progress will not all be envisioned within any single framework.

The adjustment of constructs – of theories and of policies – is facilitated by their subordination to a higher-level construct which is formulated sufficiently loosely to accommodate a variety of subordinate constructs, not necessarily mutually compatible. The permeability of superordinate constructs, to use Kelly's term (p. 79) confers resilience. Such permeability is desirable within any organisation which has to cope with change; but, as we have argued above, it is necessarily limited. Successful adaptation within an industry may therefore be dependent on the existence of a number of firms, with substantially different sets of constructs, and (quite possibly) different organisational arrangements which permit different kinds of permeability. Attempts to compel all firms within an industry to conform to a single best pattern, as judged by the perceived requirements of the current situation, may prove disastrous. However successful that pattern may presently be, we must not forget that its range of applicability is limited, and, the more closely it is tailored to contemporary circumstances (and therefore apparently the more efficient), the narrower is that range.

Sir Karl Popper reminds us that no amount of corroboration can immunise a theory against falsification. There can be no assurance that alternative conjectures will never be required; and alternative conjectures arise most readily from alternative frameworks. If we are to react effectively to the stream of events by which the universe exists (some of them the product of human action) we must avoid misguided attempts to stabilise low-level constructs, either within individuals or within firms. It is the attempt to preserve detailed subordinate constructs in the face of their growing inadequacy to cope with the phenomena which they are required to interpret which leads to human breakdown. Similarly, an attempt to preserve every firm within an industry, or even every industry within an economy, is less likely to succeed in that object than to destroy a superordinate structure which could have been preserved by greater permeability.

REFERENCES

Bradbury, F. R., McCarthy, M. C., and Suckling, C. W. (1972) 'Patterns of innovation: Part II – the Anaesthetic Halothane', *Chemistry and Industry*, pp. 105–10.

Burns, T., and Stalker, G. M. (1961) *The Management of Innovation* (London: Tavistock).

Chandler, A. D. (1962) *Strategy and Structure* (Cambridge, Mass.: MIT Press).

Coase, R. H. (1937) 'The Nature of the Firm', *Economica* (N.S.), IV, 386–405.

Hahn, F. H. (1973) *On the Notion of Equilibrium in Economics* (Cambridge University Press).

Hayek, F. A. (1937) 'Economics and Knowledge', *Economica* (N.S.), IV, 33–54.

Kelly, G. A. (1963) *A Theory of Personality* (New York: W. W. Norton).

Kirzner, I. M. (1973) *Competition and Entrepreneurship* (University of Chicago Press).

Kirzner, I. M. (1982) 'Uncertainty, Discovery and Human Action', in I. M. Kirzner (ed.), *The Contributions of Ludwig von Mises to Economics* (Lexington, Mass.: Lexington Books).

Lakatos, I. (1970) 'Falsification and the Methodology of Scientific Research Programmes', in I. Lakatos and A. Musgrove (eds), *Criticism and the Growth of Knowledge* (Cambridge University Press).

Penrose, E. T. (1959) *The Theory of the Growth of the Firm* (Oxford: Basil Blackwell).

Popper, K. R. (1972) *The Logic of Scientific Discovery*, 6th impression (London: Hutchinson).

Richardson, G. B. (1960) *Information and Investment* (Oxford University Press).

Shackle, G. L. S. (1967) *The Years of High Theory* (Cambridge University Press).

Simon, H. A. (1969) *The Sciences of the Artificial* (Cambridge, Mass.: MIT Press).
Simon, H. A. (1976) *Administrative Behavior*, 3rd edn (New York: The Free Press).
Skinner, A. S. (1979) 'Adam Smith: an Aspect of Modern Economics?' *Scottish Journal of Political Economy*, 26, 109–26.
Smith, A. (1979) 'History of Astronomy', in W. P. D. Wightman (ed.), *Essays on Philosophical Subjects* (Oxford University Press).

8 Economic Uncertainty and Business Decision-Making

MICHAEL JEFFERSON

INTRODUCTION

Uncertainty is endemic, in economic affairs no less than in other fields of human endeavour. Uncertainty intrudes heavily into decision-making, which is characterised by partial knowledge; irremediable unforeknowledge; and the exercise of hunch and judgement.

Despite the pervading mist of uncertainty there is a deeply-embedded desire in human nature to impose order on disorder; to fit recalcitrant phenomena into general theories; to speak and act as if we had knowledge where it cannot exist; to seek firm answers and 'optimum' solutions as if uncertainty could be eliminated. There is thus a tendency to live in a pretend world where by developing and applying general theories, introducing and using techniques, claiming systematic approaches and objective assessments, people can come to believe that their capacity for sound decision-making is far more robust than is the case.

Much mainstream economic theory and content of business school courses would seem to reinforce the creation of this pretend world. Traditionally, economic theory has been developed in relation to general equilibrium, perfect competition, market clearance and other notions which do little to reflect uncertainty and imperfect knowledge. Applied economics, as practised in the academic halls, normally holds fast to the presuppositions of traditional theory. Economic policy-making, at the macro level, is heavily influenced by such theory. The academic theories also exert their sway on how businessmen talk, though less so on how they act.

The mainstream academic contributions have rarely been concerned with the economics of uncertainty; of disequilibrium; of truly imperfect competition and markets; of only partial knowledge. There is insufficient realisation of the importance of context: institutional frameworks, industry history, corporate cultures, human motivations. There is overreliance on inappropriate theoretical foundations, weak historical relationships and dubious statistical data.

These weaknesses are reflected in the rather modest practical value of academic contributions to the nature of business decision-making. In the business schools themselves, economics courses tend to be of the traditional theoretical and macro variety, and little emphasis is usually placed on the microeconomics of industry or firm. Techniques are developed in relation to decision-making which, if merely treated as an aid to systematic thought, would be useful in their proper place. There is a tendency to elevate such techniques to a level where their proponents would seem to suggest they can conjure knowledge out of ignorance, precision out of vagueness, and certainty out of irremediable unforeknowledge.

Such tendencies reach their apotheosis in the widespread practice of attaching numerical probabilities to future possibilities. But such possibilities are frequently non-seriable type problems with decisions implying rival outcomes, and thus the probabilistic approach in this context is tantamount to attaching probabilities to unknowledge. Hence the word 'probability' is used in these contexts in a quite different way than that adopted by statisticians. One result is to increase the risk of disguising the true degree of uncertainty which exists, to divert attention from weak hypotheses and possibilities regarded as unlikely but liable to have serious consequences.

There is a pressing need, therefore, fully to accept the true nature of uncertainty and not to act in a manner which implies a greater degree of certainty and knowledge than the nature and circumstances of many business problems will admit. But decisions still have to be taken within a resilient strategic overview. Thus the first requirement is for a framework which both highlights uncertainty and indicates the future possibilities which are likely to emerge. This is not quite the logical impossibility that it may appear at first sight. The relevant framework is the development of multiple scenarios, about which more will be said later in relation to Shell's experience. In the development and use of scenarios, of course, the pervading uncertainty must never be overlooked.

Having instituted the framework, the next stage is the formulation and implementation of relevant strategies. These must be relevant to the existing strengths of the business, appropriate to possible shifts in supply and demand conditions, and resilient to a range of possible outcomes. Implementation of strategies, like shorter-term issues, requires decisions. It is effective linkage between scenario writing, strategy formulation and business decision-making which is the greatest challenge to businessmen. Again, Shell's experience – not always successful – is touched upon below.

At the end of the day, context is extremely important in decision-making: tradition, culture, perspective, power, the actions of others. The roles of hunch and judgement, the need for effective and speedy feedback to counter unwarranted bias, also need to be recognised explicitly. Error and subjectivity can never be eliminated.

ECONOMISTS OF UNCERTAINTY

Although traditional economic theory, and the views of what may be termed the Academic Economics Establishment, may have only limited relevance to the real world of business this is not to say relevant work has not been done. There is a small number of economists particularly concerned with uncertainty and disequilibrium.

There is, indeed, a long tradition in the economics of uncertainty. Among British economists we may say that it extends from Adam Smith to G. L. S. Shackle and others contributing to this book. It is a tradition which could no doubt be extended back in time, in Britain and elsewhere. For instance, we might compare and contrast the differing understanding of markets and implied certainty of the mediaeval scholastic tradition represented by Aquinas with the contemporaneous real world perceptions of the School of Salamanca.[1] We could pursue the trail back to Aristotle's 'Nicomachean Ethics'. But an appropriate starting-point is Adam Smith's reflections on how astronomers may refuse to believe the evidence of their senses in their desire to hold on to an outmoded theory; on the imperfections of markets; and on how businessmen may unwisely but persistently seek after stability.[2]

Then G. L. S. Shackle trying now, as he has done for more than forty years, to stretch our recognition of the bounds of unknowledge. One wonders how many academic economists and lecturers in business schools, let alone businessmen, have read Shackle's major works – notably *Epistemics and Economics: A Critique of Economic Doctrines* (1972); *Decision, Order and Time in Human Affairs*, 2nd edn (1969);

and his latest *Imagination and the Nature of Choice* (1979). In his emphasis on uncertainty, choice, imagination, the need for action, the skeins of his thoughts and words weave a manner of thinking and basis for decisions which the businessman will understand however reluctant he may be to face up to the full implications of recognising uncertainty and ignorance. Shackle has made important contributions to our understanding of why 'probabilities' should not be attached to unknowledge, why choice is an uncompletable process, and what the true implications of this incompleteness are. And while Shackle himself has not made any direct contributions to the development of multiple-scenario approaches to possible futures he has suggested that 'origination of histories-to-come' should 'take the form of compositions of elements, building-blocks of a scheme of the field and of its *potentiae*'.[3]

In this last, and some other, respects, Shackle has again made observations which businessmen act upon or are constrained by in practice. The need for a conceptual framework, such as scenarios, to which we return below. Recognition that:

> Many public pronouncements, much of the practice and the language of business and politics, suggest that unforeknowledge is an idea scarcely able to be assimilated into the foundations of modern conduct. In the thought-practice of those who conduct our affairs, unforeknowledge is treated as alien, intolerable, unbelievable. There *must* (so it would seem from the public face of politics and business) be a method and a means of foreknowledge.[4]

Here, it will be observed, Shackle is not reflecting best practice within business. He is, in fact, greatly encouraged by those examples of businesses which do attempt to recognise and cope with uncertainty, including our work in Shell. Shackle has also, perhaps, not fully exploited a practical point well within his scheme of things – that probabilities regarded with great disbelief should not be ignored because they may have calamitous consequences for the business (an extension of his critique of so-called 'subjective probabilities'). However, he has come close to this conclusion in his treatment of risk.

G. L. S. Shackle and other economists of uncertainty have also not allowed their more confident brethren of the cloth to remain above adverse criticism. In his well-mannered, finely-tuned criticisms in *The Years of High Theory* (1967), Shackle has exposed many weaknesses. Homa Katouzian in *Ideology and Method in Economics* (1980) has wielded a blunter instrument, but still to good effect. Drawing on the works of predecessors who have described economic theories as 'empty boxes', and attacked 'armchair theorising', he stridently criticises those who are driven by fashion and the dictates of the Academic Economics Establishment. He suggests:

> The modern professional academic is expected to specialise within a narrow disciplinary framework; to publish large quantities of work with relatively little consequence for the solution of real problems; to refrain from a broadly critical approach to his discipline and its established ideas . . .[5]

He dislikes the fact that:

> Without having learned much from our theories on the assumption of 'perfect foresight' we are now using mathematics in order to prove that theories which contain little or no real knowledge are also 'true' in 'conditions of uncertainty'.[6]

He deplores the fact that 'Many – and, especially, most of the more mathematical – theories are abstractions with little or no conceivable counterparts in the world of reality.'[7] And the problem that: 'The ancient preoccupation with the existence and stability of general equilibrium solutions seems to be more dominant than at any time in the past.'[8] While in conclusion he laments because:

> Modern economics is obsessed with rigorous logical or mathematical proofs, and computerised 'empirical' studies, without much success; it ignores – often with contempt – the wealth of historical experience, and qualitative evidence at its disposal.[9]

Brian Loasby has concluded that 'it is the concept of equilibrium which is at the heart of the crisis'[10] and calls for a reallocation of effort within the economics profession. In *Choice, Complexity and Ignorance* (1976), Loasby even gives the unusually practical sub-title, *An Enquiry into Economic Theory and the Practice of Decision-Making*. He points out:

> Neither the details of decision processes nor the characteristics of particular circumstances are of interest to economic theory; in modern microeconomics choice results from the application of a

well-defined preference function to a fully-specified set of available alternatives.[11]

But Loasby draws on both the economics of uncertainty and knowledge of the workings of specific firms in manufacturing, wholesaling and retailing in remarking upon the dangers of 'unforeseeable events which may have relatively low probability of occurrence, but whose impact on profitability . . . would be major', quoting Igor Ansoff in support.[12] Stress is placed upon the need for flexibility at this point, the need to guess better than your competitors at others. He wonders whether: 'Perhaps the only people fit to plan are those who do not believe in planning',[13] a view which may seem supremely sceptical, but which is fundamentally sound. At the other end of the spectrum from determinism, however, he warns: 'Although moderate ignorance may be a stimulus, ignorance which is too great to handle may paralyse decision.'[14] This is a very real challenge to businessmen: the need to avoid 'analysis paralysis'.[15]

There are, however, no easy answers to this challenge. Jack Wiseman has pointed out that there is no general pricing rule or rules which can be held unambiguously to bring about an 'optimum' use of resources by public utilities even in theory.[16] In practice the search for 'the optimum' in the sorts of business which the writer knows something about (if we exclude relatively simple scheduling tasks) is also a will-o'-the-wisp. We can open up a very large can of worms, as Jack Wiseman did in stating:

> Once we admit that the future is unknown, analysis of the behaviour of producers in terms of adaptation to *known* future conditions becomes irrelevant. . . . The task of the producer is now to decide, on the basis of *his own estimates* about likely future conditions, between the possible alternative courses of action open to him at any point in time. Present prices and conditions are relevant only in so far as they provide a basis for judgements about the future. There is now no reason to suppose that individuals in similar circumstances will make the same assessments and hence reach the same decisions.[17]

In emphasising the subjective nature of expectations, Wiseman signals the way which Shackle has travelled, beyond the point reached in the Austrian and accepted neo-Austrian tradition. As another writer here, Stephen Littlechild, summarised in his inaugural lecture, the Austrian

School differs from other theories of behaviour under uncertainty by purporting to show how it alone avoids assuming that economic agents discover all there is to know.[18] But after closer inspection, Littlechild discerns a leading and representative exponent of the neo-Austrians, Israel Kirzner, defining entrepreneurship as only altertness to existing opportunities whereas Shackle rightly allows scope for the role of imagination in entrepreneurs' creation of new opportunities.[19]

In pointing once more to this important distinction in Shackle's work, it is not the intention to dismiss the neo-Austrian contributions. F. A. Hayek's 'Economics and Knowledge', first delivered in 1936, was important and exerted a powerful influence on some who have come after.[20] Hayek's Nobel Memorial Lecture of 1974, 'The Pretence of Knowledge', is another example.[21] Nor have developments in some branches of economics occurred in isolation. Hayek himself made a notable wider contribution with *The Counter-Revolution of Science* (1952).[22] Sir Karl Popper dedicated *Conjectures and Refutations: The Growth of Scientific Knowledge* (1963) to Hayek. Popper's address on 'Prediction and Prophecy in the Social Sciences' − first delivered in 1948 − is a sharp criticism of the tendency in the social sciences to propound historical prophecies.[23]

The links between economics and the physical sciences have been forged more closely in recent years, but in what may appear paradoxical ways, as both came under the stronger sway of ideas concerning the roles of uncertainty, time and subjectivism. The initiatives taken by Lakatos and Latsis in attempting to develop a methodology of scientific research programmes for the physical sciences and economic theory alike are a case in point. Both A. W. Coats (contributing to this book) and T. W. Hutchison (speaking at another British Association function in York) contributed to *Method and Appraisal in Economics* (1976) edited by Spiro Latsis.[24] While the work of Ilya Prigogine and his colleagues in the University of Brussels emphasises how the world of physics has become one of change; irreversible processes; uncertainty; time as a subjective feeling; a new alliance between the scientist and the real world.[25]

But if many people from various disciplines are marching together through this newly-perceived (but essentially old) world of uncertainty, we should be wary not to castigate too readily those generally associated with alternative points of view. Keynes, after all, was in no doubt that 'our knowledge of the future is fluctuating, vague and uncertain'. He disliked 'pretty, polite techniques, made for a well-panelled board room and a nicely regulated market' which 'are liable to collapse'.

He pointed out that: 'The orthodox theory assumes that we have a knowledge of the future of a kind quite different from that which we actually possess. This false rationalisation follows the lines of the Benthamite calculus.' Elsewhere Keynes made adversely critical comments about 'the calculus of probability . . . supposed to be capable of reducing uncertainty to the same calculable status as that of certainty itself . . . Actually, however, we have, as a rule, only the vaguest idea of any but the most direct consequences of our acts.' Thus Keynes went on to emphasise the relevance of 'all those elements of doubt and uncertainty, interested and disinterested advice, fashion, convention and what else you will which affects the mind of the investor' in considering future prices of capital assets.[26]

Curiously though (and it is not because Keynes's *Treatise on Probability* is less clear in its messages), these are not the elements of Keynes's work most readily recalled or frequently transmitted. It is the various contributions to restoring and maintaining 'general equilibrium' which are fastened on to. There is more attention paid to treatises which aim at prediction than at highlighting uncertainty.

One of the wisest contributions to the proper role of the economist was made by John Jewkes in 'The Economist and Public Policy', published in *Lloyds Bank Review* for April 1953.[27] He was concerned at the controversy raging between economists and the waning of public respect for economists, and perceived economists to be guilty of widespread errors of omission and commission. There was abstract economic speculation treated as an end in itself, the major error of commission arising from the belief that economists can predict the future, and a host of consequential errors. Very relevant to present purposes were Jewkes's opening remarks in a Brookings Lecture the following year on 'The Economist and Economic Change':

Some time ago I published, in a journal with a specialised and limited circulation, an article in which I pleaded that economists should not claim for their science powers that it did not possess, particularly the power to predict. The economists, to whom it was directly addressed, received it somewhat coldly, which was perhaps not very surprising. Of the few commendations it received, the greater part came from those actively engaged in economic planning, from which I deduced that their experiences in placing wholehearted confidence in the predictions of economists had not been altogether happy. To me the significant thing was that the article was, in effect, ignored.[28]

Reflecting the interests, presuppositions and determination to maintain their grasp, of the mainstream Academic Economics Establishment, there are mass sales of textbooks introducing 'positive economics'. There is probably greater interest in Milton Friedman's *Essays in Positive Economics* (1953) than in F. A. Hayek's more significant and questioning contributions.

Now Milton Friedman, in his essay on 'The Methodology of Positive Economics', correctly stated: 'The ultimate goal of a positive science is the development of a "theory" or "hypothesis" that yields valid and meaningful predictions about phenomena not yet observed.'[29] But it will be clear from earlier comments and references that the idea of valid and meaningful predictions being obtainable over a broad swathe of economic problems is a delusion. To seek after a 'theory' or 'hypothesis' for this purpose is nugatory, for what is being sought is still strictly a conjecture while the search indicates an inability to comprehend the nature of irremediable unforeknowledge. Furthermore, the positivist aims at verification of his 'theory' or 'hypothesis' by empirical tests and 'direct observation', rather than accepting the Popperian requirement of falsifiability. This is a field in which several other writers in this volume have made contributions, most recently Homa Katouzian,[30] and it would be inappropriate to develop this theme further here.

However, Professor Wiseman in a delightful little paper ('Costs and Decisions') has recently warned:

Questions like: what would happen to positive economics if your arguments are conceded?, are at best contingent: let us decide where reason lies, and deal with these minor matters afterwards.[31]

THE BRITISH ASSOCIATION TRADITION

In choosing as the theme of the 1981 British Association Meeting (Section F: Economics) 'Beyond Positive Economics', Wiseman has been as good as his word. But positive economics is not a minor matter. Positive economics indicates a state of mind, a way of (not) regarding uncertainty, of perceiving the future, of analysing the real world, of advancing policy prescriptions, and of advising on decision-making, which is deeply in error.

It is highly appropriate, however, for a British Association Annual Meeting to be the occasion for returning to the general theme. The 1953

Annual Meeting of the British Association was the occasion which produced *Uncertainty and Business Decisions*, edited by C. F. Carter, G. P. Meredith and G. L. S. Shackle.[32] On the whole there was remarkable homogeneity of view among the contributors (C. F. Carter making a few effective criticisms of some of Shackle's work related to business decision-making which he was to return to in *Uncertainty and Expectations in Economics: Essays in Honour of G.L.S. Shackle*[33]). Unfortunately, a paper written by Carter in 1955 expressly for the second edition of *Uncertainty and Business Decisions*, has proved too optimistic:

> Professor Shackle opened up, in 1949, a noble prospect of work to be done; and although this prospect may so far seem aridly theoretical to the business-man, we may now not be far from the time when it will yield a harvest of practical usefulness.[34]

But it is true, as will be shown below, that many of the ideas which have found persistent expression in Shackle's writings are being applied within some business firms. The problem is that they may not always be consistently applied. Some parts of the business, some procedures or techniques in use, may simultaneously be proceeding on quite different presuppositions.

Again, however, this is not something that either the British Association or Professor Shackle are strangers to. The 1966 Annual Meeting of the British Association produced *On the Nature of Business Success* (1968) edited by G. L. S. Shackle.[35] There were the familiar views of Shackle as he wrote on 'Policy, Poetry, and Success'. Elsewhere in the same volume one had 'Economic Model-building for Control'. Here were laid out the presuppositions of positive economics: 'establishing patterns in order to predict and control events'. 'Positive and normative economic concepts must be quantifiable.' 'The subject is pressing forward in an increasingly scientific manner to reduce its region of ignorance.' 'The positive economist seeks for stable patterns of economic behaviour.' 'The estimated coefficients of the models are statistical estimates so that probabilistic criteria may be applied to attach measures of reliability both to the estimated coefficients and to the forecasts made.' Only at the end did a tiny note of hesitancy intrude: 'At the present stage of our knowledge and abilities it is probably over-ambitious to search for *the* [italics in original] model that can be used to deal with all problems'![36]

The situation then and now can be summarised thus:

- Uncertainty is endemic, but its true nature is rarely understood.
- Persistent efforts are made to propound theories, hypotheses and techniques as if uncertainty did not exist or could be effectively eliminated.
- Traditional economic theories, notably those relating to general equilibrium and perfect knowledge, buttress erroneous ideas concerning uncertainty and have few counterparts in the real world.
- The objective and pursuit of positive economics − theories that provide valid predictions − are a will-o'-the-wisp.
- Probabilities when attached to unknowledge are liable to be a snare and delusion.

But:

- There is a long tradition, especially in British economics, of some economists having a better understanding of uncertainty and the economics of the real world than the profession in general.
- In recent years this subjectivist tradition has been represented by such economists as G. L. S. Shackle, J. Wiseman, B. J. Loasby, H. Katouzian, S. C. Littlechild, and others referred to above and writing in this volume.
- There are important links between these developments in economics and parallel developments in the physical sciences, where uncertainty, time, change, order in chaos and chaos in order are matters of intensified interest.

BUSINESS DECISION-MAKING

THE NEED FOR A FRAMEWORK

Bertrand Russell, in the Introduction to his *History of Western Philosophy*, remarked: 'To teach how to live without certainty, and yet without being paralysed by hesitation, is perhaps the chief thing that philosophy, in our age, can still do for those who study it.'[37] In business we need a conceptual framework to cope with, but not to disguise, uncertainty. A framework of ideas, elements, building-blocks (as referred to by G. L. S. Shackle) which can be communicated to managers in forms which shift their personal microcosms to allow them to cope more effectively with uncertainty and change. A framework which encourages adaptability, resilience and awareness in relation to uncertainty and change. A framework which leads to appropriate action: strategy formulation and implementation, shorter-term decision-making, organisational changes suited to new conditions, and procedural changes suited to new requirements. A framework which does not close off options too quickly, sheds light on possibilities previously overlooked, widens the span of issues and consequences considered rather than contracting it. A framework which is particularly essential the larger the firm; the longer the lead-times of investment; the slower that change of direction can be achieved in activities, organisation, tradition, culture, procedures and people.

Experience in Shell suggests that the multiple-scenario approach provides the most useful framework for handling uncertainty and allowing the formulation of appropriate strategies. The approach calls for the writing of scenarios – internally consistent, sufficiently relevant and detailed stories of what may occur in the future. It is important to ensure that not too many scenarios are written; two or three can be coped with before confusion sets in and apathy rises. Effort must also be put into differentiating the scenarios sufficiently, by giving due emphasis to qualitative elements as well as quantitative ones, to avoid users drawing a line between two scenarios or merely using the middle one of three scenarios where these are partly characterised by economic growth or industry product demand paths. Where the scenarios cover, say, the next five years forward, then description of possible cyclical fluctuations can help to reduce misuse of the scenarios. For longer-term scenarios, where there is pressure in practice to move from three to two scenarios, recourse is best made to strong sub-scenario elements in order to avoid misuse. The main reasons for misuse are a widespread preference for a 'base case' which gives a greater feeling of security to the user, encourages a belief that future outcomes are more certain than is in fact the case, and is administratively convenient. Such tendencies, however natural, have to be opposed, otherwise they destroy the purpose of the multiple-scenario approach.

It is because such tendencies have to be opposed – if they were not, then major vulnerabilities of the business could get overlooked – that we in Shell have persistently refused to attach 'subjective probabilities' to particular scenarios. Essentially we would be falling into the trap that Shackle warns us against, of attaching probabilities to unknowledge.

We would be encouraging users to devote too much attention to 'high-probability' scenarios and too little to 'low-probability' scenarios. And, as already indicated, we would knowingly be overlooking the point made by Loasby and Ansoff that by that process we might be caught by surprise as a 'low-probability' outcome wreaked its devastation.

The scenarios need to be generated from the main building-blocks relevant to the business. These building-blocks are usually:

● macroeconomic growth prospects
● possible political changes and public policy developments
● societal developments affecting corporate objectives and ways of meeting them, individual values and actions, and institutions
● industry demand prospects (including energy saving, conservation and increased efficiency in use in Shell's case)
● industry supply prospects
● industry capacity, cost and price developments
● present technology, potential innovations, pace of diffusion and scope for substitution
● present and prospective competitive environment.

Under each of these headings the need is to consider what the range of credible possibilities is, within boundaries which cut off possible but calamitous global or regional disasters – such as nuclear or major conventional armed conflict. For scenario development, there are advantages in having a small, hand-picked, multinational and multi-disciplinary team. The team should be small, its key members not more than seven or eight, for effective communication and interaction. It should be hand-picked to ensure that no one person or view becomes dominant, thus leading to the premature dismissal of unwelcome or less credible viewpoints and possibilities. The multinational element is important for international operations because, for instance, per-spectives on the economic prospects for those states of North-western Europe with large public sector involvement may not be relevant to the prospects for Latin America, South-east Asia or even Southern Europe. The multidisciplinary make-up of the team is important to ensure that an appropriate range of expertise, experience and per-spective is brought to bear on the relevant issues.

It may be argued that a range of political viewpoints and attitudes towards the team's own company and corporate practices is also desir-able. In practice, certainly so far as Shell is concerned, there is a fair range of political and corporate attitudes represented among its employees, although the extreme left-wing anarchist would be a *rara avis*. More important is a willingness of team members to gain access to a wide range of external views, not necessarily represented within the company at all nor believed to be either practical or credible. There must be awareness of 'way-out' views among team members and a conscious process of accepting or rejecting them. Thus contact should be made with outstanding people in all walks of life, and through survey results of more ordinary people as well. Time should be spent with Communist Party officials in many countries as well as with their counterparts in Conservative, Liberal and Socialist parties. Regular discussions with outstanding academics — economists, sociologists, historians, physical scientists, etc. — should be maintained. Selective use should be made of consultants over a wide area. Team members need to travel, to talk with people in their own environments, to understand local conditions and to use their powers of observation.

With a high-quality scenario team, the essential value of its work lies in its qualitative assessments. Thus quantitative assessments should play a subordinate role, being handmaidens to the qualitative assessments by ensuring correspondence with perceived reality. Historic data are usually a help in forming judgements about the future, and one defence against selective perception and other biases in the exercise of judgement.[38] But there is a persistent danger of trying to quantify the unquantifiable; in believing that numerical data are invariably more precise and significant than qualitative data; and in developing models which are simultaneously too complex to be understood or used effectively and too simplistic to cope with the complexities of the real world.

Thus, unlike the mathematical economists and those who ignore the lessons of history, so severely castigated by Katouzian, within Shell's scenario team there has long been emphasis on the importance of historical insights and, after a brief foray into global energy modelling on a large scale, severe restrictions on modelling ambitions. The interest in history has been particularly concentrated on periods of social turbulence, economic instability and inflation. Insights have been sought from the later Roman Empire (say from the times of Emperor Septimius Severus), from the later Byzantine Empire (from the times of Constantine x Ducas), from various mediaeval peasants' revolts and the so-called general crisis of the seventeenth-century, as well as more modern periods. Links between inflation and social unrest have been studied over the past 2000 years. Causes of past weak economic performance have been examined. Consumer behaviour is looked at particularly closely, works such as George Katona's *Psychological Economics* being held in somewhat higher regard as a practically oriented study than would be usual in academic circles.[39]

In the main areas of our traditional concerns – the energy and chemicals business – there is obviously a large body of expertise to draw upon. When it comes to societal change, informed opinion is less widely available from internal sources, although Shell is not totally bereft of sociologists and social historians. In the societal field more reliance is placed upon maintaining access to leading thinkers in academia, in a few market research institutes and consultancies. But their views are subjected to the closest internal scrutiny and every effort is made to integrate the more robust and timely elements into the scenario framework. One of the advantages of having a multinational team, most of them with considerable international experience, and a strong historical sense is that waves of fashion and undercurrents of less practicable opinion are more effectively withstood than the more enthusiastic external advisers might sometimes wish.

At the end of the day, however, all this activity can only serve – recalling Wiseman's words quoted earlier – as the basis for judgements about possible futures. They do not provide robust forecasts, a bigger and better crystal ball than your competitors'.

People in Shell are constantly reminded of an Arab proverb: 'Those who foretell the future lie, even when they foretell the truth.'

Unforeknowledge is irremediable, as Shackle has so often pointed out. To think otherwise, to advance or to employ techniques as if it were not so, is a snare and delusion. If the necessary comprehension of uncertainty is to be communicated, understood and maintained then the scenarios themselves and the elements upon which they are based have to be transmitted by spoken and written word throughout the management (at least) of the organisation. By management we mean decision-makers at various levels. Human beings like order most of the time, their appetite for chaos and uncertainty is distinctly limited. Thus one is asking managements to shift their personal microcosms in some fundamental respects so that they both accept uncertainty and can act constructively nevertheless. Here is where the link between scenario-writing and decision-making must begin to be forged. The process calls for a high level of understanding and not a little courage among management. But if this understanding is not forthcoming then the organisation's adaptability to new circumstances, resilience when faced with threats, and capacity to take advantage of change will be severely constrained.

Fortunately, Shell's experience with scenario-writing since 1971 has been able to offer more than just communication of inherent uncertainty. First, by focusing in a systematic way on the various building-blocks it has been possible to detect a number of 'pre-determined elements' already in the pipeline. While there could be no certainty how these elements would come out at the other end, examination by the scenario team of their likely impact was found to be a great help in increasing awareness of decision-makers as to what might happen, and in preparing management for what did happen in many cases. Second, the approach was able to shed so much light and understanding on what was likely to happen that it was sometimes wondered subsequently whether the scenario team included witches on broomsticks. For if the team had been required to make forecasts then they would have exhibited an unusual degree of accuracy, and needed to remind themselves constantly of that Arab proverb. As a member of that team for five years during the 1970s, I am profoundly aware of how much may be lost in summarising the work of several people, whose perceptions of the history may at some points also differ from my own. Nevertheless, the following review may be of interest.

THE FRAMEWORK IN PRACTICE

In some quarters of the oil industry the awareness of impending oil supply problems and scope for higher prices intensified from the mid-1960s. Unease can be traced back to the mid-1950s, in the wake of the Abadan crisis, turmoil in various other Middle East countries, and demands by producer nations for higher royalties. Nevertheless, it took some years before awareness of the potential for oil crises became translated into a new framework for handling the range of envisaged possibilities.

For planning in Shell, the key year was 1971. In January of that year a document was issued internally with the long title *A Probabilistic Approach to the Forecasting of Upstream-Government Take on Crude Oil Exports, 1970–1985*. In its title and content the document represented the 1960s approach towards uncertainty and the use of techniques claimed to reduce it. There was, the document claimed, a 70 per cent probability that oil prices could move up to $3 per barrel from about $1 between 1970 and 1975. By December 1971, Shell's Group Planning division had begun to apply the multiple-scenario approach (Figure 8.1). A wider range of oil price assumptions, and of oil demand, were integrated in the four scenarios developed. The findings already began to point to a trebling or quadrupling of oil prices, and senior Shell management were from October 1971 advising OECD member governments, OECD and EEC Secretariats, on the need to plan emergency allocation schemes in the event of crisis.

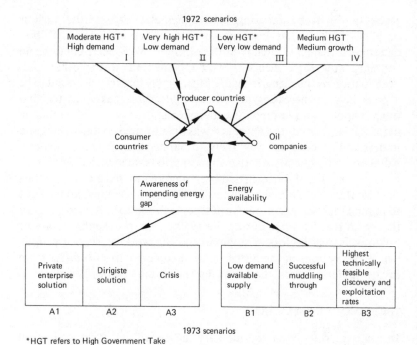

FIGURE 8.1   *1972 and 1973 scenarios (January 1973)*

In May 1972 came Shell's first considered thoughts on such concepts as the capacity of OPEC nations readily to absorb higher oil export revenues, the OPEC surplus revenue problem and 'Producer Logic' of oil production and pricing. It is worth noting that the first two problems were regarded as likely to prove only temporarily aggravating in the 1970s, as initially substantial surplus revenues quickly disappeared, and this view was confirmed by outside consultants reporting in July 1972 and again in January 1974.

By January 1973 Shell was well into its stride on scenario writing. In one sense, too much so, with a selection of six scenarios to choose from, a number which was excessive (Figure 8.1). However, under an energy crisis oil prices were expected to rise to $10 per barrel (at 1973 constant prices) in the 1970s. It was at this time that the concept of the 1970s as a period of 'rapids' through which it would be hazardous to navigate was introduced. By May 1973 attention was being concentrated on a single oil crisis scenario (Figure 8.2): 'the proposed scenario merits particular attention because it involves a threat to the economic well-being and progress of the industrialised world'. Shell

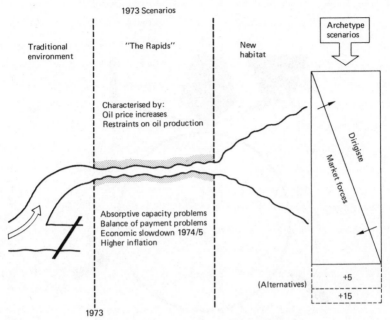

FIGURE 8.2   *The rapids in 1973 (May 1973)*

were convinced they were already in the 'rapids', although not every part of the organisation was equally quick to adjust perceptions and actions to fit new circumstances and challenges.

Despite outstanding work in building up relevant scenario elements, there remained some odd lacunae. The full significance of the work done for adjustment of future economic growth, industry oil demand and inflation prospects was not quickly understood. The perception of economic slowdown in 1974/5 which was recognised in late 1973 was not immediately carried forward into the realisation that longer-term prospects had changed markedly, despite the comments made early in 1973. From the beginning of 1974 there was therefore a persistent effort by the economists involved in the scenario work to get the economic growth assumptions down and the inflation assumptions up. Acceptance of higher inflation assumptions came quickly. Lower growth assumptions and with them lower oil demand assumptions came more slowly, although major downward adjustments were accepted internally from July 1974.

These issues played a significant part in propelling Shell into fuller consideration of medium-term scenarios, built around possible

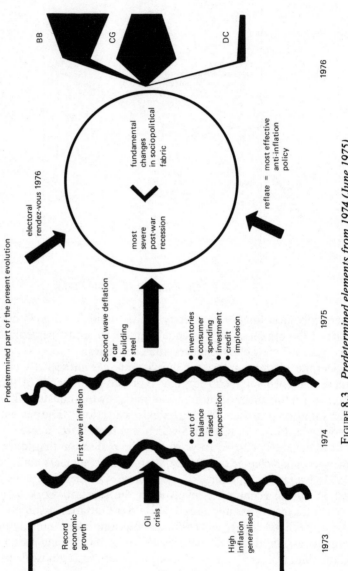

FIGURE 8.3 *Predetermined elements from 1974 (June 1975)*

macroeconomic developments five years forward. This consideration began in the autumn of 1974 and fully-developed medium-term scenarios have been issued internally at regular intervals since June 1975. The emphasis was placed from the outset upon forces making for 'constrained growth' in the longer run after examination of various 'predetermined' elements (Figure 8.3). Growth assumptions for the longer term were reduced, emphasis was given to a low-growth 'world of internal contradictions' scenario, and doubt was expressed about the viability of a higher-growth 'belle epoque' scenario before the end of this century. Particularly close attention was paid to consumers' ability to pay higher oil prices (say $21 per barrel by 1980), the scope for Saudi Arabia to guide OPEC oil price developments, and the importance of energy saving in reducing pressure on oil supplies.

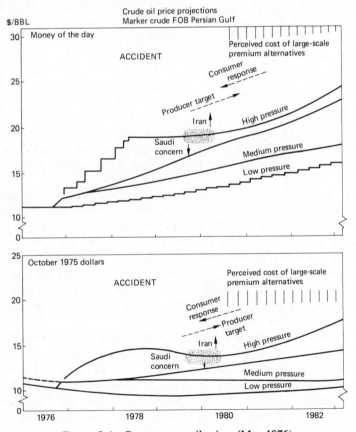

FIGURE 8.4   *Pressures on oil prices (May 1976)*

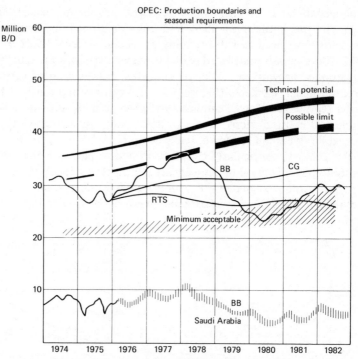

FIGURE 8.5   *OPEC oil production possibilities under constrained growth (CG), recovery turns sour (RTS) or boom and bust (BB) scenarios (May 1976)*

It was the 'recession' effect on energy saving rather than 'pure' savings which was emphasised from 1975, combined with concern at the possibility of 'producer logic' combining with 'accidents' to drive up the price of OPEC oil somewhere around 1979/80 (Figure 8.4). Scope was seen as early as May 1976 for OPEC oil production to fall to 25 million barrels per day or below in 1980/1 (Figure 8.5). This idea was linked with the concern felt in late 1976 that OPEC producers might miscalculate their capacity to raise oil prices and the consequences thereof in the period 1978/80 (Figure 8.6).

This theme of 'producer miscalculation' was elaborated upon during 1977 but it cannot be claimed that events in Iran and their consequences from late 1978 were clearly foreseen. However, it is interesting to note that the concept of producer miscalculation was linked to the 'relapse' scenario issued in May 1977, which was 'regarded as having a more compelling logic when applied to the weaker West European economies'.

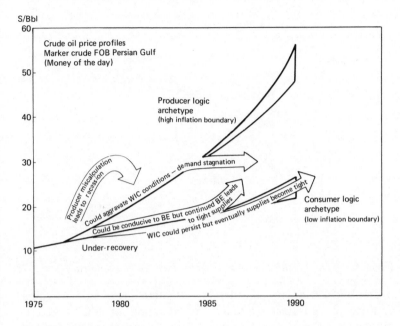

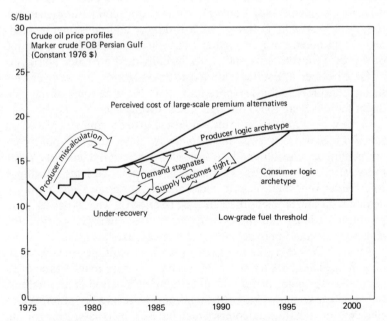

FIGURE 8.6 *Scope for producer miscalculation? (January 1977)*

The business environment

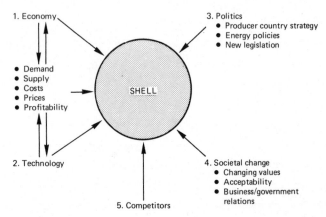

FIGURE 8.7   *The widening perception of the business environment (June 1978)*

The mid-1970s saw considerable attention being paid to vulner-abilities in consumer nations. Consideration of Shell's external business environment had extended from narrow economic and tech-nological elements into political, societal and competitor elements (Figure 8.7). Public policy of both producer and consumer govern-ments had taken on even greater importance than heretofore, while pressures on institutions and shifts in individual attitudes and goals attracted closer attention. This led to investigation of the problems facing consumer nations (Figure 8.8) about the time some of the pro-ducer nations were to go through severe turbulence.

In the generation of scenarios, and the degree of emphasis placed on specific scenario elements, there is always liable to be in-built con-servatism, an unwillingness to consider sufficiently seriously some more extreme possibilities. There may at one point be some reluctance to consider very high oil price possibilities, at another very weak oil demand. At one moment there may be fixation on what is occurring in producer nations, and the consequences after due lapse of time for consumer demand may be temporarily overlooked.

All in all, however, the record of a decade of multiple-scenario plan-ning in Shell has been a remarkable success. The approach has enabled people to cope much better with uncertainty in a period of unusual tur-bulence. The scenarios have shed light on a large number of important elements and possible outcomes which have come to pass. Recognition of uncertainty, awareness of some 'predetermined' elements and

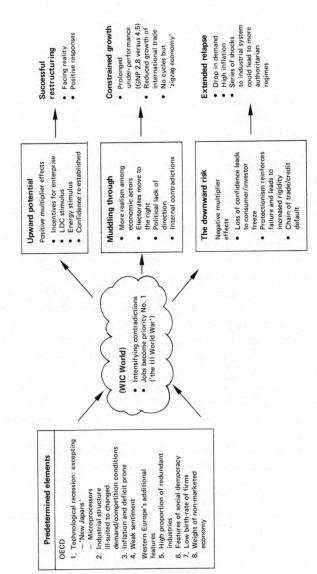

Predetermined elements

OECD

1. Technological recession: excepting
   - 'New Japans'
   - Microprocessors
2. Industrial structure ill-suited to changed demand/competition conditions
3. Inflation and deficit prone
4. Weak sentiment

Western Europe's additional features

5. High proportion of redundant industries
6. Features of social democracy
7. Low birth-rate of firms
8. Weight of non-marketed economy

(WIC World)
- Intensifying contradictions
- Jobs become priority No. 1 ('the III World War')

Upward potential

Positive multiplier effects
- Incentives for enterprise
- LDC stimulus
- Energy stimulus
- Confidence re-established

Muddling through
- More realism among economic actors
- Electorates move to the right
- Political lack of direction
- Internal contradictions

The downward risk

Negative multiplier effects
- Loss of confidence leads to consumer/investor freeze
- Protectionism reinforces failure and leads to increased rigidity
- Chain of trade/credit default

Successful restructuring
- Facing reality
- Positive responses

Constrained growth
- Prolonged under-performance (GNP 2.8 versus 4.5)
- Reduced growth of international trade
- No cycles but 'zigzag economy'

Extended relapse
- Drop in demand
- High inflation
- Series of shocks to industrial system could lead to more authoritarian regimes

FIGURE 8.8 *Failing industries, unemployment and the non-marketed economy (June 1978)*

forewarning of the direction of possible changes, have all been achieved. It would have been astonishing if, amid all the successes, there had not been a few weak points or phases.

THE FRAMEWORK APPLIED

A framework which is not applied is of no practical value however brilliant the speculation by, and however stimulating the intellectual exercise for, those directly involved in scenario development. The framework must lead to appropriate action – whether in the fields of strategy formulation and implementation, everyday decision-making, organisational or procedural changes. This calls for a high order of communication and understanding between all parties involved, from the scenario-writers to decision-makers at all levels of the organisation. It is rarely and then only partially, achieved. The reasons for failure are numerous.

Too many planners, including those involved in generating scenarios, are remote from business problems. In some cases this may be due to lack of experience, interest or temperament; in others, because planners may be kept away from involvement in the day-to-day business or strategic decision-taking, for instance by being kept outside the main management team. Too many decision-makers, on the other hand, get overwhelmed by day-to-day problems, even at the highest levels, where such problems should be capable of satisfactory delegation. They become too quickly dismissive of planners and the contribution planning can make, and too resentful or deaf when planners point to the very costly errors which neglect of that contribution has caused. (As the writer has both planning and operational responsibilities, a privileged and unusual position, he can be fairly unbiased in these comments.)

Another source of failure is unhappiness with any approach which illuminates uncertainty rather than purporting to reduce it. Most people want to know what *the* future will be, what *the* result of a decision will be, and dislike being confronted with the realities of uncertainty. Even where those realities are grudgingly recognised they may be put on one side because administrative convenience, or unwillingness to take responsibility, call for a single set of assumptions to be handed down from above. For many people the opportunity of working with more than one scenario, for instance, is not perceived as offering scope for choice and responsibility but as opening up the risk of error.

There are various means whereby the incidence of failure can be reduced, though it cannot be entirely eliminated. The scenario writers need to be continually in contact with people around the organisation, discovering what the main problems and vulnerabilities of the business are and sifting them for robust scenario elements. The decision-makers must be able to communicate their concerns, and their reactions to scenarios, directly to the planners. In Shell, for instance, several hundred managers – decision-makers – and planners throughout the organisation receive oral presentations of the scenarios each year. This is in addition to the circulation of scenario books containing the scenario elements and both qualitative and quantitative work on their implications.

Other means are through the various internal courses that Shell runs, for people of every level from new entrants to senior managers. Many of these courses include contributions from planners who explain the philosophy of multiple-scenario planning and its applications. At the most senior level, beyond even what Shell calls its Advanced Management Study Group course, there is a Decision Processes Seminar. In this seminar the nature of uncertainty is highlighted; the role of hunch and judgement is extolled alongside the more apparently systematic approaches derived from decision theory; biases in judgement and perception scrutinised; blocks to creativity and new ways of thinking and acting examined; and decisions taken within specific contexts looked at. At many points the objectives of the seminar coincide with the arguments being advanced here, and are therefore reproduced as Figure 8.9.

By shedding light on future possibilities or key issues, scenarios, or some of their main elements, give important insights into the lines along which corporate strategy should proceed. In Shell's case it has been indicated how the early work shed light on possibilities of oil price rises, oil supply disruptions, international political and financial issues, and the likely economic consequences if these possibilities came to pass. Investment in oil exploration, and improved methods of finding and exploiting oil reserves, were given important new dimensions. Better, because more efficient, processes of converting crude oil into higher-value oil products became more necessary. But widespread and prolonged economic stagnation was likely to undermine growth prospects for oil products, including petrochemicals, and in some important respects inhibit the rapid development of alternative energy. In the oil business, therefore, there were fundamental implications for the exploration and production of crude oil, shipping it in tankers,

Traditionally, business organisations have assumed that uncertainty is minimised and knowledge maximised by detailed quantification of relevant factors, objective appraisal of the results, and rational decision-making based on these efforts which are assumed to approximate to reality. But in a business environment undergoing major, and often unforeseen, changes these assumptions are undermined by uncertainty and ignorance. The application of imagination and hunch may shed more light on possible future developments and the means of coping effectively with them. Decisions which allow scope for hunch, and procedures which recognise that excessive quantification is counter-productive, may be more appropriate to the challenges of the 1980s.

The seminar begins by illustrating and demonstrating that a fact or reality exists principally in the mind and perception of the individual. Thus an individual's 'hunch' may be a more reliable 'fact', or sixth and 'higher' sense, than commonly assumed. In this context judgement is of critical importance, and relies not only upon individual character but also breadth of vision and experience. Broad experience, including the ability to use apparent chaos to achieve higher orders of perception and reality, are important buttresses to sound judgement.

In an era of severe challenges to business and businessmen it is necessary to place problems in their historical and cultural perspective, hold fast to some perennial truths, and come forward with positive responses. In this context some of our standard tools and ways of thinking are defective. Economics is normally concerned with states of general equilibrium in theory; whereas in practice disequilibrium, uncertainty and partial ignorance are the order of the day. The distinction between statements of fact and statements of value (the latter regarded by logical positivists as unscientific, if not meaningless) is seen to be blurred and unreal.

Technology is often viewed either as a cataclysmic threat or as an unbounded opportunity, rather than with closer discrimination. Bureaucracies, public and private, are regarded as uncreative whereas − sometimes with a struggle − they can be creative, and with effort can be made even more so.

In moving towards improvements in strategy formulation and implementation and better business decisions more generally, it is necessary to go beyond the existing state of affairs: whether the corporate culture, or received opinion, or the information given. Conscious recognition of the role of judgement and hunch may reduce the burden of unnecessary or spurious quantification, model-building, and such like. More emphasis can then be placed upon imaginative and positive responses to the challenges of our times. There will be presentations on selecting optimum strategic positions and practical exercises in business decisions, as well as coverage of the other issues raised in this outline.

FIGURE 8.9   *Objectives of the decision-processes seminar (May 1981)*

manufacturing it (i.e. refining or converting it into oil products), and marketing the products. Not all these implications were seen as quickly, or acted upon, by some parts of the business as they were by others.

Thus, it has been very noticeable how much lower Shell's growth and demand assumptions were after 1974 in the scenarios than those of competitors, national governments, international institutions and forecasting institutes in general. Shell therefore allowed themselves some advance warning on what not to spend money on building or acquiring, and how much might suitably be spent on building or acquiring something else. Selective strategies were encouraged, geared to weak overall demand but within which lay more buoyant and profitable sectors. Indications were also given of what to close down or rationalise in other ways. These often sombre warnings and indications have not always gone down well or quickly with the more venturesome or traditional spirits geared to the ways of thinking and acting appropriate to the high-growth 1950s and 1960s. Shell has not avoided all the problems of overcapacity which have inflicted the oil and chemical industries in recent years, although, without the scenarios, this problem would certainly have been even worse and remedial action further delayed.

In its traditional fields of activity, the scenario work has often added weight to other, more technical, arguments for investing in what have proved to be profitable ventures: in the introduction of enhanced oil recovery techniques, which greatly improved the recovery of heavy oil reserves in particular (e.g. the processes of steam drive and steam soak); in raising the success ratio of hydrocarbon finds and speeding up accurate evaluations of drilling activity (e.g. bright spot analysis and interactive log data-processing); in the drive for additional conversion capacity in our refineries (from thermal cracking units to hydro-demetalisation); and in the drive for higher value added as a key element of marketing strategy, hence the emphasis placed on preferred sectors and the rationalisation and withdrawal from others.

In less traditional activities the record is more patchy, as our nuclear misfortunes demonstrate, but care should be taken in assessing what lessons can appropriately be drawn. In the nuclear example, most of the scenario elements were and are robust, yet failure resulted. The logic of Shell's entry into nuclear included oil supply and price uncertainties; pressure for the 'noble uses' of oil; high potential for the nuclear generation of electricity; the safety and environmental attractions of high-temperature gas-cooled reactors and fusion research by our chosen partners, General Atomic; and the large orders being placed for new generating capacity. Unfortunately a large number of problems arose: reduced electricity demand growth and generating requirements; controversy over nuclear and shifts in federal policy in the United States; underperformance of a demonstration plant and budget overruns; technical, licensing and contractual problems; and legal issues surrounding uranium supplies. Yet nevertheless, the main scenario elements are still there, and the high-temperature gas-cooled reactor retains major potential advantages in safety, environmental conservation and resource utilisation.

In the area of alternatives to oil more generally, commercial viability is persistently the problem, however robust the scenario elements and technological feasibility.

The scenario work, applied at a national level and taking full account of local conditions, may again raise fundamental issues. It may suggest that the maintenance of traditional scales and methods of operation are liable to prove unprofitable to the company and unacceptable to third parties. This may be because in the local political or social environment the traditional logic of a major multinational oil corporation, however justifiable in a global context, is simply incompatible with the logic now acceptable to local interests. Or it may be because in a particular national context smaller operations generally survive better, or offer a smaller hostage to the rapacity of state entities, or may be more resilient to changing political regimes and policies. There can be no doubt that Shell's scenario approach, especially where it has highlighted political or social factors, has offered useful guidance for strategic choice. In some cases it has been the relevance of key scenario elements, rather than the scenarios *per se*, which have proved particularly valuable.

By setting the scene or scenes, scenarios are an important aid to formulating appropriate strategies. Once an appropriate strategy can be formulated, its implementation has some chance of success. The prime question is: What do we want to be in year X? The next question is: How do we get there? Another question (often overlooked, but well understood by the military strategist) is: Where do we go from there? (i.e. what are the terminal conditions, can we perceive a line of advance or retreat?). Answers to these questions are the basis for the long-term plan.

With scenarios and a long-term plan there should be useful antidotes to the deep-rooted tendency to cope with today's problems rather than sitting back to take the longer view. An oil supply crisis may cause consternation and encourage the payment of excessive prices for supplies. Placed in the context that underlying demand conditions are weakening, oil companies may be more cautious in the payment of premia to obtain their perceived requirements of crude. This broader perception may have a critical and beneficial influence on financial results, because domestic oil price regimes frequently allow only slow or partial recovery of costs in the market-place.

For an organisation as large and as decentralised as Shell, the scenario approach has other benefits. The scenarios provide a global framework for thought and action, without imposing too much influence from the centre on local decision-making. The scenarios themselves can be refined, or re-developed, to suit local circumstances. They provide a common way of viewing uncertainty, possibilities, challenges and opportunities without imposing too rigid and restrictive a structure. And the scenario approach allows a wide variety of subordinate techniques to be used as and when appropriate. For a company employing over 150 000 people, despite the fact that it is capital-intensive, with operating companies in over 100 countries, the framework applied is an excellent vehicle for aiding communication while retaining flexibility.

Relatively little has been written about Shell's experience in the application of multiple-scenario planning for outside audiences. Pierre Wack, who has led Shell's scenario team for the past decade, has published the occasional article. André Bénard, a Managing Director of the Royal Dutch/Shell Group, wrote 'World Oil and Cold Reality' in the November/December 1980 issue of the *Harvard Business Review*. Peter Beck, when concerned with strategic planning in Shell International Petroleum's Group Planning Division, wrote on 'Strategic Planning in the Royal Dutch/Shell Group' in 1977; and he has recently written about his planning experiences within a UK context. The present writer has touched on the subject at a previous British Association Annual Meeting (Bath University, 1978) and elsewhere; and two articles by Christopher Lorenz in the *Financial Times* are particularly well informed.[40] But it is work which is in a continuous process of evolution. There is a strong desire to ensure the more effective application of the multiple-scenario approach, to assist in improving the overall strategic thrust of our business, to develop and maintain a *leitbild* which will carry Shell through successfully into the twenty-first century. That may seem a long-term perspective, but in the energy, chemicals and metals businesses in which Shell is engaged the lead-times are very long.

IMPLICATIONS FOR ECONOMISTS

The introduction to this contribution made it clear that mainstream economic theories and the work of most academic economists have only limited relevance to the economics of the real world, and to the problems of businessmen. To the extent that there is a tradition, a body of work, and a group of people active, relevant to the real world of business, then — as the section on 'Economists of Uncertainty' indicated — this tradition and work are well represented by other contributors to this volume. Their adverse criticisms of mainstream economic theory, the lack of relevance to the real world of much academic work, the role of uncertainty, the defects of the positivist position, are all closely relevant to the challenges facing businessmen.

Regrettably, there have been few academic contributions to the frameworks as developed and applied here. The technique of scenario writing is not new. Erich Jantsch wrote up its essentials in 1967 for the OECD publication: *Technological Forecasting in Perspective*.[41] Jantsch touched on the subject five years later in *Technological Planning and Social Futures*.[42] Herman Kahn and his associates at the Hudson Institute were leading practitioners in the late 1960s and early 1970s with *The Year 2000* and *Things to Come*.[43] Such academics as interested themselves in scenario development tended to be cool in their reactions. A group at the Science Policy Research Unit in the University of Sussex, writing in *The Art of Anticipation: Values and Methods in Forecasting*, felt unable to assess the success of scenario development in comparison with other techniques (though the scenario approach can incorporate many techniques in a subordinate role, this is one of its virtues) and concluded: 'No sound means exist for identifying the impact of scenarios on real, live decision-makers in making them aware of an increased range of options.'[44]

Some of the same group contributed to *World Futures: The Great Debate* (1978) in which twelve global scenarios were outlined. Not surprisingly, one author remarked: 'these twelve scenarios throw up a bewildering variety of prospects for the future'.[45] Nevertheless, this contribution had the merit of refusing to attach probabilities to the different scenarios because: 'we would argue that such an approach is wrong both in principle and in practice'.[46]

It is disappointing, and perhaps a suitable subject for contemplation, that the contributions of the academic halls to either the comprehension of uncertainty or the study of disequilibrium or the role of scenarios, have been so modest. We are told that academics are now devoting much attention to the modelling of uncertainty, change, disequilibrium. The issues are real, but the means chosen to achieve them suggest that there is still a search after that illusory Philosopher's Stone. Mainstream economists would do well to shift their attention to the work of the economists of uncertainty, to go beyond general equilibrium theory.

Yet it will not be enough to comprehend uncertainty. There must be a re-evaluation of the worth of general theorising. This is an uncomfortable demand, seeming to strike at the heart of the role of the academic and of the intellectual more generally. Yet the importance of context cannot be overstated. The roles of time, place, circumstances, tradition, institutional framework, industry norms, corporate cultures are vital.

When a large number of academic economists and university students of economics began to take an interest in oil matters after the 1973 crisis, the absence of an understanding of context was widespread. The history and politics of the Middle East, for instance, did not seem well understood. Oil was not infrequently considered like any other commodity; it could have been groundnuts − or cocoa or bananas − for the purposes of much of the academic analyses. Because US-based academics were in the forefront of vociferous attacks on OPEC as a cartel, it was too readily assumed that in the early days OPEC fulfilled all the necessary conditions of a cartel and all cartels collapsed quickly, just like US trusts had done. In reality, however, OPEC for most of its history to date has not fulfilled all the conditions of a cartel. Furthermore, those with a knowledge of the history of cartels in Europe know many examples of cartels lasting several decades, and in a few cases on and off for periods of up to 200 years.[47] Lack of proper context caused much ill-founded debate and speculation in the mid-1970s.

The importance of context is even more obvious when looking at the oil industry within the framework of the energy industry more generally, between oil products, between these products and actual or potential substitutes, or between oil companies themselves. The structure of Shell, for instance, is quite different from that of any other oil company. For a start it is more multinational and − as mentioned earlier − decentralised in its staffing and structure, and encompasses a variety of subcultures within its corporate culture. It is very difficult in such circumstances to advance general theories. It is particularly difficult to do so from a foundation of general equilibrium, perfect knowledge and markets, and other notions which have little or no counterpart in the real world.

This is a rather sad conclusion for mainstream economics and economists, but unlike unforeknowledge it is not irremediable. The way forward is to go beyond positive economics.

Fifteen years ago G. L. S. Shackle believed there were links between policy, poetry and business success. Surely they are still there. Life is a continuum (or should be) through time and across human activities — poetic, academic and business. Is not business 'Burnt Norton':

> Time present and time past
> Are both perhaps present in time future
> And time future contained in time past.
> If all time is eternally present
> All time is unredeemable
> What might have been is an abstraction
> Remaining a perpetual possibility
> Only in a world of speculation.
> What might have been and what has been
> Point to one end, which is always present.
> Footfalls echo in the memory
> Down the passage which we did not take
> Towards the door we never opened . . .?

and 'East Coker':

> There is, it seems to us,
> At best, only a limited value
> In the knowledge derived from experience.
> The knowledge imposes a pattern, and falsifies,
> For the pattern is new in every moment . . .
> To arrive where you are, to get from where you are not,
> You must go by a way wherein there is no ecstasy.
> In order to arrive at what you do not know
> You must go by a way which is the way of ignorance.
> . . . And so each venture
> Is a new beginning . . . and now, under conditions
> That seem unpropitious. But perhaps neither gain nor loss.
> For us, there is only the trying . . .?

and 'Little Gidding':

> We shall not cease from exploration
> And the end of all our exploring
> Will be to arrive where we started
> And know the place for the first time?[48]

Uncertainty!

NOTES AND REFERENCES

1. Marjorie Grice-Hutchinson, *The School of Salamanca. Readings in Spanish Monetary Theory, 1544–1605* (Oxford University Press, 1952) and *Early Economic Thought in Spain, 1177–1740* (London: Allen and Unwin, 1978).
2. Thus: 'it is a mark of the trained mind never to expect more precision in the treatment of any subject than the nature of that subject permits; for demanding logical demonstrations from a teacher of rhetoric is clearly about as reasonable as accepting mere plausibility from a mathematician.' Aristotle, *The Ethics of Aristotle: The Nicomachean Ethics*, trans. J. A. K. Thomson (Harmondsworth: Penguin, 1976) p. 65.

   Though Adam Smith's *Wealth of Nations* and even *The Theory of Moral Sentiments* are widely read, his *The Principles Which Lead and Direct Philosophical Enquiries: Illustrated by the History of Astronomy* is less well known. It is most conveniently found in W. P. D. Wightman, J. C. Bryce and I. S. Ross (eds), *Adam Smith: Essays on Philosophical Subjects* (Oxford University Press, 1980) pp. 31–105. It is discussed in Andrew S. Skinner, *A System of Social Science: Papers Relating to Adam Smith* (Oxford University Press, 1979) pp. 25–41.
3. G. L. S. Shackle, *Imagination and the Nature of Choice* (Edinburgh University Press, 1979) p. 13. The other two works referred to in this paragraph are published by Cambridge University Press, as is *The Years of High Theory: Invention and Tradition in Economic Thought, 1926–1939* referred to three paragraphs later.
4. Ibid., pp. 57–8.
5. Homa Katouzian, *Ideology and Method in Economics* (London: Macmillan, 1980) p. 133.
6. Ibid., p. 189.
7. Ibid., p. 205.
8. Ibid., p. 204.
9. Ibid., p. 210.
10. Brian J. Loasby, *Choice, Complexity and Ignorance: An Enquiry into Economic Theory and the Practice of Decision-Making* (Cambridge University Press, 1976) p. 209.
11. Ibid., p. 115.
12. Ibid., p. 164. Loasby here refers to H. Igor Ansoff, *Corporate Strategy: An Analytic Approach to Business Policy For Growth and Expansion* Harmondsworth: Penguin, 1968) p. 56 in this edition. Other, similar references occur in this book, e.g. on p. 157.
13. Loasby, *Choice, Complexity and Ignorance*, p. 171.
14. Ibid., pp. 162–3.
15. One of the many *mots justes* of Carlo Brumat, of INSEAD and the Free International University in Rome.
16. Jack Wiseman, 'The Theory of Public Utility Price – an Empty Box', in J. M. Buchanan and G. F. Thirlby (eds), *LSE Essays on Cost* (London: LSE Weidenfeld and Nicolson, 1973) pp. 247–8.
17. Jack Wiseman, 'Uncertainty, Costs and Collectivist Economic Planning' in ibid., pp. 233–4.

18. S. C. Littlechild, *Change Rules, OK?* (Inaugural Lecture, University of Birmingham, 28 May 1977) p. 7. See also S. C. Littlechild, *The Fallacy of the Mixed Economy: An 'Austrian' Critique of Economic Thinking and Policy* (London: Institute of Economic Affairs, 1978) pp. 73–4.

19. S. C. Littlechild, 'Comment: Radical Subjectivism or Radical Subversion', in Mario J. Rizzo (ed.), *Time, Uncertainty and Disequilibrium: Exploration of Austrian Themes* (Lexington, Mass.: D. C. Heath & Co., 1979) pp. 44–6. Littlechild is here commenting on G. L. S. Shackle's *Imagination, Formalism, and Choice*, pp. 19–31. Israel M. Kirzner's work is set out in *Competition and Entrepreneurship* (Chicago University Press, 1973) and *Perception, Opportunity, and Profit: Studies in the Theory of Entrepreneurship* (Chicago University Press, 1979).

20. Friedrich A. Hayek, 'Economics and Knowledge', in Hayek, *Individualism and Economic Order* (London: Routledge & Kegan Paul, 1949) pp. 33–56.

21. F. A. Hayek, 'The Pretence of Knowledge', in Hayek, *New Studies in Philosophy, Politics, Economics and the History of Ideas* (London: Routledge & Kegan Paul, 1978) pp. 23–34.

22. F. A. Hayek, *The Counter-Revolution of Science: Studies on the Abuse of Reason* (Glencoe, Ill.: The Free Press, 1952).

23. Karl R. Popper, 'Prediction and Prophecy in the Social Sciences', in Popper, *Conjectures and Refutations: The Growth of Scientific Knowledge*, 4th edn 1972 (London: Routledge & Kegan Paul, 1963) pp. 336–46. See also Karl R. Popper, *The Poverty of Historicism* (London: Routledge & Kegan Paul, 1957, paperback edn 1961).

24. A. W. Coats, 'Economics and Psychology: the Death and Resurrection of a Research Programme' and T. W. Hutchison, 'On the History and Philosophy of Science and Economics', in Spiro J. Latsis (ed.), *Method and Appraisal in Economics* (Cambridge University Press, 1976). Hutchison's contribution is reprinted in T. W. Hutchison, *Knowledge and Ignorance in Economics* (Oxford: Blackwell, 1977). A. W. Coats, in introducing *The Classical Economists and Economic Policy* (London: Methuen, 1971) pp. 1–32 has many relevant things to say about the claims made by, and on behalf of, the classical economists for the robustness and practical relevance of their theories (and the way in which 'research in economic thought and policy has hitherto been seriously inhibited by the professional jealousies of scholarly specialists', p. 22).

25. Ilya Prigogine and Isabelle Stengers, *The New Alliance: Part One – From Dynamics to Thermodynamics: Physics, the Gradual Opening towards the World of Natural Processes* (Scientia, vol. 112 5th–8th, 1977) pp. 319–32; *The New Alliance: Part Two – An Extended Dynamics towards a Human Science of Nature* (Scientia, vol. 112 9th–12th, 1977) pp. 643–53. See also Ilya Prigogine, *From Being to Becoming: Time and Complexity in the Physical Sciences* (San Francisco: W. H. Freeman, 1980). An important related work is Richard L. Gregory, *Mind in Science: a History of Explanations in Psychology and Physics* (London: Weidenfeld and Nicolson, 1981).

26. All the quotations in this paragraph are from J. M. Keynes, 'The General Theory of Employment', *The Quarterly Journal of Economics* (February

1937). This article is reprinted in Donald Moggridge (ed.), *The General Theory and After: Part II, Defence and Development*, The Collected Writings of John Maynard Keynes, vol. xiv (London: Macmillan for The Royal Economic Society, 1973) pp. 109–23. Keynes's *Treatise on Probability*, referred to in the following paragraph, is most conveniently found as vol. viii of *The Collected Writings*, 1973 (but first published 1921).

27. John Jewkes, The Economist and Public Policy', *Lloyds Bank Review* (April 1953). Reprinted in Jewkes, *A Return to Free Market Economics? Critical Essays on Government Intervention* (London: Macmillan, 1978) pp. 12–25.

28. John Jewkes, 'The Economist and Economic Change' in var. *Economics and Public Policy: Brookings Lectures, 1954* (Washington D.C.: The Brookings Institution, 1955) pp. 81–99. Reprinted in *A Return to Free Market Economics?* pp. 26–38. Jewkes here answers the question 'why predictions continue on such a wide scale':

> The simple answer is that there is a market, a demand, for them. Nearly every one of us has to take action that is coloured by our guesses about the future. Certainly every business and every government is in that difficult position, and it is not surprising that they should be prepared to clutch at straws. It is melancholy that men and communities should be exposed to the anxieties and dangers of the unknowable future. But that is one of the facts of life. It is my thesis that, in the last resort, the burdens that fall upon the men of action cannot, in fact, be lifted off their shoulders by economists who hold themselves out as capable of providing a service that they cannot, in fact, perform' (p. 87).

29. Milton Friedman, 'The Methodology of Positive Economics' in Friedman, *Essays in Positive Economics* (Chicago, 1953; Phoenix Edition, 1966) p. 7.
30. Katouzian, *Ideology and Method in Economics*, pp. 45–84.
31. J. Wiseman, 'Costs and Decisions', Paper presented at the Conference of the Association of University Teachers of Economics, 1978 (University of York: Institute of Social and Economic Research, Reprint Series: Economics, No. 289). Reprinted in David A. Currie and W. Peters (eds), *Contemporary Economic Analysis*, vol. 2 (London: Croom Helm, 1980) p. 473.
32. C. F. Carter, G. P. Meredith, G. L. S. Shackle (eds), *Uncertainty and Business Decisions*, 2nd edn (Liverpool University Press, 1962).
33. C. F. Carter and J. L. Ford, *Uncertainty and Expectations in Economics: Essays in Honour of G. L. S. Shackle* (Oxford: Basil Blackwell, 1972).
34. Carter, Meredith and Shackle (eds), *Uncertainty and Business Decisions*, p. 152.
35. G. L. S. Shackle (ed.), *On the Nature of Business Success* (Liverpool University Press, 1968).
36. Ibid., p. 181.
37. Bertrand Russell, *History of Western Philosophy, and its Connection with Political and Social Circumstances from the Earliest Times to the Present Day* (London: Allen and Unwin, 1946) p. 11.
38. See Robin M. Hogarth, *Judgement and Choice: The Psychology of Decision* (Chichester: Wiley, 1980) chap. 9 for an excellent check-list on

biases in information processing, pp. 166–70. The same topic is covered in Robin M. Hogarth and Spyros Makridakis, 'Forecasting and Planning: An Evaluation', Management Science 27, 2 (February 1981) 115–38. The reader is warned, however, that Hogarth's book does not always follow the author's stress on the need to accept uncertainty. A good, very readable little book in the same field is James L. Adams, *Conceptual Blockbusting: A Guide To Better Ideas*, 2nd edn (New York. W. W. Norton, 1980). Previously published in 1974 in the Portable Stanford series.
39. George Katona, *Psychological Economics* (Amsterdam: Elsevier, 1975).
40. For example: P. Wack, 'The Future of Jobs', *de ingenieur, Koninklijk Instituut van Ingenieurs*, Den Haag, 91, 5 (1 February 1979); André Bénard, 'World Oil and Cold Reality', *Harvard Business Review* 58, 6 (November/December 1980) 91–101; Peter Beck, 'Strategic Planning in the Royal Dutch/Shell Group', a paper presented on 1 March 1977 to a Conference on Corporate Strategic Planning, New Orleans (London: Shell Centre, 1977); Peter Beck, now Planning Director, Shell UK Limited, has recently written, 'Scenario Development and Corporate Planning for an Uncertain Future' (Shell UK Ltd, April 1981); Joop L. de Vries (of Shell) with D. N. Michael, A. Mitchell, W. S. Royce, P. Schwartz, 'Values and Strategic Planning', *VALS Report*, No. 15, Stanford Research International (October 1980) draws *inter alia* on Shell's societal scenario work, especially pp. 50–3; Michael Jefferson, 'A Post-Industrial Future? Some Cautionary Comments', Proceedings of Section X, British Association Annual Meeting, Bath (1978); Michael Jefferson, 'Historical Perspectives of Societal Change and the Use of Scenarios in Shell', in Brian Twiss (ed.), *Social Forecasting for Company Planning* (London: Macmillan, 1982) pp. 188–209; Christopher Lorenz, 'Shell Strikes a Refined Way of Exploring the Future', *Financial Times*, p. 19 (4 March 1980); Christopher Lorenz, 'How Shell Made its Managers Think the Unthinkable', *Financial Times*, p. 13 (5th March, 1980).
41. Erich Jantsch, *Technological Forecasting in Perspective* (Paris: OECD, 1967). Especially pp. 180–1.
42. Erich Jantsch, *Technological Planning and Social Futures* (New York: Wiley 1972) pp. 86–7.
43. Herman Kahn and Anthony J. Wiener, *The Year 2000. A Framework for Speculation on the Next Thirty-Three Years* (New York: Macmillan, 1967). Especially pp. 262–4 on the use of scenarios. Herman Kahn and B. Bruce-Briggs, *Things To Come: Thinking About The Seventies and Eighties* (New York: Macmillan, 1972). Especially the definition of scenarios on pp. 176–7. More recent studies are Herman Kahn, William Brown and Leon Martel, *The Next 200 Years: A Scenario for America and the World* (New York: William Morrow, 1976); and Herman Kahn, Irving Leveson, Garrett Scalera, Jimmy Wheeler, *World Economic Development: Projections from 1978 to the year 2000* (Boulder, Colorado: Westview Press, 1978). The latter work discusses scenario techniques on pp. 65–6. It should be pointed out, however, that the Hudson Institute's work should be approached with some circumspection, and on energy matters their insights have been of very limited value.
44. Solomon Encel, P. K. Marstrand, W. Page (eds), *The Art of Anticipation:*

Values and Methods in Forecasting (London: Martin Robertson, 1975) p. 87. But the authors subsequently conclude: 'to the extent that scenarios do open up new horizons to decision-makers and provide a broader framework in which to make decisions, they are a good thing'. Ibid., p. 89.

45. Ian Miles, 'Worldviews and Scenarios', in Christopher Freeman and Marie Jahoda (eds), *World Futures: The Great Debate* (London: Martin Robertson, 1978) p. 277.

46. Ibid., p. 278.

47. At a time, shortly after the 1973 oil crisis, when American academics and other experts loudly forecast the imminent demise of the OPEC cartel, because cartels always had collapsed quickly, an internal paper entitled 'How Quickly Do Cartels Collapse?' was circulated in Shell. It drew on over thirty major studies in industrial history and applied economics (it could, of course, have drawn on many more) to demonstrate that the historical evidence pointed in a different, and generally less satisfactory, direction. Among the long-lasting cartels referred to were: the Newcastle Vend; the London Coal Ring; early agreements between English and between Welsh ironmasters; the Siegerland ironmasters' cartel; the Neckar Salt Union; the Oberlahnstein Association for the sale of Neckar pig-iron; the German bismuth, tinplate and potash cartels; the Rhenish-Westphalian Coal Syndicate; the international steel rail cartel; the international Borax Syndicate, Quinine Syndicate, Acetic Acid Syndicate, Carbide Syndicate, and various similar syndicates in the explosives industry; shipping cartels; the Incandescent Lamp Cartel; the Soap Makers' Association; the Cable Makers' Association; and IATA.

48. T. S. Eliot, 'Four Quartets', in *The Complete Poems and Plays of T. S. Eliot* (London: Faber and Faber, 1969) pp. 171, 179, 181, 182 and 197.

AUTHOR'S NOTE

It should be clearly understood that the views and opinions expressed in the foregoing are entirely my own and are not in any way to be construed as committing Shell International Petroleum Company Limited or any associate member of the Royal Dutch/Shell Group of Companies to endorsement (or rejection) of any of the views which I have put forward or contested. In other words, it is not to be inferred that I am, in any sense, speaking on Shell's behalf, or that I am representing Shell views and practices in respect of the concept of 'uncertainty'.

9 Towards Double Negative Economics

JOHN D. HEY

Present-day positive economic theory essentially views the world as being a relatively simple place, certainly in relation to the decision-making capabilities of the human beings who populate that world: however complex the decision problem facing the individual, he or she always takes the best decision with respect to that problem.

While this may be a convenient way of viewing the world when we are wearing our 'economic theorist' hats (or when we are looking through our special rose-tinted 'economic theorist' spectacles), it is not a view of the world we would recognise as mere actors in it. As we know all too well in our real-life selves, the real world is not simple and we human beings are not infallible. While there may be some problems sufficiently simple for us to take the best decisions, many more problems – particularly those which have significant repercussions elsewhere in the economy or in our future lives – are sufficiently complex for human fallibility to play a crucial role.

Positive economics assumes that the world is sufficiently simple for humans to behave infallibly. In contrast, Double Negative economics assumes that the world is *not* simple, and that humans are *not* infallible. While positive economics has reached a highly sophisticated level of development, double negative economics is merely in its infancy. It is the purpose of this paper to describe the birth pains of the new infant, and to speculate on its early life. I trust that it will not experience infant mortality, but whether it will become a David to the Goliath of positive economics, I hesitate to say.

In marshalling my thoughts on the appropriate modelling of decision-making, I find it useful to imagine a *spectrum of complexity* of decision-problems. In my mind I picture this spectrum as ranging from extremely simple, essentially trivial problems on the left, through moderately complex problems in the middle, to extremely complex, essentially insoluble problems on the right. (I should hasten to add that there is no political significance intended by this representation!) Such a portrayal would command widespread intuitive agreement, though it might be difficult to capture in a single variable the degree of complexity of a decision-problem; indeed, how one might actually measure the complexity of a particular problem is a far from trivial task. Fortunately, such issues are not central to the theme of this paper.

While the precise measurement of the complexity of a particular problem may be open to debate, there should be general agreement about the factors which make some problems more complex than others: for example, a greater number of variables involved; a larger number of time periods to take into account; a greater number of possibilities to consider; more calculations to be made; more difficult calculations to be made; more time to be spent thinking about the problem; and so on. Of course, if the actual process of decision-making takes no time and imposes no costs on the decision-maker (however well he carries out the relevant calculations), then all problems become essentially trivial — and are thus located at the extreme left-hand end of my spectrum. This is the view taken by positive economics — which regards all problems as being located at that extreme. At this extreme all problems can be solved optimally.

At the opposite extreme, problems are so horrendously complex that there is absolutely no way of deciding whether one decision is any better than any other. At this extreme, the only thing to do is to choose a decision at random. (Before purists leap in, let me remark that I am fully aware of the difficulties involved with defining, let alone specifying, a problem sufficiently complex for it to be located at this extreme., My spectrum should not be taken too literally.)

Most problems lie somewhere between the two extremes. In contrast, our theories relate to the two extremes themselves. Clearly some kind of reconciliation is necessary. Given that we have some theory relevant to the two extremes, two ways of approaching the middle (rather than just jumping into it 'cold', which may be rather difficult) are from the two extremes. In the next two sections, I discuss these two possibilities, beginning with the approach from the more familiar left-hand end. In the final section, I discuss the big unknown: will the missionary parties from the two extremes make contact in the middle?

IN THE BEGINNING, THERE WAS OPTIMALITY . . .

Before beginning our adventure into the relative unknown, it should prove useful to describe the key features of our starting-point. This starting-point is the familiar construct of positive economics, the ultra-rational economic man, as embodied (or, perhaps, disembodied) in subjective expected utility theory – henceforth SEU theory. This theory envisages an individual facing a decision-problem in which he or she has to choose one choice from a set of choices $\{C_j; j = 1, \dots, J\}$, this set being certain and known. There is possibly some lack of certainty inherent in the problem in that, at the time the choice is made, the individual does not know definitely which 'state of the world' will prevail. However, the theory assumes that the individual can specify the set $\{S_i; i = 1, \dots, I\}$ of all possible states of the world; again this set is certain and known, though which of the S_i will eventually occur is not necessarily known. Moreover, for each (choice, state of the world) pair, the individual can specify the precise consequences as far as he or she is concerned. I denote by A_{ij} the consequence if C_j is chosen and S_i occurs. Note again that the *set* $\{A_{ij}; i = 1, \dots, I; j = 1, \dots, J\}$ is certain and known.

Subjective expected utility (SEU) theory starts from the familiar and innocent-sounding assumption that the individual has a preference-ordering over the set of all possible C_j, and that this preference-ordering has the usual properties (that is, it is complete, transitive, reflexive and antisymmetric). The most important of these properties are the completeness (which means that for any pair of possible choices the individual either prefers one to the other or is indifferent between them) and the transitivity. To modern economists, transitivity plays a crucial role in that it captures what is generally understood by *economic* behaviour. (In contrast, intransitivity implies uneconomic behaviour, in that the individual can be continually, but willingly, milked of money by a cynical exploiter of his cyclical preference structure.)

Given this starting-point, it follows that there exists a function $U(.)$, with choice as the argument, which encapsulates the individual's preference. Thus, $U(C_1) \geqslant U(C_2)$ if and only if C_1 is at least as preferred as C_2. The next stage of the SEU theory is to show that, if certain axioms hold, then there 'exists' a set $\{p_i; i = 1, \dots, I\}$, and a function $u(.)$, with the final consequences (the A_{ij}) as the argument, such that the following relationship holds for all j:

$$U(C_j) = \Sigma_{i=1}^{I} p_i u(A_{ij}). \tag{1}$$

The p_i can be interpreted as the individual's subjective probabilities of the S_i, and the function $u(.)$ as the individual's utility function; thus equation (1) states that the utility of an uncertain choice is equal to the expected value of the utility of the possible final consequences. Hence the name of the theory.

As I have already mentioned, equation (1) (and thus the theory) relies for its validity on certain axioms. Some of these relate to the 'existence' of the p_i, and others to the 'existence' of the $u(.)$ function. Let me briefly comment on these, beginning with those in the second category. As is well known, the most contentious of these axioms is that referred to as the 'independence of irrelevant alternatives' axiom; this requires that, if the individual is indifferent between choices C_1 and C_2, then he should also be indifferent between choices $(C_1, C_3; p)$ and $(C_2, C_3; p)$ where C_3 is an arbitrary choice (and where $(C_i, C_j; p)$ denotes a risky choice which yields C_i with probability p and C_j with probability $1 - p$).

Viewed appropriately, this axiom seems self-evident and hardly contentious; indeed, one may be tempted to conclude that the violation of it must constitute irrational behaviour. Consider the following representation, where

represents a choice node and a chance node:

(I have deliberately omitted details of C_1 and C_2 so as to focus attention on the generality of the argument.) Suppose that the individual is indifferent between C_1 and C_2 (the argument still works, appropriately modified, if one or other is strictly preferred). Now tack on an irrelevant extra:

Presumably our individual, if he gets to box (*a*), will declare that he is indifferent between C_1 and C_2. Now suppose he has to commit himself to a choice, as to what he would do *if* he did get to box (*a*), before he knows whether he gets to box (*a*) or not. Presumably again he will say he would be indifferent between C_1 and C_2. Let me denote by C_1' (C_2') the choice of C_1 (C_2) conditional on getting to box (*a*). Then my argument suggests that, if the individual is indifferent between C_1 and C_2, then he will also be indifferent between C_1' and C_2'. Now note that the choice between C_1' and C_2' can be expressed in the following alternative fashion:

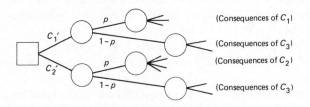

The axiom thus appears innocuous.

In essence, this axiom ensures that the utility of a specific final consequence is not affected by the context in which it appears. A 'parallel' axiom ensures that the 'probability' attached to a specific state of the world is not affected by the specific implications of a particular choice-problem. For example, consider the simple choice-problem below, in which the table entries are the *utilities* of the relevant consequences, and suppose that we determine for our individual the value of u (call it $u^*(a)$ to emphasise its dependence upon (*a*) at which the individual is indifferent between C_1 and C_2. (Presumably for $u <(>) u^*(a)$ the individual strictly prefers C_1 (C_2).)

	S_1	S_2
C_1	a	0
C_2	u	u

Then implicit in the individual's preference structure is the subjective probability of

$$u^*(a)/a$$

for the state of the world S_1. (The expected utility of C_1 is p_1a; the expected utility of C_2 is u; indifference implies equality — that is, $p_1a = u^*(a)$.) Clearly, consistency requires that

$$u^*(\lambda a) = \lambda u^*(a). \tag{2}$$

A similar argument to that used above with respect to the 'independence of irrelevant alternatives' axiom suggests that 'rational' behaviour requires that (2) does in fact hold. Thus the axioms underlying (1), and hence SEU theory, appear to be the embodiment of 'rational' behaviour.

Unfortunately, there is a large body of empirical evidence (admittedly mostly based on 'laboratory-type' experiments) which suggests that individuals do not actually behave in accordance with SEU theory — even in relatively simple decision-problems, and even with the added 'simplification' that the subjects are told the relevant probabilities. (Useful references include Allais and Hagen (1979), Kahneman and Tversky (1979) and Schoemaker (1980).) While one may dismiss some of this evidence on the grounds that it is based on 'laboratory-type' experiments, and while one may wish to use this evidence to argue for more statistical education in schools, one can hardly deny the implication that there exists a large number of people who do not behave in accordance with SEU theory, particularly if the choice problem is at all complex.

What can/should the theorist do about such people? Starting from the position of ultra-rationality as embodied in SEU theory, the theorist can gradually relax the assumptions underlying the model. This can be done in stages. To begin with, we can maintain the assumption that the individual has a preference-ordering over the $\{C_j\}$ with the usual properties; this would, as I have already argued, appear to constitute a minimal requirement for 'rational' behaviour. If we maintain this, but dispense with some or all of the axioms underlying SEU theory, we continue to have a function $U(.)$ defined over the C_j which encapsulates preference, but it no longer takes the simple form given in (1).

Two familiar examples, which continue to enjoy some popularity, particularly in financial circles, are mean-variance analysis and the safety-first approach. In the former, the function $U(.)$ is given by:

$$U(C_j) = v(\mu, \sigma^2), \tag{3}$$

where μ and σ^2 are the mean and variance of the univariate consequence set. In the (pure) form of the latter, the function $U(.)$ is given by

$$U(C_j) = \text{Prob}\{X \geqslant 0\}, \tag{4}$$

where X is the single consequence variable. There are also a number of extensions to this pure form. However, both of these $U(.)$ functions suffer from a number of problems as contenders for sensible representations of preferences. As these problems are well known (see, for example, Hey (1981a)), I will not discuss them further here.

In general, (3) and (4) are inconsistent with SEU theory, though at the same time they can be regarded as less general (more specific) than SEU theory. A very recent alternative, which is a generalisation of SEU theory, at least in the utility domain, is 'expected utility analysis without the independence axiom' as developed and presented by Machina (1981). Since Machina's theory contains SEU theory as a special case, it follows that it requires less stringent assumptions for its validity. In fact, Machina's analysis starts simply from the assumption that there exists a function $U(.)$, defined over all possible C_j, which encapsulates preference, and is 'smooth' in a technical sense.

As I have already noted, Machina's work is a generalisation of SEU in the *utility* domain; indeed, to simplify his analysis he assumes that the (subjective) probabilities, the p_i, are already known. The remaining interest lies in the function $u(.)$. Machina shows that, under his (less restrictive) assumptions, there exists a utility function with the final consequences *and the probability distribution* as arguments, such that the preference ordering over the C_j is given by the function $U(.)$ defined by:

$$U(C_j) = \Sigma_{i=1}^{I} p_i u(A_{ij}; \mathbf{p}). \tag{5}$$

Here $\mathbf{p}$ denotes the vector $(p_1, \dots, p_I)$, and I hasten to add that this is *my* interpretation of Machina's paper (which is all framed in terms of distribution functions); he is not to be blamed for my sloppy mathematics.

In comparing (5) with (1), it is clear that Machina's generalisation consists of replacing the utility function $u(.)$ by a set of *local* utility functions $u(.; \mathbf{p})$. As such, it is a formal representation of intuitive ideas expressed earlier by Bernard (1974), by various writers in Allais and Hagen (1979), and by others. Interestingly, Machina demonstrates that much (though not all) of the 'laboratory-type' evidence mentioned earlier can be explained by this more general formulation. However, his explanation is not vacuous, since it employs two restrictions on the form of the function u (for details, see Machina (1981)).

In Machina's analysis, the p_i are given. If the p_i are not given, then the obvious way forward is to follow the technique used in SEU theory (to determine the p_i), but to relax the assumptions in much the same way as Machina relaxes the assumptions in the utility domain. This would appear to lead to an encapsulation of the preference ordering over the C_j by the function $U(.)$ as given by:

$$U(C_j) = \Sigma \, {}^I_{i=1} p_i(\mathbf{A}) u(A_{ij}; \mathbf{p}), \tag{6}$$

where $\mathbf{A}$ denotes the matrix of the A_{ij}. I must emphasise the words 'would appear' in the above sentence, as I have not formally proved this assertion. In (6), which appears to be the 'natural' further generalisation of Machina, and hence of SEU theory, the $p_i(\mathbf{A})$ is a *local* probability – the appropriate counterpart of the local utility function $u(.; \mathbf{p})$.

Although Machina's generalisation of SEU theory (and my proposed further generalisation) appear to explain a large part of observed 'laboratory-type' evidence, there still remains some evidence left unexplained. (In addition, it should be remembered that most of these laboratory experiments were very simple, and therefore located towards the left-hand end of my complexity spectrum. There is still much of the spectrum left unexplored.) Much of this remaining evidence concerns *instransitive* behaviour – that is, behaviour excluded by Machina's assumptions.

Economists have long been averse to the idea of intransitive behaviour: in an obvious sense, as I have already noted, it is synonymous with uneconomic behaviour. Indeed, some economists would argue that if intransitivities are present, prediction becomes impossible. This would appear to me to be going too far; true, more information is needed before predictions can be made, but they can still be made nonetheless. (The nature of the prediction may well change too – from deterministic to stochastic – but that should please the econometrician.)

The very recent past has seen two important new developments in this direction. Both of them arose out of the 'laboratory type' experiments mentioned above. The earlier, and now quite familiar, development is that called *prospect theory* by its originators Kahneman and Tversky (1979). The distinguishing feature of prospect theory is the notion that decision-making consists of two separate phases: an *editing* phase and an *evaluation* phase, carried out in that order. The evaluation phase proceeds along relatively familiar lines, with the edited prospects being evaluated by a function of the form

$$U(C_j) = \Sigma_{i=1}^{I} w(p_i)v(A'_{ij}). \tag{7}$$

In this, $w(.)$ is a weighting function applied to the probabilities, while $v(.)$ is a utility function applied to the *edited* prospects (denoted by A'_{ij}).

Possible intransitivities arise during the editing phase; crucial to this process is the way that the choices are presented to the individuals. According to Kahneman and Tversky, an important role is played by the individual's *reference point* (relative to which gains and losses are assessed); this may well vary depending upon the way prospects are presented. To my mind, this idea of a two-stage decision-process is attractive; I have long felt that, when faced with a complex problem, individuals tend to simplify the problem and then attempt to behave optimally with respect to the simplified version. The simplification part corresponds to Prospect Theory's editing phase, while the optimisation part corresponds to the evaluation phase. In practice, there may well be a third, and final, phase: the adjustment of the apparently optimal decision in the light of the relationship between the actual problem and the simplified abstraction.

An alternative 'intransitive' theory, but one which contains just one (an evaluation) phase, is that very recently proposed by Sugden and Loomes (1982). At the heart of their theory is the notion of *pairwise* choice (which is the source of possible intransitivities). Two elements are involved: a certainty utility function, and a 'regret/rejoicing' function. They are used as follows. In a choice-problem between C_1 and C_2, preference is determined by the larger of $U(C_1)$ and $U(C_2)$ as given by:

$$U(C_1) = \Sigma_{i=1}^{I} p_i[u(A_{i1}) + r(A_{i1}, A_{i2})]$$

and $\tag{8}$

$$U(C_2) = \Sigma_{i=1}^{I} p_i[u(A_{i2}) + r(A_{i2}, A_{i1})].$$

In this, $u(.)$ is the certainty utility function (defined over the final consequences), while $r(.,.)$ is the 'regret/rejoicing' function defined over the actual final consequence (given the actual choice) and the foregone final consequence (what would have been the final consequence if the other choice had been made). Presumably, $r(A, B) \gtreqless 0$ according as $A \gtreqless B$.

As Sugden and Loomes show, the precise implications of their theory depend upon the particular functional form for the 'regret/ rejoicing' function $r(., .)$. However, they do show that under some quite plausible assumptions about this functional form, much (though not all) of the 'laboratory-type' evidence mentioned earlier can be 'explained' by their theory. Combined with the fact that the basic formulation (8) is intuitively attractive, this approach has much to commend it. The main problem, however, as Sugden and Loomes themselves emphasise, is that it deals only with *pairwise* choices. Some suggestions for possible extensions to n-wise choices are made by the authors, but their thinking is clearly at a tentative stage. Whether this is likely to constitute a serious difficulty is not yet clear. (One can anticipate that the same kinds of criticisms will be levelled at the Sugden and Loomes approach as were levelled at Savage's Minimax Regret criterion; but then this new approach is more general, and more intuitively satisfactory, than Savage's approach.)

It should be noted also that Sugden and Loomes take probability as given, and thus operate under the same rules as do Machina and Kahneman and Tversky. While Machina's approach appears to have a 'natural' generalisation to the unknown-probabilities case (as discussed above), this does not appear to be so with the Sugden and Loomes approach.

A further paper with the same general implications as Sugden and Loomes is a recent one by Fishburn (1981). In this, preference is represented by a bivariate function $U(., .)$, with $C_1 \geqslant C_2$ if and only if $U(C_1, C_2) \geqslant 0$. Intransitivities can arise.

While the Machina generalisation, the Sugden and Loomes approach, the Fishburn approach and Prospect Theory all offer different explanations of choice under risk, they are all concerned with essentially the same kind of choice-problem. It would be interesting to carry out some more detailed tests to try to discover which of the four approaches appears to be the best. Possibly the independently-generated data of Schoemaker (1980) might be useful in this respect. Schoemaker's conclusions might also help to point the way to a more general theory.

At the time of writing, the various approaches discussed above were the best-developed departures from SEU theory. However, they are clearly not the end of the story. A number of other further generalisations of, and possible greater departures from, SEU theory appear potentially hopeful.

One interesting avenue is one partially travelled above — namely the route to a deliberately intransitive theory. As I have already noted, intransitivities may arise in both Prospect Theory and in the Sugden and Loomes approach — in the former because of the editing phase, in the latter because of the pairwise nature of choice. In conventional theory, intransitivities are ruled out — because of the distaste most economists feel about such apparent manifestations of irrational behaviour. But perhaps this distaste simply arises because of the nature of the mathematical tools that economists habitually use. For example, consider some features of a preference structure as typically encapsulated using set theory. An economist may define three sets with reference to a given commodity bundle b, say: $P_b \equiv \{x: x \succ b\}$, $I_b \equiv \{x: x \sim b\}$, and $N_b \equiv \{x: b \succ x\}$, where x denotes a generic bundle, $\succ$ denotes strict preference and $\sim$ denotes indifference. Given any bundle y, then y belongs to one and only one of P_b, I_b and N_b. It cannot belong to two simultaneously; moreover for each of the three sets, P_b, I_b and N_b, y is either a member of it or not.

This all-or-nothing feature of set membership is a feature of conventional set theory — the theory habitually used by economists. But this is not inevitable: instead, we could use the theory of *fuzzy subsets*. In this theory, membership is not an all-or-nothing matter; instead, some element y could be .9 a member of some set, or .4 a member, and so on. The use of the theory of fuzzy subsets would appear to open up a whole new way of encapsulating preferences. For example, it would appear to be possible to encapsulate the following very real set of preferences: consider a set $\{C_j; j = 1, \ldots, J\}$ and suppose that C_j and C_{j+1} are so 'close together' that the individual cannot distinguish between them, and so is indifferent between them. If this is true for all j ($= 1, \ldots$, $J - 1$) conventional logic would require the individual to be indifferent between C_1 and C_J. But C_1 and C_J may be sufficiently 'far apart' for the individual to say that he definitely prefers one of them. The theory of fuzzy subsets should be able to deal with this quite reasonable set of preferences, whereas conventional set theory cannot. (For further details, see Gupta, Ragade and Yager (1979), which also contains some theories of decision-making based on fuzzy subsets.)

In thinking about transitive and intransitive behaviour, it is instructive to reappraise the arguments underlying the alleged rationality of the former and irrationality of the latter. On reflection, it is clear that these arguments ignore the problems of computational complexity and computational cost. If the actual process of decision-making imposes a cost on the decision-maker, then it is no longer clear that intransitivity is irrational. (Suppose, for example, that you are faced with pairwise choices between C_1 and C_2, C_2 and C_3, and C_3 and C_1. Suppose further that you know that the magnitude of the difference between the payoff to you of C_i and C_j (for any i and j) is at most £5, but to determine the *actual* magnitude of the payoff of C_i (for any i) would cost you £20, in computational cost. Then it is perfectly sensible for you to determine your pairwise choices by tossing a coin. The outcome could then very well be intransitive.)

Indeed, if the actual process of taking a decision imposes a cost on the decision-maker, then it is by no means clear that there is such a thing as an optimal decision. (To decide is costly; therefore one needs to decide whether to decide; but to decide whether to decide is costly; therefore one needs to decide whether to decide whether to decide; and so on . . . for ever.) This seriously undermines any approach from the left-hand end of my spectrum.

I now briefly return to some more specific issues before concluding this section. My general framework involved a set of choices $\{C_j\}$, a set of states of the world $\{S_i\}$, and a set of consequences $\{A_{ij}\}$. I have spent some time discussing the first of these three sets; let me now mention the other two sets. First, the set $\{S_i\}$. A common objection to the assumption that this set is certain and known is the notion that there may be some residual, totally unknown category – which, definitionally, is indescribable. I suppose logic requires one to admit this possibility, but I am not sure what one should do about it. My gut feeling is that one should ignore it – as presumably this is what individuals do themselves when taking decisions. If one cannot even conceive of some possible states of the world, how can one take them into account in one's decision-making? I suppose one could say that some decisions involved a greater residual unknown than other decisions, but here again, unless one invoked some kind of lexicographical procedure, it is not clear how one should proceed.

Unease about the assumption that the set $\{S_i\}$ is certain and known could be translated into unease about the assumption that the set $\{A_{ij}\}$ is certain and known. Certainly my own unease is particularly strong with respect to this latter assumption. I fully appreciate the formal arguments which bolster this assumption, either through the requirement that the $\{C_j\}$ be fully specified *strategies*, or through the requirement that, if the choice problem under consideration is merely the first stage of a sequence of choices, then the $\{A_{ij}\}$ are the consequences assuming that the remainder of the sequence is solved in an optimal fashion. This latter is rather a clumsy way of saying that the method of *backward induction* should be employed in the optimal solution of a sequential choice-problem. If one is faced with a choice-problem involving n stages, one first solves the final stage, then one solves the $(n - 1)$th stage conditional on carrying out the final stage optimally, then one solves the $(n - 2)$th stage conditional on carrying out the final two stages optimally, and so on. The logic is elegant, and has paved the way to many insights.

Unfortunately, the method of backward induction, because of its logical elegance, has become a real barrier to progress. It has caused our thinking to run in a preordained channel, and one has genuinely to 'struggle to escape' from its siren call. In practice, it is often simply impossible, because of computational complexity and overpowering uncertainty, to apply the method of backward induction. In demonstrating this heretical assertion, I find the following analogy helpful. Imagine yourself dropped in the middle of open country in a totally unknown area. Imagine that you have been told to get to a specified objective which is, say, 10 miles due north of your initial position. Imagine, finally, that it is foggy. How would you set about your task? *Would you employ the method of backward induction?*

Of course not – even though 'logic' and 'optimality' insist that you do. No, instead, you would use some kind of *forward* (rather than backward) procedure. This would necessarily imply that you might make mistakes (something which is impossible using backward induction); moreover, you would be unable to specify, in advance of making a particular move, the precise consequences of that move.

To my mind, this argument points the way forward: we must dispense with backward induction and replace it with some kind of forward procedure. My ideas on how this might be done are still in a rather primitive state, but some preliminary discussion can be found in Hey (1979 and 1981a); one possible avenue mentioned in that discussion is that opened up by the flexibility/robustness approach.

IN THE BEGINNING, THERE WAS RANDOMNESS . . .

In the section above, I discussed how we might reach the middle of the complexity spectrum by starting our journey from the extreme left-hand end: that is, by starting with familiar optimality theories. As I hope I have demonstrated, it does appear possible to venture out quite far into the jungle in this fashion. After a point, however, it becomes virtually impossible to retain any vestiges of optimality, and the link with the left-hand end becomes broken. The obvious thing to ask now is whether we can pick up the links by approaching from the opposite direction. This is the concern of this section.

At the extreme right-hand end, problems are so complex that the only thing to do is to pick a decision at random. Thus, we begin with randomness. Actually this is not as bad as it appears: if there are constraints in the problem (which there almost always will be in any meaningful economic problem) then the constraints will impose a pattern on the outcome of the random decision-making process. This has been demonstrated by Becker (1962).

However, it is clear that, towards this right-hand end of the spectrum, there is the serious danger that theorising may simply degenerate to saying that 'people do what they do because they do it'. If this happens, then one has recourse only to empirical evidence, and economics degenerates to empiricism. This would be undesirable. However, there is a way forward.

At the left-hand end of the spectrum, the use of optimal strategies implies that there will usually be a uniquely best decision rule to use in any given circumstance. At the right-hand end of the spectrum, there can be no such unique best rule; instead, there is a whole set of possible 'rules of thumb' that individuals may employ. Nevertheless, even though individuals cannot pick the uniquely best rule from this set, *they can often discard rules that are manifestly inferior*. Having done this, they are left with a set of 'reasonable' rules of thumb. While this may be quite a' large set, it is smaller than the set of all possible rules; thus prediction is possible. That is, even if we assume only that individuals behave *reasonably* rather than *optimally*, predictions can still be made. True, such predictions might be less strong, but, on the other hand, they may be more general.

In Hey (1981b) I investigated this 'reasonable' approach in the context of search theory. There I showed that some very simple criteria for reasonableness were sufficient to generate all the major conclusions of (optimal) search theory. This would appear to demonstrate the potential of this approach.

Of course, one is also interested in the actual 'rules of thumb' that individuals use. The determination of the actual rules should point the way forward to further theorising about actual decision-processes. In Hey (1982), a follow-up paper to that mentioned in the paragraph above, I found that a set of five simple rules was sufficient to 'explain' almost all the observed behaviour in a simple 'laboratory-type' investigation. Interestingly, these rules – some of which I had not even considered as serious candidates before I began my investigation — turned out to be remarkably good. Obviously, they did not perform as well as the fully optimal rule, but they did do reasonably well, and, more importantly perhaps, were reasonably robust.

A development along similar lines is that pioneered by Radner and Rothschild (1975). The basic idea of this development is that decision-makers do not have the time or the resources to optimise; rather, they live their lives going from crisis to crisis — 'putting out fires' as Radner and Rothschild graphically put it. Thus, at any one time, the individual devotes his attention single-mindedly to the problem that is most pressing at that time. This procedure obviously comes into the category of 'reasonable rules of thumb'. One almost inevitable implication of these types of models is that the predictions are stochastic. This is in stark contrast to optimality theory in which (conditional) predictions are deterministic; but this would appear to constitute a strength of the former and a weakness of the latter.

A more systematic treatment of the idea that decision-makers have limited information-processing capabilities can be found in the various psychological theories of information processing. Of particular interest to economists is the development of *production systems*. The use of the production-systems approach facilitates a formal characterisation of decision-making as a set of possibly conflicting rules of thumb, with conflicts resolved by a higher-level interpreter. A useful discussion of the role of production systems in economics can be found in Rae and Reynolds (1981). More generally, it would appear that economists have much to learn from psychologists about the processes of decision-making, though the economists' interest is probably less 'fine-grained' than that of psychologists.

LINKING UP . . .

Starting from either end one can venture quite far into the middle. The problem, of course, is whether the two approaches will link up. If one is thinking in terms of a spectrum of complexity, then one would ideally like a smooth gradation from reasonable rules of thumb, through to the optimal rule, as the complexity of the problem reduced from infinity to zero. If one picks rules out of thin air, there is no guarantee that this will happen. Indeed, there is no guarantee that the rules actually employed by individuals will display this desirable pattern.

What we clearly need is some higher-level theory, which shows how rules are modified in the light of experience. Of necessity, this learning process would have to be non-Bayesian; but equally it could not be one of those rather depressing psychological theories of learning which imply that people never behave optimally however much experience they have. What this new learning theory will look like, I do not know; but there are rich rewards to be gained from it.

REFERENCES

Allais, M., and Hagen, O. (eds) (1979) *Expected Utility Hypothesis and the Allais Paradox* (Dordrecht: Reidel).

Becker, G. S. (1962) 'Irrational Behaviour and Economic Theory', *Journal of Political Economy* 70, 1–13.

Bernard, G. (1974) 'On Utility Functions', *Theory and Decision* 5, 205–42.

Fishburn, P. C. (1981) 'Nontransitive Measurable Utility', discussion paper.

Gupta, M. M., Ragade, R. K., and Yager, R. R. (1979) *Advances in Fuzzy Set Theory and Applications* (Amsterdam: North-Holland).

Hey, J. D. (1979) *Uncertainty in Microeconomics* (Oxford: Martin Robertson).

Hey, J. D. (1981a) *Economics in Disequilibrium* (Oxford: Martin Robertson).

Hey, J. D. (1981b), 'Are Optimal Search Rules Reasonable? And Vice Versa? (And Does it Matter Anyway?)', *Journal of Economic Behavior and Organization* 2, 47–70.

Hey, J. D. (1982) 'Search for Rules for Search', *Journal of Economic Behavior and Organization*, forthcoming.

Kahneman, D., and Tversky, A. (1979) 'Prospect Theory: An Analysis of Decision under Risk', *Econometrica* 47, 263–91.

Machina, M. J. (1981) '"Expected Utility" Analysis without the Independence Axiom', *Econometrica* forthcoming.

Radner, R., and Rothschild, M. (1975) 'On the Allocation of Effort', *Journal of Economic Theory* 10, 358–76.

Rae, J. M., and Reynolds, M. L. (1981) 'Information Processing and Economic Decision Making', University of York, discussion paper.

Schoemaker, P. J. H. (1980) *Experiments on Decisions under Risk* (Boston: Martinus Nijhoff).

Sugden, R., and Loomes, G. (1982) 'Towards a New Theory of Rational Choice under Uncertainty', *Economic Journal*, forthcoming.

10 The Consumer in his/her Social Setting – a Subjectivist View

PETER EARL

INTRODUCTION

The aims of this paper are both critical and constructive, in keeping with the general theme of the conference. It will be argued that positive economics, as it is conventionally practised, is particularly weak in the area of consumer theory because its methodology prevents it from generating any practically applicable results. This will be followed by an attempt to show that it is possible to go 'beyond positive economics' with a subjectivist analysis of consumer behaviour which can actually be used by economists in industry when, for example, they are called upon to advise on appropriate strategies for launching new products in oligopolistic markets.

The subjectivist view presented in this paper has been synthesised by the author from the works of many academics in diverse disciplines, who seem to view the world through almost identical sets of blinkers but refer to each other hardly at all. These scholars include the following: Boulding (1956), Scitovsky (1981) and Shackle (1943, 1979) in economics; Kuhn (1970), Popper (1976, especially p. 48) and Adam Smith (see Skinner (1979) on Smith's study of the history of astronomy) in the philosophy of science; Garfinkel (1967), Schutz (1943) and Thompson (1979) in sociology and social anthropology; Steinbruner (1974) in political science; and Kelly (1963) and Bannister and Fransella (1971), leaders of the personal construct school of personality theorists, in psychology. Limitations of time and space prevent any discussion of how so many researchers have come to see human behaviour from an almost uniform perspective. Nor is there room for detailed explanations of whose ideas are being used at each point. Readers are asked to take the 'whole' on trust and are encouraged to investigate the prime sources − which make fascinating reading − for themselves.

The analysis we offer may seem somewhat shocking in an age when the liberal consensus in economics is so pervasive. Our suggestion is that if economists investigate the nature of human motivations rather more deeply than they have hitherto been willing to do, they will gain insights on how firms may manipulate consumer behaviour to suit their goals. We make no attempt to consider whether or not such manipulation is socially desirable, but do not expect to come under fire from positive economists for this omission, since their methodology prevents them from saying anything on normative welfare matters. However, the theory proposed is not only useful as an aid to firms, who may wish to manipulate consumer choices in a socially undesirable way. It can also be used by economists who advise on consumer protec-. tion legislation, even in situations where 'undesirable' sales practices have not actually been formulated with the aid of the theory itself.

POSITIVE ECONOMICS AND CONSUMER THEORY

Practitioners of positive economics, unlike subjectivists, are reluctant to cross the conventionally accepted boundaries of their subject. They make no attempt to borrow from psychologists or sociologists ideas that might form a detailed and solid foundation for their investigations of the behaviour of consumers and firms. This is hardly surprising. It would be a very time-consuming activity, and any emergent theories would be likely to be difficult to express in mathematical terms or test with econometric techniques. The choice of basic building-blocks would not be an easy one, either, for these unfamiliar disciplines are, just like economics, full of factional squabbles. Moreover, there would always be the danger that the components selected might later be shown to be flawed and thus, by implication, as 'unrealistic' as any of the assumptions actually used by positive economists.

To avoid such anxieties, and to hasten the construction of precise and hopefully testable models, positive economists prefer to assume that the world functions as if it is populated by isolated, omniscient individuals whose every action can be seen as conforming with 'utility maximis-ation', a short-hand term under whose heading one supposes must be subsumed all the more complex sources of motivation proposed in other disciplines. They see no need to complicate matters by attempting to give any substance to the notion of utility maximisation so long as they can get adequate predictions by using the assumption that people have convex preference-orderings. The standard positivist defence of the use of unrealistic assumptions is the suggestion that, in a world of partial knowledge, any theorising must involve simplifications if specific hypotheses are to be derived and what matters is whether or not realistic predictions can be generated. All too often it seems to be forgotten that past predictive success is no guarantee of good predictions in the future, and that, as a result, *a priori* plausibility might usefully be examined as a guide to a theory's likely range of convenience.

A positivist approach to consumer theory necessarily stands or falls according to its success in generating testable hypotheses about consumer choices. These hypotheses should either be of relevance to policy-makers or add to knowledge for its own sake, while academic prestige demands that they should not already be found on the list of 'common-sense truths which everyone knows'. Unfortunately, the simple axioms of orthodox consumer preference theory, which form part of the hard core of the positivist research programme, can be used to generate the 'Law of Demand', and little else.

The Law of Demand (which the person on the Clapham omnibus would regard as common sense) states that when the relative price of a commodity is reduced consumers will, other things equal, buy more of it – except when they do not. The other-things-equal clause turns out to be rather important. It is quite possible that behaviour at odds with the axioms of consistency and transitivity is a result of shifting consumer preferences and perceptions, which would make a nonsense of the notion of a demand-function of the usual sort. But positive economists will not ask consumers the sorts of questions that might reveal whether such preference shifts were actually taking place, even though this might enable them to map the direction of such changes and obtain better predictions. Their methodology restricts them to dealing only with independent observations. This rule for the avoidance of subjective bias inevitably renders inadmissable all questionnaire data, no matter how replete it might be with cross-checking responses.

The lack of specific results in modern consumer theory once drove E. J. Mishan (1961, p. 1) to suggest, cynically, that 'After all the display of technical virtuosity associated with such theorems, there is nothing that the practising economist can take away with him to help him come to grips with the real world. Indeed, he would be no worse off if he remained ignorant of all theories of consumers behaviour, accepting the obviously indispensable Law of Demand on trust.'

So-called positive economists who wish to conduct econometric investigations in this area rather seem to have taken this leaf out of Mishan's article. As Brown and Deaton (1972, pp. 1150–2) have observed, much empirical work on consumer choice does not attempt to *test* hypotheses about consumer behaviour at all. Rather, it is aimed simply at estimating demand relationships; i.e. it is not so much positive economics as measurement without theory. Most of this econometric work deals only with demand at the industry level in the context of fairly stable market structures. This is because positive economics, even in such a restricted form, must remain silent while a market is undergoing a structural shift, or if attempts to obtain new data to test hypotheses in advance of a policy decision would undermine an existing structure.

In the case of a new product no independent sample yet exists from which even a demand relationship might be estimated. Of course, existing, related products might offer similar characteristics in different proportions, and the economist might attempt to use this data to estimate a likely pattern of demand. However, the positive economist can only do this by presuming how consumers will perceive the new and old products, and the criteria they will use for evaluation. Once again, her methodology's insistence on using independent data precludes asking the kinds of questions that market researchers would use to find out. But there is no guarantee that the economist's own introspection with regard to opportunity-costs will bear any close correspondence to actual consumers' perceptions of competing products, a difficulty whose general ramifications are explored in detail in Buchanan and Thirlby (1973).

Once a new product has been launched, data about its market performance can be gathered. This time the problem is that shifts in sales are often due not to relative price changes so much as to the effects of the diffusion of information about the product between consumers (Bain, 1964; Ironmonger, 1972) and changes in income levels (Pasinetti, 1981). The process of structural change thus prevents the discovery of a demand curve, whether rooted in theory or even merely estimated.

In oligopolistic markets firms cannot experiment to discover price/quantity relationships without the prospect of inducing structural change. To lower a price may spark off an irreversible price war, while, in initially setting a price, they will usually feel constrained by the threat of entry from actual or potential producers of (near) duplicate products. It thus often seems wise to set, and keep to, a price that will deter entry, based on expected 'full costs' at a 'normal' level of capacity utilisation (in so far as it is believed that rivals have fairly similar production costs). As Andrews (1949, 1964) has observed, in such situations it is somewhat misguiding to think in terms of individual firm demand-functions.

The firm contemplating the launch of a new product in a price-constrained, oligopolistic market needs to have an idea of the quantity that could be sold, through time, at a price that will not attract entry, and to what extent this might be affected by the choice of a particular sales campaign (whose extra costs, if any, would be passed on into the price). It is not possible to estimate such quantities without investigating consumer motives in detail or engaging in fieldwork with questionnaires. Positivists are horrified by such activities and regard those who undertake them not as applied economists but as members of the less respectable profession known as marketing. The positive economists prefer to restrict their attention to those issues which their methodology can handle, even if this means little more than the estimation of demand equations for static market structures against a theory that seems to proclaim little more than 'consumers buy what they like' (or even, bearing in mind the circular definitions they offer for utility, 'consumers buy what they buy').

A SUBJECTIVIST WORLD VIEW

The common starting-point for the subjectivist authors cited in the introduction seems to be a view that what drives people into action is ignorance, wonder or enchantment with aspects of the world of which they have not yet obtained what they feel to be an adequate grasp. Perfect knowledge, such as is commonly assumed by positive economists, is seen as leading to a state of stupifying boredom, a state of indolence rather than enterprise. Instead of regarding people as 'utility seekers', subjectivists see them, in effect, as agents attempting to discern patterns in, and impose order upon, the complex and uncertain world in which they find themselves.

People are seen as forming theories about, or imagining relationships between, what they believe to be connected features of the world (features which can, in turn, only be described in relativistic terms). They can then use their resources and choices of activity to discover whether or not their theories are adequate representations of how things really are, or, in the absence of any better explanation, whether their perceptions can be forced into conformity with their expectations. Success in doing this means that a person can predict and control things, and has escaped from the nightmarish situation of being at the mercy of events, a situation where any random action would seem as likely to produce any outcome as the next. Having acquired an ability to predict and control part of the world a person can use her resources to explore new areas, to refine her comprehension of areas already explored, or to surround herself with the familiar and cocoon herself from the unexpected at the cost of not being able to broaden her perceptual field.

It is easier to get the feel of the subjectivist world-view by 'seeing' people as if they are generalised scientists, researching in what might be called the 'laboratory of life'. Just as scientists within a more narrowly-defined disciplinary area are more interested in finding out about, and feel more competent to investigate, some things rather than others, so inquiring people generally will be keener, or under greater pressure, to explore some areas of mystery than others. This is just as well, since only a limited number of the theories competing for someone's attention can be uplifted from being mere daydreams and actually be subjected to testing.

The relationships which people conjecture or attempt to impose are most conveniently labelled as images. For most people the first priority will be to clarify their self-image, to test their theory of how they fit into the scheme of things. When, for example, we hear people speak of 'having an identity crisis' what they are really talking about is an inability to form an acceptable theory of themselves. An inability to sustain any self-image except that of a person who is a fool and cannot cope will represent a grave cause for anxiety, an emotion for which we shall later provide a subjectivist definition with a practical application. So, too, will evidence which destroys a prevously conjectured self-image without seeming to point towards an acceptable alternative. The risk of uncovering inconvenient evidence is present whatever a person chooses to investigate, though there is also the possibility that no relevant information at all will be generated by an activity, or that what is discovered merely heightens ambiguities instead of clarifying an image.

To summarise the picture so far, we can say that people choose activities because they may help them cope with the world by enabling them to:

(1) explore, directly or indirectly, an unfamiliar situation (e.g. employment in a job that is not boring enables a person to test certain skills while earning the wherewithal for exploring new consumption activities);
(2) refine their understanding of something of particular interest (connoisseurship);
(3) preserve a set of conjectured relationships in a familiar pattern, thus removing uncertainty (e.g. the act of tidying up, which imposes order upon chaos, or the situation where a parent attempts to restrict the behaviour of her children).

Subjectivists see the process by which people come to terms with the world – like academic science – as very much a social affair. History, a person's upbringing in a particular social situation, 'common-sense' knowledge, opinions of others and the 'state of the news' all play vital parts in shaping a person's ideas about what it is reasonable to expect and in the interpretation of experience. It is this aspect of behaviour, and its implications for corporate policy, upon which we shall concentrate our attention for the rest of this paper. Conventional positive economists deprive themselves of the ability to say anything about how social factors and past actions affect current behaviour, or what the policy implications of these factors might be, since they treat consumers as if they have no past experiences and live isolated existences, interacting with each other only in order to make market transactions.

THE BENEFITS AND COSTS OF SOCIAL INTERACTION

There seem to be five main reasons why we bother to interact with other members of society:

1. Other people can help us form theories about the nature of things by offering advice and information.
2. Other people can help us test theories, either directly (e.g. 'What do you think of . . .?'), or indirectly (e.g. where we can observe their experiences in particular circumstances).
3. We find some people particularly interesting and wish to clarify our images of them.

4. In industrial societies social interaction in the workplace is necessary if we are to obtain income with which to explore other activities, or test our skills.
5. If we are prepared to accept on trust what others have told us to be 'common-sense things which every knows' we can confidently proceed to more adventurous activities. Social codes and customs, as well as the legal framework and reputations of people and products, enable us to save time and take a lot for granted.

But there is an important price to pay for enjoying the benefits of social interaction. In seeking to form and test *their* theories, including, possibly, theories about ourselves, other people may ask us why we have done certain things or demonstrate publicly that the *justifications* we have so far offered for our actions are, in some sense, inadequate. If we offer demonstrably inadequate justifications for our behaviour we reveal ourselves to be fools. Worse still, if we cannot provide any justification at all for the views we hold or the decisions we take, we demonstrate to other people that we do not understand how the world works, and that our actions have not been based on any well-thought-out choice criteria. If we cannot justify our choices or, to put it somewhat differently, if we cannot preserve or clarify our images of things, we cannot be acting rationally. We must be acting randomly rather than according to reason. If we view ourselves as capable, articulate and reasoning beings, we will be alarmed by the prospect of not being able to justify to others what we do or think.

Even if we do have justifications for our actions we may be reluctant to articulate them because we realise that to do so would display inconsistencies in our world-views; the preservation of one image seems to require the destruction of others. In order to preserve consistency in our frameworks of belief we have to ignore certain activities and situations, if it is possible to do so, or judge the adequacy of our theories and interpret evidence in a way which preserves our most important, core presumptions. As the experiments surveyed by Steinbruner (1974, chap. 4) clearly show, people preserve their world views by turning a blind eye to inconsistencies or fudging things where this is permitted by ambiguities.

The implication of this analysis of the costs of social interaction is that people will only buy products if they will be able to justify their decisions to purchase them, or will not be called upon to justify their purchases because they are the approved subjects of 'common-sense' knowledge as means to particular ends, or because they will be kept away from the public eye. How necessary a person will find it to justify a decision to purchase something will depend on her reference group, the social grouping to which she attempts to be attached in order to reap the benefits that such an association may offer. Continued membership of a given social group may require that a person presents an image that is neither at odds with the group's views as to how private a life-style may be enjoyed, nor at odds with its conventions with regard to consumption behaviour or beliefs that may be held.

People such as students, who live very public life-styles, and are expected by members of their reference group to be able to assess complex technical information for themselves or argue with sales persons if a product is faulty, would be expected, other things equal, to be particularly likely to feel it necessary to use discount shops to obtain a low price. They will then be able to preserve their self-images as capable shoppers when called upon to justify their purchases by those with whom they mix. A relatively insular group (e.g. middle-aged working-class people) would be expected to be rather more concerned with the prospect of losing face at the point of purchase rather than in the presence of friends and neighbours. They might have identical budgets, yet be prepared to pay for a friendly before and after sales service at the cost of only being able to afford a lower-grade model.

The problem of not being able to justify our behaviour or preserve our self-images is evidently one that will concern us most when we have to make choices outside our usual frames of reference. In such situations we may be alarmed that our actual choice criteria are of the kind we would find unconvincing or inappropriate if other people offered them to us as justifications for choices similar to our own. The choices we make we will only be able adequately to justify with the benefit of hindsight (i.e. with evidence as to how things seem to be related) or if we are provided with suitable information by another party. But the knowledge that a person has useful information does not guarantee that a consumer will attempt to obtain it: to do so might involve asking questions that she thinks will be construed as inane, and such behaviour might be at odds with her self-image.

If firms fail to appreciate the concern of consumers with regard to their often complex purchases, and fail to analyse the characteristics of their customers' usual reference groups, they are likely to sell less of their products than it might actually have been possible for them to sell. In particular, when selling to novice consumers they may lose out unnecessarily to those rival brands which are commonly known to be acceptable performers. For this reason it seems appropriate to spend the next, and final, part of the discussion considering how firms may put some of these ideas to practical use and gain insights on what is happening in their markets so that they can better manipulate consumer behaviour.

IMAGES, EMOTIONS AND BUSINESS POLICY

In order to affect consumers' behaviour by their choices of selling techniques, firms must manipulate their potential customers' expectational environments so as to produce images which will deter them from switching away from, or make them switch to, their products. To see how they might be able to do this, and when such action will be particularly necessary, we need to analyse two things: first, why consumers persist with or cease buying certain things; and second, the nature of consumer emotions, as seen from the subjectivist standpoint, with reference to which firms can design their product images. Let us consider these in turn.

In general we can say that people will cease to purchase a product if the activity with which it is associated has become boring — i.e. when sufficient evidence has been acquired to make it seem less enchanting than another activity — or when the person no longer finds an activity necessary to preserve a familar image and keep the unexpected at bay. However, people will not willingly adopt a form of behaviour which they cannot justify. Hence, even if they are bored, they will not venture into new areas or allow interesting things to happen to them if they expect to be unable to understand what is going on and what consequences might follow, or if they have doubts about whether their reference group would regard their behaviour as consistent with the images they see themselves projecting to the world.

Extensions of this basic idea about behaviour dynamics may help explain not only the common tendency for people to refuse to treat sunk costs as so much water under the bridge, but also sudden changes in consumption behaviour of the kind highlighted in studies by Katona (1960) and Smith (1975). Both of these kinds of behaviour are inconvenient to firms, as well as being at odds with orthodox preference theory.

Neo-classical positivist economists must frequently become perplexed when they see people, firms and governments persisting in activities seemingly because of, rather than despite, sunk costs. Their usual rationalisation, that people taking the decisions sadly do not understand economic theory, is not a positive one. It is rare to find economists actually proposing theories which recognise this 'misguided' behaviour, though the articles by Thaler (1980) and Wolf (1970, 1973) are notable exceptions. We offer the following subjectivist rationalisation of this kind of behaviour.

If people make public statements justifying the choice of a particular activity they will remain committed to it afterwards as they wait in the hope that experience will eventually throw up evidence upon promise of which their justification was based. If things presently seem to be going in the opposite direction a person may chance everything on events coming out right in the end, no matter how implausible such an outcome may seem to others at the moment, in order to prevent being humiliated by someone who presents an image of relative superiority by saying 'I told you so'. So long as the incremental returns to persisting with a particular activity are even slightly ambiguous there is scope for our minds to distort our perceptions with wishful thinking. Thus an outcome which would not have been possible had particular costs not been sunk in the past may be made to appear highly plausible. If the outcome actually occurs, past behaviour which others have attempted to condemn can be shown, with the benefit of hindsight, to have a very high pay-off. So long as the experiment is continued, judgement of the hypothesis under test must be suspended and, meanwhile, critics might forget the outcomes that have been promised and turn their attention elsewhere. In the long run we may be pouring good money after bad, but in the short run our continued expenditure buys the right to delay someone else's judgement of our behaviour.

Our explanation of the sunk costs issue rests quite clearly upon the idea that people use the actions of others as reference-points when trying to preserve and clarify their self-images. Relativity concerns are all-important to people attempting to decide where they fit in, what position they occupy in the scheme of things. This means that when the rate of conspicuous consumption by an individual's reference group changes, the amount of spending she needs to undertake to preserve a given image changes too, and in the same direction. For example, if everyone else in her reference group is replacing their cars she will be presenting an image of relative poverty or one who is willing to accept second best if she does not replace her vehicle also. If such an image conflicts with her self-image she will need to follow suit, regardless of whether her existing vehicle has become boring or is wearing out, in order to preserve her view of herself. However, if members of the reference group stop buying cars she has no need to replace her car unless it has become boring or worn out.

This analysis, and the fact that consumer durables are usually replaced before they are worn out, which means that their replacement can be postponed, means that the sales of 'positional' goods can be very unstable. It only takes a withdrawal of expenditure for a minority of individuals more concerned with the prospect of embarrassment at not being able to meet commitments in the future (e.g. due to fear of redundancy), than with current images as people who cannot 'keep up with the Joneses', to spark off a kaleidoscopic contraction in sales. Neither 'the Joneses' nor third-ranking consumers, who constitute 'the Joneses' for still lower levels, will feel such a pressing need to spend. The shift in spending spreads along the chain of reference groups. Evidently, the policy implication is that the marginal return to sales expenditure designed to stop the initial minority breakaway (or start one in an upward direction) can be quite considerable.

Sales strategies to produce or disturb persistent patterns of behaviour may be designed in the light of a knowledge of the participants' emotional responses to features of their environment. Obviously firms cannot analyse the particular cognitive processes of each potential customer but they can attempt to map, by a process known as psychographics, the ways in which their markets are segmented into groups of people with common world-views or life-styles (cf. Engel *et al.*, 1978). To economise on space, however, we will confine ourselves in the present paper to some general remarks about emotions and business policy, in the light of subjectivist definitions of emotions suggested by Bannister and Fransella (1971, pp. 34–41).

They define *anxiety* as a person's awareness that the events with which she is confronted lie mostly outside the range of her theory-forming system. That is to say, the person feels as if life is becoming akin to a series of examinations in unfamiliar subjects. A natural response will be to avoid those activities which involve anxiety, just as a student will not willingly attempt subjects where failure seems likely. A firm attempting to expand (or maintain) its sales should do so in a way which suggests that people who continue to refrain from (or cease) purchasing its products will find their abilities to anticipate events, and their self-images, undermined. Furthermore, the firm must ensure that its products will not cause potential purchasers to feel they might be stepping out of their depths. It will thus need to make things easy for inarticulate and inexperienced members of society to use without the fear of throwing up evidence at odds with their (often over-optimistic) self-images.

To give some examples: by displaying prices, retailers can remove the prospect of embarrassment from the customer who is unwilling to ask for price details in the belief that subsequently to decline to purchase may present an image as someone who is unable to understand what is valuable, or who is relatively poor. 'No quibble guarantees' will attract the custom of those who fear the prospect of having to return faulty goods because it might involve a somewhat humiliating argument. Similarly, property developers who promise to find mortgages and handle solicitors for their customers remove the anxiety from unfamiliar situations. The most obvious example of how the creation of anxiety can lead to business success is the 1970s body freshness revolution. The easy availability of antiperspirant and deodorant sprays was effectively used to show that there was no justification for a person to allow her normal bodily functions to bring her into conflict with a socially acceptable image, whose importance advertising campaigns had sought to increase.

Hostility can be seen as the continued effort by a person to extort validational evidence in favour of a type of social prediction which has already been recognised as a failure by her reference group. Hostility manifests itself in attempts by people to persuade others to conform with their expectational norms in order to prevent their previously acquired images from being destroyed. It is thus a result of anxiety. Obvious examples of people often subjected to exhortations to conform with other people's images of normality are: teetotallers, alcoholics, hippies, skinheads, punk rockers, nuclear power lovers and friends of the earth, fascists and Marxists, positive and subjectivist economists. Hostility, in this sense, is inherent whenever there is a clash of world-views, whenever one group claims another's values are rubbish.

A firm attempting to cause customer anxiety in a particular area must be careful not to overstep the mark and produce hostility instead. The risk of doing this is most acute when consumers are placed in a situation in which they are being shown that their core tenets are misplaced. It is simply no use to design a product which dominates at a low level but which, if chosen, would cause anxiety at a higher level by threatening key images. If confronted with such a prospect consumers will simply filter the product from their attention unless they are already in a face-to-face situation with a sales person.

In the latter case there is the possibility of success despite hostility due to the consumer fudging things in order to remove inconsistencies and avoid the destruction of a vital image. For example, if a person cannot conceive of a way of saying 'no' which is not at odds with her self-image she may buy something simply to save face against, say, a doorstep salesman whom she has unwisely allowed into her home. With less captive customers a firm is most likely to succeed in displacing its rivals if it shows potential purchasers how easy it is even for people supposed to be experts to make the kind of mistake it is implied they have been making. The strategy used in some current British Leyland advertisements, where press reports expressing surprise at improvements are cited, is one way of doing this.

The arguments we have advanced may be drawn together as we consider, finally, *aggression*, defined as the active elaboration of a person's perceptual field. People will attempt to expand the scale of their understanding and control over the world, but only so long as further exploration does not threaten to destroy, without providing an acceptable alternative, their hitherto cherished beliefs about themselves and the world. Where a consumer has not yet experienced its product, or an activity that requires its purchase, the firm's task is to direct her aggressive tendencies towards it. The firm can provide ammunition for the construction of beliefs about which characteristics really do combine to form the product it is selling, and display evidence to show how rival products will not conform with common expectations. By doing this the firm enables consumers to justify purchasing it and avoid anxiety, even if such a purchase might be rather at variance with the world-views of their reference groups. However, the firm must make some slightly implausible claims about the product, for only that which is in some degree mysterious can be other than boring and thus be deemed worthy of attention.

CONCLUSION

We began by arguing that positive economics lacks a practically applicable theory of consumer choice. We then went on to propose a subjectivist analysis which clashes with the positive economist's image of economics since it draws freely upon ideas from other disciplines, and suggests that, in order to formulate successful business policy, it may be necessary to engage in fieldwork which investigates consumer perceptions. For these reasons the paper is likely to get a hostile reception from positive economists.

But the proof of any pudding lies in the eating. Psychographics, one form of application of the ideas we have outlined, is increasingly being used by firms to find out how their markets are segmented into groups with different views of their products. Eden *et al.* (1979) have found another application in the study of organisational design. The theory also seems to offer promise in the study of labour market behaviour and, through its emphasis on the importance of relativities, reference groups and shared expectations, in many ways complements the work of Baxter (1980) and Wood (1978). With further development in these areas it may survive any hostility and one day become one of the main-stream economist's tools for coping with a world of complexity and structural change.

REFERENCES

Andrews, P. W. S. (1949) *Manufacturing Business* (London: Macmillan).
Andrews, P. W. S. (1964) *On Competition in Economic Theory* (London: Macmillan).
Bain, A. D. (1964) *The Growth of Television Ownership in the United Kingdom Since the War: A Lognormal Model* (Cambridge University Press).
Bannister, D., and Fransella, F. (1971) *Inquiring Man: The Theory of Personal Constructs*, 1st edn (Harmondsworth: Penguin Books).
Baxter, J. L. (1980) 'A General Model of Wage Determination', *Bulletin of Economic Research* 32, 3–17.
Boulding, K. E. (1956) *The Image: Knowledge in Life and Society* (Ann Arbor: University of Michigan Press).
Brown, A., and Deaton, A. (1972) 'Surveys in Applied Economics: Models of Consumer Behaviour', *Economic Journal* 82, 1145–236.
Buchanan, J. M., and Thirlby, G. F. (eds) (1973) *LSE Essays on Cost* (London: LSE/Weidenfeld and Nicolson).
Eden, C., Jones, S., and Sims, D. (1979) *Thinking in Organizations* (London: Macmillan).
Engel, J. F., Blackwell, R. D., and Kollat, D. T. (1978) *Consumer Behavior* (Hinsdale, Illinois: Dryden Press).
Garfinkel, H. (1967) *Studies in Ethnomethodology* (Engelwood Cliffs, New Jersey: Prentice-Hall).
Ironmonger, D. S. (1972) *New Commodities and Consumer Behaviour* (Cambridge University Press).
Katona, G. (1960) *The Powerful Consumer: Psychological Studies of the American Economy* (New York: McGraw-Hill).
Kelly, G. A. (1963) *A Theory of Personality* (New York: W. W. Norton).
Kuhn, T. S. (1970) *The Structure of Scientific Revolutions*, 2nd edn (University of Chicago Press).
Mishan, E. J. (1961) 'Theories of Consumer Behaviour: A Cynical View', *Economica* 28 (N.S.) 1–11.
Pasinetti, L. L. (1981) *Structural Change and Economic Growth* (Cambridge University Press).

Popper, K. R. (1976) *Unended Quest: An Intellectual Autobiography* (London: Fontana/Collins).

Schutz, A. (1943) 'The Problem of Rationality in the Social World', *Economica* 10 (N.S.) 130–49.

Scitovsky, T. (1981) 'The 'Desire for Excitement in Modern Society', *Kyklos* 34, 3–13.

Shackle, G. L. S. (1943) 'The Expectational Dynamics of the Individual', *Economica* 10 (N.S.) 99–129.

Shackle, G. L. S. (1979) *Imagination and the Nature of Choice* (Edinburgh University Press).

Skinner, A. S. (1979) 'Adam Smith: An Aspect of Modern Economics?', *Scottish Journal of Political Economy* 26, 109–26.

Smith, R. P. (1975) *Consumer Demand for Cars in the U.S.A.*, Cambridge University Department of Applied Economics, Occasional Paper 44 (Cambridge University Press).

Steinbruner, J. D. (1974) *The Cybernetic Theory of Decision* (Princeton University Press).

Thaler, R. (1980) 'Toward a Positive Theory of Consumer Choice', *Journal of Economic Behavior and Organization* 1, 39–60.

Thompson, M. (1979) *Rubbish Theory: The Creation and Destruction of Value*, with a foreword by E. C. Zeeman (Oxford University Press).

Wolf, C., Jr. (1970) 'The Present Value of the Past', *Journal of Political Economy* 78, 783–92.

Wolf, C., Jr. (1973) 'Heresies About Time: Wasted Time, Double Duty Time and Past Time', *Quarterly Journal of Economics* 87, 661–7.

Wood, A. J. B. (1978) *A Theory of Pay* (Cambridge University Press).

11 From 'Dismal Science' to 'Positive Economics' – a Century-and-a-Half of Progress?[1]

TERENCE HUTCHISON

In the title suggested for this paper by the Recorder of Section F the most significant component seems to be the question mark at the end: '. . . Progress?'

For a baffling initial problem in trying to review the last 150 years of change, growth or perhaps 'progress', in political economy and economics, is presented by the uncertainty and ambiguity of the criteria for assessing growth or progress in this context. The problem is somewhat similar to the index-number problem familiar to economists, but considerably more complex and controversial. It is also considerably more complex and controversial to try to assess progress, or the growth of knowledge, in economics and the social sciences, than it is in the natural sciences. This is because economics and the social sciences have a crucially significant, though often overlooked, historical dimension, which the natural sciences do not possess to anything like the same extent: that is, they are not complicated, as economics is, by historical and institutional changes in their subject-matter, and in the significant questions and answers about it.

Certainly, in economics, one can confidently point to vast increases in the stock and flow of factual knowledge, historical and statistical, and also in the range and refinement of analytical, and especially mathematical, techniques and abstract models. But, though growth in these two respects is probably necessary, it is surely not sufficient for progress in an empirical science, and especially one in which most of the practitioners have entertained, and continue to entertain, as a prime aim and claim, the guidance of policy or a significant contribution to less unsuccessful policy-making. For increases *simply* in factual knowledge, and/or in the range and refinement of analytical techniques, do not necessarily yield the kind of progress in explanation, or − in some at least minimal sense − in predictive potential, which is necessary for a science with the aims and claims which political economy or economics has had, and is having, made for it.

Indeed, the much enlarged stock of factual knowledge, and the much more numerous, powerful or refined techniques available in 1981, as compared with 1831, *may* be of relatively little use for reaching scientific explanations of the main, real-world problems at the later date, and *may* even explain these problems less adequately, and provide less useful predictions, than the much smaller stock of factual knowledge, and the much smaller range of techniques available in 1831, helped to provide at the earlier date. This may be the case if the economic world has, in the meantime, become more complex, unpredictable and difficult to explain.

Of course, if the aims and claims made for economics by its practitioners are rejected or reduced, then the requirements for 'progress' in the subject may become much more flexible. Sir John Hicks has recently observed: 'There is much of economic theory which is pursued for no better reason than its intellectual attraction; it is a good game' (1979, p. viii).

In so far as this is the case, the assessment of 'progress' in economics may well become even more uncertain and relaxed. Indeed such claims might become comfortingly irrefutable.

The attempt might also be made to apply Lakatos's concept of how, in the progress of a scientific subject, a 'growth of knowledge' can be said to take place, when a new theory not only explains and predicts all that the previous theory explained and predicted, but *more*. It may be that Lakatos's concept of the growth of knowledge is less difficult to apply to the physical sciences, in terms of which it was developed. But it seems doubtful how successfully, or unambiguously, it can be applied to the development of *historical* subjects, concerned, that is, with material which has an historical dimension such as real-world economics undoubtedly has. For, in such subjects, *two* kinds of changes are important, which render highly problematic any assessment of the growth, let alone 'progress', of scientific knowledge or of a scientific discipline. Not only are there vital changes in valuations regarding the interest or importance of different problems, which, in economics, would derive mainly from changes in policy importance.

There are also significant, positive, historical or institutional changes, which alter economic reactions and behaviour, particularly via changes in experience, information, expectations and processes of learning and unlearning, which may crucially transform, or complicate, economic processes, and render obsolete, or more inadequate, previous explanations and theories.

A more or less adequate explanation or theory, at an institutionally or historically earlier, and perhaps simpler and less complex stage, may become quite inadequate and misleading as experience, information and institutions change.[2] To meet such changes, what are earlier put forward as 'general' economic theories have increasingly to be adapted or qualified by *ad hoc* stratagems, to the point perhaps of virtual taxonomic emptiness. For with subjects that possess a significant historical dimension, the task is not, as with the more developed natural sciences, one of giving fuller and fuller explanations or answers regarding the more or less constant, stable or unchanging behaviour of the physical world: the generalisations and explanations of political economy and economics, except for the flimsiest and least substantial, have frequently to be adapted to historical, institutional, informational and expectational changes, or to new or growing complexities in the subject-matter. Economists share, in significant measure, the fate of Sisyphus.

The progress or regress of economics and economic knowledge, in so far as it may be regarded as both a scientific and historical subject, must be distinguished from the (not entirely unrelated) processes involved in the ups and downs in public prestige and influence which economics and its practitioners have undergone, depending on whether or not they appear to be able to provide convincing answers to the main policy problems of the day. In periods of economic success in Britain, like the 1850s and 1860s, and, somewhat similarly, the 1950s and 1960s, there will be a tendency for economists to claim, and be granted, credit for this success, on behalf of a politico-economic theory around which a convincing range of consensus is likely to have gathered, with fundamental disagreements in abeyance. In periods, on the other hand, of striking economic *un*success, like the 1970s, there are more likely to be fierce and fundamental disagreements, so that the subject and its practitioners suffer in influence and prestige, either because they do not seem to have an adequate answer to current problems, or because they have too many sharply conflicting answers. Previously orthodox theories may have become institutionally obsolete and the new challengers may not have established their credibility.

With this brief warning about the difficulties of attempting an answer to the question-mark in the title of this paper, we shall now examine a set of four snapshots, posed at roughly half-century intervals, that is, at around 1831, 1881, 1931 and 1981. This is all that can be attempted by way of setting up the issues for those bold enough to attempt an answer regarding the 'progress', over the last century and a half, of Section F's subject.

Section F was not a founder section of the BA. According to Adam Sedgwick, the President of the Association at its 1833 meeting in Cambridge, 'this self-formed section' was created, that year, with some 'irregularity' (British Association, 1834, pp. xxvii–viii; see also Royal Statistical Society, 1934, pp. 4–8). The leading founders (or culprits) were Richard Jones, Malthus and Babbage. The title of the new section was simply 'Statistics', of which economic statistics was simply a part. 'Economic Science' was not allowed into the forefront of the title until 25 years later, in 1856, at a time when the prestige of the new science of political economy had reached something of a peak.

At its foundation, the ground which the Association's President somewhat grudgingly conceded to Section F comprised: 'What may be called the raw material to political economy and political philosophy; and by their help the lasting foundations of those sciences *may be perhaps ultimately laid*' (1834, p. xxviii, italics added).

Sedgwick was afraid that in admitting a human, moral, political or social subject, the British Association would be deserting 'the secure ground' which it had marked out for itself. He argued:

> The things with which the Association had to do were the laws and properties of matter and with these alone; the nature of the human mind was utterly beyond their province; the sciences of morals and politics were elevated far above the speculations of their material philosophy . . . When we enter on these higher generalisations, that moment they are dissevered from the objects of the Association, and must be abandoned by it. (1834, p. xxviii)

Those among the early pioneers of Section F who were primarily interested in political economy, were surely not as negatively sceptical as Sedgwick regarding the longer-run scientific possibilities of their subject. But several of them, like Richard Jones and Malthus, *were* highly sceptical of the new, abstract, deductive method of Ricardo, and also were very dubious about the extremely confident claims for their new doctrines put forward by James Mill and McCulloch, for example. In helping to found Section F, Jones and Malthus were expressing an emphasis on the need to build up the empirical and statistical base of their subject. They may at some points have moved towards a kind of 'naive' empiricism, in questioning the excessive Ricardian claims. But it is surely incontrovertible that they were thoroughly justified in seeking to develop economic statistics, and thus to build up the empirical foundations of the subject. Anyhow, in Section F, they were balanced by Nassau Senior, who upheld the method of deduction from a few fundamental assumptions, but was much more cautious than the Ricardians about applications to policy.

Thus at the time when the Section was launched, three views may be distinguished regarding the possible programme and prospects for a science of political economy:

First, there was the negativist scepticism of Adam Sedgwick regarding the possibility of any 'scientific' treatment of economics, or of other human, moral or social subjects, in anything like the same ways, or in accordance with the same criteria, as those upheld by the main branches of natural science, around which the British Association had been founded.

Secondly, at the other extreme, there was the pretentious confidence of the Ricardians and McCulloch about their new science, with their claim of epistemological parity with the most advanced natural sciences.

Thirdly, and in the middle, there were the mainly, but not entirely, empirical economists, prominent in the foundation of Section F, who rejected, on the one hand, extreme negativist scepticism regarding the possibilities of economic science, and, on the other hand the excessive pretensions and abstractions of Ricardo, James Mill or McCulloch.

Whatever may be concluded today regarding the longer-run balance of wisdom between these three programmes or viewpoints, there is no doubt that it was the second view which flourished over the next two or three decades. Outside Section F, among political economists, and increasingly among the public elite, much of this period was a time of growing confidence in the new science of political economy. Smith was acknowledged as the great founder. But in the ensuing half-century since *The Wealth of Nations*, immense progress was held to have taken place. That was the view of the two Mills and McCulloch, who exercised such a powerful influence. Admittedly there were some deep disagreements on value and distribution between the Ricardians and the

Oxford–Dublin school of Senior and Whately, who were much closer to French and German theories. But – except for Malthus – there was widespread agreement on classical macroeconomics, as well as on the deductive method and, above all, on the general principles of policy. Of course, in the background – or the 'underworld' as Keynes called it – there were socialist and historical critics. But thanks largely to the influence of the Mills and McCulloch, a version of classical orthodoxy was gaining great influence and authority. To some extent this authority was obtained, not by weight of numbers, for those were very small, but by a kind of circular, self-sealing argument: the orthodox, authoritative doctrines were those of the serious, responsible economists; while the serious, responsible economists were identifiable as those who held the orthodox, authoritative doctrines. James Mill fairly explicitly adopted such an argument in his remarkable paper of 1836 entitled 'Whether Political Economy is Useful?' – to which question his answer was, of course, an extremely confident affirmative (1966, pp. 371 ff.).

Especially ambitious claims came from the followers of Ricardo, and from McCulloch, who insisted on intellectual parity between the laws of physics and the laws of distribution of the new science of political economy. As McCulloch claimed:

> The errors with which Political Economy was formerly infected have now nearly disappeared, and a very few observations will suffice to show that *it really admits of as much certainty in its conclusions as any science founded on fact and experiment can possibly do.* (McCulloch, 1824, p. 75, italics added)

Moreover, the doctrines of the new science were regarded as so indisputably well founded that they could suitably be imparted to children. Indeed, Mrs Marcet's *Conversations on Political Economy*, which went through numerous editions between 1816 and 1839, was prescribed by Ricardo for his daughters. This work, as Schumpeter has observed, 'presents many of the most important tenets of the Ricardian school' (1954, p. 477). As Schumpeter (writing in the 1940s) goes on:

> Not for a moment did Mrs Marcet doubt not only that the definitive truth about economics and economic policy had been discovered at last, but also that this truth was so delightfully simple as to be capable of being taught to every schoolgirl. This frame of mind was then common and is highly characteristic of that age – exactly as a

similar frame of mind is common among modern Keynesians and not less characteristic of our own age.

However, in 1831, though well on the upswing, classical political economy had not yet come to full fruition or the peak of its prestige in this country. That was to come in the three decades following the great reform of the franchise in 1832. The structure of the classical free market economy was completed, through, notably, the new Poor Law of 1834, the Bank Act of 1844 and the abolition of the Corn Laws in 1846. A relative peak of prosperity for the British economy was to follow in the 1850s.

Some further features of this 1831 snapshot may be noticed:

First, everything was, quantitatively, on a miniature scale compared with today. The number of economists in the country – depending, of course, on how this somewhat problematic term is defined – would perhaps hardly have equalled the number today in a single, medium-sized modern university department. The same applied to the number of publications. There were no specialist journals, and not to be any for decades. As regards the stocks and flows of factual material, these, compared with today, were minute, whether in the form of historical and institutional material, or of economic statistics, which were confined mainly to certain trade returns and to the three or four population series after 1801.

Secondly, among the founders of Section F, and among economists generally, academics, though prominent, were not dominant. Chairs of Political Economy had been founded at Oxford in 1825, in Cambridge in 1828, and in Dublin in 1832. But academics did not dominate the subject to anything like the extent they were to do a century later, in the 1930s.

Thirdly, at this period, just when the British economy was achieving a unique supremacy in the world, so British economists were pre-eminent in the field of political economy, certainly in their own eyes, but in the eyes of others too. In fact, as Schumpeter has said of this period, 1790–1870: 'Barring a few lonely peaks abroad, England easily comes out first in the period's performance. In fact that period was the specifically English period in the history of our science', (1954, p. 382). Or, as T. H. Huxley put it (1868), political economy was 'an intensely Anglican subject'.

Two further points to be noticed at this stage refer to different aspects of the title of this paper.

The term 'positive economics' has come to possess a rather varied and uncertain content. But what might be regarded as the initial, core principle involved in the concept of 'positive' economics is the insistence on a fundamental distinction between positive and normative. This distinction, though not always easy to observe, and in some senses perhaps impossible to maintain, remains, as far as it goes — which is quite a long way — essential for that clarity which it is an intellectual and professional duty to strive after.

The introduction of this positive–normative distinction into political economy dates from just those years of the early 1830s when the BA, and Section F, were being launched. In Smith and Ricardo, the adjective 'natural' had shed a kind of normative–positive ambiguity over much of early classical political economy, which it was surely an important step forward to begin to dispel. This fundamental clarificatory work was due, in the first instance, mainly to Whately and Senior, both prominent in the early years of Section F (Whately 1832, pp. 20–4). 'Positive economics', in this important initial sense, was, therefore, a classical and not a neo-classical innovation.

Another sense of this multifaceted concept of 'positive economics' is concerned with the view that economics can be, and is, a science in the same full sense as the most advanced natural sciences, and has already produced fully comparable theories and laws. We have noted above the two extremes, of Sedgwick, on the one hand, doubting whether such an epistemological possibility could, or would, ever be realised regarding human, moral, political or social subjects; and, on the other hand, the extreme claims of the Ricardians and McCulloch for the laws of their new science, and for full epistemological parity with the natural sciences. But here distinctions and discriminations are vital: between, on the one hand, claims to full epistemological parity of *already achieved results*; and, on the other hand, the moderate views, shared by the economist founders of Section F, that the empirical 'methods', discipline and criteria of the natural sciences can and should be followed in political economy, as far as the material allows, which is significantly far — without, of course, it being claimed, or hoped, that theories, laws, explanations and predictions, on a par with those of the natural sciences, were being, or would be, achieved.

A decade later, political economy was described by Carlyle — (in *Past and Present*, 1843) — as 'The Dismal Science'. However, over the next couple of decades, the policies of 'dismalness', or austerity, were to be followed by the British economy achieving a *relative* strength in the world unequalled before or since, while the living standards of the British people, at least by conventional standards, rose well above those of comparable countries. Of course, one may reject this kind of 'success', as conventionally measured, or one may deny that the application of the theories of the 'dismal science' played any effective part in achieving these outstanding results. But most economists would not find all the implications of such rejections, or denials, easy to accept.

Moving on half a century to 1881, one finds that the subject has gone through a large part − though not quite all − of a kind of cycle.

English classical political economy had moved to the climax of its prestige and influence in the 1850s and early 1860s. By means of a simple but effective *post hoc ergo propter hoc* argument, the extraordinary success of the British economy as 'the workshop of the world' had been more or less credibly transferred to boost the prestige of the dominant 'Anglican' version of the science of political economy. Pointing to the world leadership of the British economy at this time, Nassau Senior, who at different periods of his career played a prominent part in Section F, proclaimed to an admiring Frenchman: 'It is the triumph of theory. We are governed by philosophers and political economists' (Senior, 1878, vol. I, p. 169).

Meanwhile, the intellectual foundations for the prestige of the subject with the intelligent elite of the day, was provided by J. S. Mill's lucid, authoritative and masterly exposition of its principles.

However, quite suddenly in the middle or late 1860s, there had come a collapse in confidence and credibility. The causes may be found in various directions. Long-standing theoretical inadequacies were rendered more acutely serious by historical and institutional changes, at the same time as what was taken to be the subject's simple policy message of *laissez-faire* was being increasingly called in question by new political forces, which began to take their share of electoral power as a consequence of the second reform bill of 1867.

The point of departure for this 'revolution', or turning-point, is often taken to be Jevons's utility theory of value. Jevons, a great BA man, who delivered several of his most important papers to Section F, had first expounded his utility theory at the 1862 meeting of the Association. But no notice of Jevons's arguments was taken until they appeared in his *Theory of Political Economy* of 1871.

In fact, it seems that it was the problems raised by the increasingly serious institutional obsolescence of the classical distribution theory, which was probably the prior and more important theoretical cause of the collapse in credibility, and of the rapidly mounting crisis, of classical political economy. In particular, institutional changes were calling in question the significance of both the natural wage theory and the wages fund doctrine. When, in 1876, the centenary of *The Wealth of Nations* came round, profound disagreements were expressed about the state of the subject in respect of its theory, methods and policy doctrines. Jevons himself declared 'the state of the science to be almost chaotic'. J. E. Cairnes, often described as 'the last of the classicals' discerned in 1870, 'signs of a belief that Political Economy had ceased to be a fruitful speculation' − a complete reversal of James Mill's confident claims of a generation earlier. Later Walter Bagehot, in the 1870s, contrasted the prestige of, and enthusiasm for, political economy in the earlier part of the century: 'At that time economists indulged in happy visions; they thought the attainment of truth far easier than we have since found it to be' (Hutchison, 1953, pp. 5−7).

Indeed, such was the distrust of the subject that in 1877 Francis Galton published a paper in the *Journal of the Royal Statistical Society* entitled 'Considerations Adverse to the Maintenance of Section F', in which he castigated the 'unscientific' nature of the Section's discussions and complained that they lacked the degree of consensus requisite in a scientific subject, which should reach conclusions 'that all minds are obliged to accept'.

In a notable presidential address to Section F at Dublin the following year J. K. Ingram agreed that:

> An important crisis in the history of our Section has taken place . . . and this is what lends a peculiar gravity to the incident − such a step could hardly have been taken if the general mass of the intelligent public entertained strong convictions as to the genuinely scientific character of political economy. (1878, p. 41)

This intellectual crisis, or depression, of the 1870s was mainly a British phenomenon, just as classical political economy itself had been. In other countries, where English classical theories had never achieved the same dominance, the subject moved into the neo-classical era without the kind of 'revolution', or crisis in credibility, which occurred in Britain − though a major *Methodenstreit* ensued in Austria and Germany.

Anyhow, by 1881, signs of a new upswing were (or are, with hindsight) discernible, centred round what came to be called 'neo-classical' theory. Jevons died in 1882. But Alfred Marshall was already at work on his *Principles* and took over the Cambridge chair in 1885. A generation change had taken place, usually an important element in fundamental new developments in the subject.

But political economy, or 'economics', as it was about to be called, could no longer be described as an 'intensely Anglican' subject. British predominance was beginning relatively to decline. Important new schools of economic theory had begun to emerge in the 1870s in Vienna and Lausanne. Moreover, the academic influence was about to increase significantly, both as regards numbers of personnel, and intellectual criteria, a development marked in this country, a decade or so later, by the foundation of the London School (1893) and by the specialist Economics Tripos in Cambridge (1903). Numbers, however, were still very small. Cairnes, back in 1870, had estimated that there were fewer than 100 students of political economy in the whole of London.

The stock and flow of statistical and historical factual material was growing, thanks especially to some of the pioneer neo-classicals, notably Jevons, with the great advance he achieved in price index numbers. Moreover, economic history was emerging as a specialist subject. But unfortunately, this development was largely separate from economics; so that, apart from Marshall's own individual efforts, a mutual, two-way enrichment of history and theory failed to ensue.

In due course, the theoretical advance was not confined to micro-economics. By the 1880s, concern with cyclical fluctuations and with irregularity of employment as a cause of poverty, was increasing markedly in Britain. In the second half of the nineteenth century much of the pioneer work on cyclical fluctuations and macroeconomic instability had been done in France and Germany – for example, by Juglar, a visitor to Section F. But 1886 was notable for two events in this field in Britain. First, there was the publication by Foxwell, Marshall's lieutenant in Cambridge, of his study of irregularity of employment, in which he described this problem as the most serious policy problem of the day. Secondly, in the same year, Joseph Chamberlain circularised local authorities recommending the setting up of relief works in times of high unemployment. Quantitatively, the effects of Chamberlain's measure were trivial. But intellectually, it marked an important break with Ricardian policies and was cautiously approved by Marshall.[3]

Before coming to the present day, I would like to glance rapidly at the BA centenary year, 1931, when, because of the great economic crisis of that year, some of the more elderly of today's economists were, perhaps overoptimistically, first getting engaged with the subject of Section F.

Again, over the previous half-century since 1881, something of an intellectual cycle can be discerned as having taken place, though this does not stand out as clearly as in the preceding and succeeding periods. 1931 came just about halfway through that era of almost continuous violent upheaval between 1914 and 1945, when First World War, post-war, great slump, pre-war and Second World War followed one another with only fleeting interludes in between – a period, incidentally, which coincided almost exactly with the career of Keynes as an economist.

The economic world of the inter-war years was dominated by the breakdown of the monetary standard, together with very serious instability and unprecedented levels of unemployment (for which official statistics were now regularly available). As we have seen, for several decades before 1914, increasing concern had been shown with the business cycle and the unemployment problem. But this had been against a background of *comparative* economic stability, and 'a stable general culture', as Pigou had called it – in particular, the kind of stability provided by a more or less accepted and assured monetary framework and standard. For a time, in the 1920s, an attempt was made to get back to this framework of monetary stability. 1931 saw the end of this attempt.

Economic theory in this country in the 1920s, though hardly itself in a state of explicit crisis, was not manifestly mastering the fundamental and massive changes taking place in the political economy of the post-war world. Neo-classical microeconomics, and, in particular the treatment of monopolistic, oligopolistic and imperfect markets, was, in Cambridge, being shunted away from the historical and institutional methods of Marshall's *Industry and Trade*, into a *cul-de-sac* of increasingly arid geometrical abstraction. As regards macroeconomics, though progress was being made with the study of cyclical fluctuations, the subject was not equipped to confront with credibility the tornado which struck in late 1929. Moreover, there were fundamental ambiguities and inadequacies in the logical links between the two branches of theory ('micro' and 'macro' as they were soon to be described).

Nevertheless, with hindsight, it is clear that by 1931 what was to be known as 'the Keynesian Revolution' was already underway, though it only came to full fruition, with the first 'Keynesian' budget, ten years later in war-time Britain. But already by 1929 Keynes had claimed, without *much* exaggeration, that the majority of British economists supported his opposition to the Treasury or classical view that public works would then simply 'crowd out' private investment, and do little or nothing to relieve unemployment.

For some years after 1931, thanks to the intellectual confidence and optimism generated by Keynes, economists could plausibly convince themselves that they were on their way to solving the basic economic problems confronting mankind – unemployment and economic instability. The kind of excited euphoria generated by such an intellectual upswing is demonstrated in the quite rhapsodic, Wordsworthian terms in which one of the senior Nobel Laureates has described the 1930s. In the midst of the great Depression, with unemployment everywhere at unprecedented levels, and with Stalin and Hitler gaining alarmingly in power, nevertheless, so rosy were the intellectual–political vistas then opening up, Professor Paul Samuelson tells us, that:

> Bliss was it in that dawn to be alive.
> But to be young was very heaven.

In any event, in the 1930s, an expansion in the numbers of economists in Britain was underway, considerable in relation to previous low levels, but still relatively very small compared with what was to come two to three decades later. But more than at any other time, in the years before the Second World War in Britain, the subject was dominated by university economists. At the time of 'the Keynesian Revolution', outside the universities, in government, banking and industry, there were in Britain only one or two isolated individuals described as 'economists'.

Finally, we reach 1981. Again, in the preceding half-century, since 1931, part of an intellectual cycle is discernible, more clearly so than in the case of 1881–1931, and having some similarities with the cycle of, roughly, 100 years previously. In the 1950s and 1960s there was certainly a remarkable intellectual boom of confidence in the subject, comparable with the English classical boom of about a century before. Again in the 1970s there was something of an intellectual depression or even a persisting 'crisis'. Whether by 1981 the elements of a new upswing, in one direction or another, are now discernible – as could be claimed regarding 1881 – remains rather debatable.

The remarkable period of real-world economic success, throughout most western countries, which lasted from shortly after the Second World War down to about the middle 1960s, was certainly *post* Keynes, and was widely acclaimed, by Keynesians, to be *ergo propter* Keynes. In Britain the spectacular fall in unemployment, compared with the inter-war period, generated more confidence in the validity and operational power of the prevailing economic doctrines than had existed for 100 years. This optimism regarding the solution of the unemployment problem was then extended – by, for example, Sir Roy Harrod, Lord Kaldor and other Keynesians – to the long-standing, if, by many, newly-discovered problem of Britain's relatively lower rate of economic growth, which was also confidently expected to yield to the ministrations of 'the New Economics' (see Hutchison, 1968, especially chaps 3 and 4).

Certainly this New Economics had shed, with contempt, all the puritanical, protestant-ethical 'dismalness' of English classical political economy. Spending one's way out of unemployment and low growth into the new age of affluence and plenty became an influential message, just at the moment when democratic appetites were coming to exercise more and more influence on economic policy through the electoral process. Even more clearly than the Keynesian doctrine proclaiming the power of governments to reduce unemployment, the new 'growthmanship' message seemed to provide the answer to politicians' prayers. In unprecedented numbers, economists began to be welcomed into Whitehall, Downing Street and the House of Lords.

The expansive, liberating policy message was matched by an expansive, liberating methodological message. At this time – roughly describable as that of the 'silly sixties' – the 'positive' restraint and discipline, called for by a regard for the normative-positive distinction, as had been upheld in Cambridge by such past masters and disciplinarians as Marshall, Sidgwick and J. N. Keynes, was, in some fashionable circles, cast aside as an outmoded, 'positivist' repression, in favour of the liberating methodological doctrine that 'anything goes'.

Anyhow, the huge upsurge in the number of economists reduced all previous figures to insignificance. The expansion reached out far beyond the university base, which was itself then growing at an unprecedented pace, and proceeded backwards into the schools, on an immense scale, and forwards into the civil service, finance and industry. However, though Keynes had revived the Anglican contribution to the subject, British economics was rapidly becoming a much smaller part of the world profession, which was dominated more and more from the USA.

Then, quite suddenly, in the late 1960s, came the collapse, in a manner comparable in *some* respects with the slump in the English classical doctrines of just 100 years previously.

Again, significant institutional changes had been accumulating, on this occasion affecting employment conditions, the powers of trade unions and inflationary expectations. These changes seriously aggravated long-standing theoretical limitations in the prevailing doctrines. Moreover, at this point, alarming and unprecedented economic phenomena began rather suddenly to appear, notably the combination of more and more serious inflation with a marked rise in unemployment. The question arose as to how far such new phenomena, long held to be more or less incompatible, called for revisions in the prevailing, confidently, and even some cases dogmatically, held theories and policy doctrines, in which such quantities of intellectual capital had been invested over the previous decades. Just how fundamental were the revisions required by the new institutional and expectational facts? Of course, it is always possible, indeed almost easy, for *a priorists* impervious to empirical evidence, to add on another *ad hoc* patch to a cherished pair of general theoretical trousers. Pending a generation change, such will often be a widespread reaction in such intellectual crises.

Meanwhile, however, the theory and policy doctrines now challenging 'Keynesian' orthodoxy (which orthodoxy, in the form widely prevalent a quarter of a century after his death, Keynes himself might well have largely rejected) harked back, in some respects, to the classical model. The previous degree of consensus, which had been held together in the late 1950s and early 1960s to an important extent by the prevailing appearance of real-world economic success, proceeded to disintegrate. Disagreements were soon magnified. In times of economic difficulty or crisis, economists are usually ready to ascribe great infuence to their opponents. Adherents of one 'general theory' began to accuse the other side of being responsible for unemployment; while adherents of the alternative 'general theory' accused the first of being responsible for inflation – or for 'Keynesian inflation', as it was called by one authority.

After about a decade of 'crisis' (this term was still being authoritatively applied to the state of the subject in 1980), can it now be said, in 1981, that a new intellectual upswing is discernible – as might have been claimed in 1881? As with the economy itself, downswings seem to have been followed fairly regularly by upswings. But it does not follow that a new upswing, or one resembling previous upswings, will follow on cue, on this occasion. Perhaps, for some time, a kind of persistent depression may ensue. But, of course, optimists of different persuasions discern the approach of dawn (unfortunately, at diametrically opposite points of the compass).[4]

Anyhow, it might be worthwhile to enquire just how far the kind of boom of prestige and influence enjoyed by the subject in the 1850s and early 1860s, and again in the 1950s and early 1960s, is either possible or desirable. In the real-world economy a boom, in spite of some inflation, brings more employment and makes many people better off than previously. But in intellectual booms, overconfident, inflated pretensions run the danger of causing more harm, in fostering subsequent political disillusion, than the gains, which may accrue from a growth of knowledge, do good. It should not, however, be denied that the great English classical and Keynesian 'booms' *did* produce, or were based on, *some* genuine growth of knowledge both of specially valuable relevance for a few decades, and even of *some* permanent significance. Unfortunately, however, the serious limitations of the original, general theoretical claims were overlooked in the course of the initial success and intellectual euphoria, and this, in turn, led on (with the epigoni taking over from the original founders), to dogmatic inflexibilities and over-simplifications, which were then undermined and rendered seriously obsolete by historical, institutional and expectational changes.

Therefore, what does *not* seem a promising line of advance is a new intellectual upswing based on a new exclusivist 'general theory'. We have had the classical and neo-classical general theories, and the Keynesian general theory. Also, for over 100 years, through the eras of Stalin and Mao, the Marxian general theory has gained adherents among economists. Something in the way of synthesis may be possible, but not in terms of a significant new general theory. What may rather be needed is not some 'general theory', adjusted in all directions to the possibilities of all times and places, but rather a much greater recognition of the historical and institutional dimensions of the subject, together with the development of a range of alternative theories appropriate for changing historical and institutional conditions.

Meanwhile, through all the booms and slumps of the last 150 years, the stock of factual material, historical and statistical, and the range and sophistication of analytical techniques and models, has continued steadily to grow, probably at an increasing pace over the last half-century.

If scientific progress consisted simply of growth in these two components, or is defined in these terms, then progress has surely been

208   *Beyond Positive Economics?*

continuing, and may confidently be expected to continue. But if, as we
suggested above, economics has a significant historical dimension, as
well as a heavy commitment to policy application, then whether 'progress' has taken place is a much more problematic question.

The President of the Royal Economic Society claimed last year, with
perhaps not quite completely justifiable euphoria, that today 'economists are technically streets ahead' of those of a generation or two ago;
and that 'the tools on offer to the policy-makers are getting more and
more sophisticated' (Stone, 1980, p. 732). But, with historical and
institutional change, new and unprecedented problems confront
theory and policy. What if the 'streets-ahead' techniques, and the
'more and more sophisticated' tools are of limited, and perhaps
increasingly limited, relevance for answering the new questions, both
of theory and policy, which historical or institutional changes are
producing? And what if, in spite of all this 'streets-ahead' sophistication, no reasonable degree of consensus − in fact, much less than
existed earlier − emerges regarding the answers to what are considered
the most important theoretical and policy problems?

Certainly it may be inappropriate to deny the progress of a subject
simply because new policy problems are being created, or aggravated,
in the real world, by the excessive appetites of politicians and public,
which prove insusceptible to anything like agreed solutions − even if,
in some cases, these excessive appetites have been stimulated by
economists.

But can significant progress be claimed, if the subject provides less
adequate answers, to what are regarded as the main problems of both
theory and policy than earlier economists provided for the problems of
their day − even though it might be claimed that the problems of
today, especially the policy problems, but also some theoretical
problems, are much more complex and intractable than those of earlier
periods?

The precise answer to that particular conundrum may well not be of
much importance. But what *are* of the greatest importance are
questions of the nature and extent of economic knowledge and ignorance, and of what growth or progress in them it is realistic and responsible to suggest is likely. Such questions are not simply of
academic, philosophical interest, though it would be philistine and
obscurantist to neglect them even if that is all they were. It is of considerable public and political importance, if dangerous political disillusion is to be prevented, to assess how far any hopes for less
unsuccessful economic policy-making can realistically and responsibly

be based on the state and possible progress of economic knowledge. Such clarification may be considerably more feasible, and possibly just as valuable, as new theoretical work in economics, certainly than that considerable part of it which is apparently pursued simply as 'a good game'. It is an eminently suitable task for Section F.

Finally, let us recall that triangle of contrasting views about the scientific nature of Section F's subject, which was apparent at the time of the Section's foundation. First, outside Section F, there were the extremely excessive claims of the Ricardians for full epistemological parity with the most advanced natural sciences, not only regarding aims and 'methods', but in already achieved laws and results. Though somewhat similar pretensions were being advanced 20 years ago in the 1960s, at the peak of the mathematical and 'Keynesian' boom, such claims today have become very muted. More danger today is perhaps contained in the other kind of extreme, represented in 1833 by the then President, Adam Sedgwick, and today by a vocal group of sociologists, social philosophers and 'social scientists', as well as by some economists. Sedgwick suggested the kind of view, that it is not simply pretentious, in human and social subjects, to hope for similar laws, and the same degree of consensus as in the natural sciences, but that it is wrong even to attempt to pursue the same kind of 'methods' *and discipline* as far as they will go − which, over the last 150 years, has not been a negligible distance, even if *far* less than has often been claimed. The dangers of such an attitude are that it represents an over-reaction to the present 'crisis', and, more seriously, that it may encourage the abandonment of the element of scientific discipline − which should be common to natural and social sciences − in favour of the anarchy of 'anything goes'. Moreover, those who entertain such an attitude must *either* show satisfactorily just how it is compatible with the traditional aims and claims of the subject, still very widely upheld, to provide significant guidance for policy, including less unreliable predictions, *or* they must explicitly jettison these traditional aims and claims.

So, in 1981, the moderate programme of the economist founders of Section F, 150 years ago, seems to retain its superior validity against its two competitors: that is, the programme of rejecting the pretentious claims and hopes for epistemological parity with the advanced natural sciences, in terms at any rate of explanations and predictions; and of seeking to continue building up the often-changing empirical foundations of the subject, in accordance with, and in acceptance of, the disciplines of scientific method, common to both social and natural sciences.

210   *Beyond Positive Economics?*

NOTES AND REFERENCES

1. This paper, in an abbreviated form, was delivered on 2 September 1981 at one of the special Symposia held to celebrate the 150th anniversary of the founding of the British Association for the Advancement of Science at York.
2. The labour theory of value, as treated by Adam Smith, provides a classical example of how a comparatively powerful theory is rendered obsolete, and deprived of its original power, and has increasingly to be qualified and complicated, in the face of institutional changes. The labour-embodied theory can be said to work powerfully 'in the early and rude state of society which precedes both the accumulation of stock and the appropriation of land'; that is, in a hand-to-mouth, hunting economy, where labour can reasonably be treated as homogeneous. As soon as the ideally simplified conditions of such a very primitive economy are complicated by institutional developments, including private property in land, the use of capital, and the emergence of different qualities of labour, then endless qualifications and adjustments have increasingly to be introduced into the theory, until it becomes either false or virtually empty.
3. See T. W. Hutchison (1978), chap. 5, section VIII. In the history of macroeconomics in England, 1836, 1886 and 1936 are highly important dates. 1836 is the date of the second edition of Malthus's *Principles*, the concluding paragraph of which – Malthus's last word, so to speak – emphasised the 'serious sum of human misery' caused by economic instability or cyclical fluctuations. Then the classical view, as represented, for example, by J. S. Mill, came to dominate in England, to the effect that macroeconomic instability was not a serious problem. It was just 50 years later that Foxwell, in Cambridge, stressed the great social significance of economic fluctuations and 'irregularity of employment' as 'the root evil of the present industrial régime' (and just another 50 years, of course, to *The General Theory*).
4. See, for example, the contrasting pronouncements of Lord Kaldor (1978) and Professor Minford (1980) referred to in Hutchison (1981), pp. 258–9.

REFERENCES

British Association for the Advancement of Science (1834) *Report of the Third Meeting, 1833*.
Foxwell, H. S. (1886) 'Irregularity of Employment and Fluctuations of Prices', in *The Claims of Labour*, ed. J. Burnett *et al.*
Galton, F. (1877) 'Considerations Adverse to the Maintenance of Section F', *Journal of the Royal Statistical Society* (September) 468 ff.
Hicks, Sir John (1979) *Causality in Economics* (Oxford: Blackwell).
Hutchison, T. W. (1953) *A Review of Economic Doctrines, 1870–1929* (London: Greenwood Press).
Hutchison, T. W. (1968) *Economists and Economic Policy in Britain, 1946–1966* (London: Allen & Unwin).
Hutchison, T. W. (1978) *On Revolutions and Progress in Economic Knowledge* (Cambridge University Press).

Hutchison, T. W. (1981) *The Politics and Philosophy of Economics* (Oxford, Blackwell).

Ingram, J. K. (1878) 'The Present Position and Prospects of Political Economy', reprinted in *Essays in Economic Method*, ed. R. L. Smyth (1962) pp. 41 ff (London; Duckworth).

Lord Kaldor (1978) *Further Essays in Economic Theory* (London: Duckworth).

McCulloch, J. R. (1824) *A Discourse on the Rise, Progress, Peculiar Objects and Importance of Political Economy*.

Malthus, T. R. (1836) *Principles of Political Economy*, 2nd edn.

Mill, J. (1966) 'Whether Political Economy is Useful?' (1836) in *Selected Writings*, ed. D. Winch, (Oliver & B., 1966) pp. 371 ff.

Minford, P. (1980) 'The Nature and Purpose of UK Macroeconomic Models', *Three Banks Review* (March) 3 ff.

Royal Statistical Society (1934) *Annals 1834–1934*.

Samuelson, P. A. (1946) 'Lord Keynes and the General Theory', reprinted in *The New Economics*, ed. S. Harris (London: Dobson, 1948) pp. 145 ff.

Schumpeter, J. A. (1954) *History of Economic Analysis* (London: Allen & Unwin, 1965).

Senior, N. W. (1878) *Conversations with M. Thiers, M. Guizot, and other Distinguished Persons during the Second Empire*.

Sir Richard Stone (1980) 'Political Economy, Economics and Beyond', *Economic Journal* 90 (December) 732 ff.

Whately, R. (1832) *Introductory Lectures on Political Economy*, 2nd edn.

Index